" ...AND ECONOMIC JUSTICE FOR ALL"

"...AND ECONOMIC JUSTICE FOR ALL"

Welfare Reform for the 21st Century

MICHAEL L. MURRAY

M.E. Sharpe

Armonk, New York
London, England

Poetry on page 25 is an excerpt from *The People, Yes* by Carl Sandburg,
© 1936 by Harcourt Brace & Company and renewed 1964
by Carl Sandburg, reprinted by permission of the publisher.

Song on page 107 is an excerpt from "Work for the Night Is Coming,"
verse 2, in *The Methodist Hymnal*, The Methodist Publishing House,
Nashville, TN, 1939, p. 293.

Library of Congress Cataloging-in-Publication Data

Murray, Michael L., 1937–
. . . and economic justice for all : welfare reform for the 21st century /
Michael L. Murray.
p. cm.
Includes bibliographical references and index.
ISBN 1-56324-988-X (hc : alk. paper). —
ISBN 1-56324-989-8 (pbk. : alk. paper)
1. Public welfare—United States.
2. Guaranteed annual income—United States.
3. Distributive justice. I. Title.
HV95.M87   1997
362.5′82—dc21
96-48442
CIP

Printed in the United States of America

The paper used in this publication meets the minimum requirements of the
American National Standard for Information Sciences—
Permanence of Paper for Printed Library Materials,
ANSI Z 39.48-1984.

BM (c)   10   9   8   7   6   5   4   3   2   1
BM (p)   10   9   8   7   6   5   4   3   2   1

Contents

LIST OF TABLES

ACKNOWLEDGMENTS

I wish to acknowledge my good fortune in having been blessed with so many of the characteristics which are helpful in becoming a success in our economic system, and without which this book could not have been written.

I also express my appreciation to those—family, friends, colleagues, students, chance acquaintances—who have been willing to discuss my ideas over the years. I particularly appreciate those whose views did not correspond with mine, but who were willing to consider these as issues on which reasonable people could reasonably disagree (and to give me the benefit of the doubt on the ''reasonable'' criterion).

This book is dedicated to Paula J., who shared with me some of her life story during a discussion on a pedestrian overpass in Baltimore, Maryland. Paula epitomized those millions of good people who suffer from, and struggle to make up for, the fact that they possess very few of the advantages necessary for success in our economic system.

Introduction

Nothing irritates me quite so much as things that don't make sense. I think our current welfare system doesn't make sense. I believe that most proposals to change it don't make sense. It seems to me that the "guaranteed adequate income" makes a great deal of sense.

How did I, a Professor of Insurance in a College of Business Administration, come to write a book on economic justice with a proposal for dramatic change in our economic system? This may seem particularly out of character when you realize I have been well treated by the economic system in this country. Well, what happened was I extended my basic area of interest (insurance) to teach a course on Social Insurance. In this course, topics such as Social Security (more precisely the Old Age, Survivors, Disability and Health Insurance [OASDHI] program), Unemployment Compensation, Medicare, and Workers Compensation are routinely discussed. In the process of these discussions, I came to the realization that, in order to understand the role these programs play, one must also understand public assistance programs. This category includes Aid to Families With Dependent Children (AFDC), Food Stamps, Supplemental Security Income (SSI), and Medicaid. It didn't take many years of studying and teaching these programs before I concluded there is something drastically wrong with the system of public assistance in the United States.

For example, my conservative side recognized that far too much money is being spent administering the system. I ultimately realized that, while most people agree there is something wrong with the system, there is little agreement on what should be the remedy. Any inquiry into the basis for the disagreements over the possible solutions requires an examination of the issue of economic justice.

In my case, that led to the development of an honors course titled "Economic Justice/Income Distribution." The focus of the course was criteria for determining the preferred allocation of scarce resources. Over the years of teaching that course, I discovered a fundamental difference in the way students viewed their fellow human beings, which accounted to a great degree for their opinions on economic justice. This difference related to the issue of fault, and whether those in poverty should be held responsible for their status. I came to realize that this position depended to a great extent upon whether one regarded human behavior as "determined."

In my research for these courses, I encountered an idea which made such good sense I couldn't see why it hadn't been widely accepted. This idea is the guaranteed income.[1] In this book I describe in detail the various guaranteed income/negative income tax proposals. Suffice to note now that the idea emanated from those representing a wide range of the political spectrum, from liberals to conservatives. The security aspect particularly appeals to me. I had long recognized that economic security is a prime concern for all of us (this is why insurance is such a valuable tool). However, only with a guaranteed adequate income can true economic security be achieved.

MY POLITICAL HISTORY

My search for alternatives to our current welfare system was influenced by my fundamental political and social attitudes. My politics, to some extent, are summed up in my choices for president. The list includes Barry Goldwater (a fiscal conservative who believed in a limited role of government), George McGovern (a liberal with an apparent genuine concern for the plight of the less fortunate), and one or two libertarians, who advocated limiting the government sector to just those activities which protect us from others and from each other. As may be apparent, I haven't been too good at pickin' 'em. Oh yes, I did vote for Bill Clinton—my first winner. While he wasn't my first-choice Democrat, I did feel he represented a deeper concern than did George Bush for those less fortunate in our society.

You can interpret this voting pattern in a number of ways. I hope to convince you that it is the voting pattern of one who believes that government is best which governs least, but does not trust the invisible hand of market forces to bring about economic justice. That is important, because I intend this book to build on the best of alternative political philosophies and provide a means of reconciling some differences.

MY INTELLECTUAL HISTORY

Comments by, and details on, the people who have influenced my thinking in this area are in the body of the book. Perhaps the most influential was Robert Theobald, who edited a small volume (and wrote a chapter for it) in the 1960s, titled *The Guaranteed Income*. While I was not at the time familiar with Theobald, his book provided innovative and forward-looking insights. An author of one chapter in that book, Robert Davis, describes how the advance of cybernation will eventually lead to a significant decline in the size of the work force. The major point is that if we don't have enough jobs on which to base incomes, we must find an alternative method of providing incomes.

In Theobald's introduction, he referred to John Maynard Keynes's contention that mankind is on the verge of solving the problem of adequacy of resources. Keynes then described how the challenge will become that of distributing these resources. In arguing for a guaranteed income, Theobald noted:

> The ideal of private enterprise can . . . be preserved only if the guaranteed income is introduced.[2]

As a believer in the merits of private enterprise, this struck me as a compelling point. In another chapter of this book, C. E. Ayres, in what he referred to as "An Institutionalist View" discusses the critical need for security by members of society. Since I have studied, for twenty-five years, the use of insurance to help provide security, I was well aware of the limitations of insurance.[3]

A major concern is that all productivity might be lost in the presence of a guaranteed income. Erich Fromm, a psychoanalyst, in a chapter of Theobald's book titled "The Psychological Aspects of the Guaranteed Income" stated:

> It is a fact that man, by nature, is not lazy, but on the contrary *suffers* from the effects of inactivity.[4]

This recognition that most people want to be productive allayed my reservations in this regard.

I also encountered the writings of Milton Friedman, economic advisor to Barry Goldwater and member of the conservative Chicago School of Economics, who made a compelling case for a "negative income tax." This represents a dramatic departure from the current welfare scheme and is a form of guaranteed income. His arguments are particularly attractive since they're founded on a goal of minimizing government activity. In his book *Capitalism and Freedom*, Friedman describes the shortcomings of our current social welfare measures, including the OASDI program. His primary focus is on the extent to which all our programs involve considerable government activity and intrusion in people's lives. Efficiency and effectiveness are his goals. In a chapter titled "The Alleviation of Poverty," he states:

> Two things seem clear. First, if the objective is to alleviate poverty, we should have a program aimed at helping the poor. . . . Second, so far as possible the program should, while operating through the market, not distort the market or impede its functioning.[5]

With respect to the first point, he argues against programs which are targeted at only certain segments of the poor population, and concerning the second, he points out the undesirable characteristics of such programs as minimum wage laws and price supports. Recommending a negative income tax, he notes:

In this way it would be possible to set a floor below which no man's net income . . . could fall.[6]

These arguments make great sense to the conservative side of my nature.

Ayn Rand, whose arguments I found well thought out, contributed to my appreciation of the private enterprise system and forced me to be careful about support for government intrusion. The realization that I could accept the essence of her arguments and still be a proponent of a guaranteed income was a revelation. She felt a great antipathy toward collectivism and an unswerving support for capitalism.[7]

I concluded that the guaranteed adequate income is the best method for keeping faith with my conservative/libertarian ideals. It allows us to minimize the influence of government in individuals' lives, while still recognizing we must do *something* through government to help everyone to a reasonable shot at success in the capitalist system.

Rand also convinced me that all of human behavior is based on motivations which are essentially selfish. According to her view, when we oppose programs which would cause a reduction in our wealth, we are motivated by the same drive as one who contributes to a charity. Having money makes some feel good; giving to others makes others feel good. Of course, most of us get some pleasure out of both. I conclude that our natural tendency to want to keep what we have is no more to be criticized than our natural tendency to want to give to others. If our neighbor wishes to share more than do we, this does not make her a better person.

However, as a society we are better served to foster the sharing instinct. All of us, acting through government, encourage each of us to share.[8]

The liberal in me was impressed by the case made by B. F. Skinner, particularly in the book *Walden Two*. In this novel, Skinner provides some compelling insights into the nature of work and criteria for compensating members of a society.

The existence of a real poverty problem in the United States was driven home to me by Michael Harrington, in his book *The Other America*. He forcefully argues that Americans tend to ignore the problems of poverty because it is so well hidden from them. Harrington notes, for example, that our modern freeways tend to skirt the areas of poverty so that most of us rarely see them.

Daniel Moynihan, in his book about the Family Assistance Plan proposed by President Nixon, chronicles in detail the various forces tugging the welfare system in various directions.[9] He describes the decision to pursue a guaranteed income and its political obstacles, which were never overcome. One of his most telling points is that the proponents of dramatic change may be the worst enemy of that change, if it doesn't go far enough for them.

I feel it is important at this point to discuss my communist or socialist side. I find those who initially dislike the guaranteed adequate income proposal wish to dismiss it with one of these, to them, pejorative labels. In truth, the proposal is neither. The primary characteristic of socialism is the ownership of the means of production by the state, rather than by private parties. I am proposing just the opposite. I want to get government *out* of the welfare business. The current bureaucracy handling our complex welfare system is an example of the inefficiencies associated with government enterprises. The guaranteed annual income would need no such enterprise.[10]

When many people think of communism, they think of the slogan "From each according to his ability, to each according to his need." This is not what I'm proposing. In the first half of this statement, the communists refer to a person's contribution to society, in the form of work effort. The GAI incorporates no such requirement. It does not meet the second test, either, because the GAI is not based on "need." My proposal is no more communist than is our current welfare system.[11]

THE BOTTOM LINE

As indicated above, I am impressed by the arguments of a wide range of thinkers on this issue, and my own political persuasions run the gamut from conservative to liberal. I conclude that there are thoughtful, concerned, well-informed people who, nonetheless, close their minds to a discussion of so dramatic a reform as a guaranteed adequate income. What is the fundamental difference of opinion which separates these camps?

I conclude there are two underlying viewpoints which separate the two positions. First, some feel poverty is a necessary spur to productivity. Accordingly, without the threat of poverty, too many people would choose to not contribute. While I acknowledge the need for incentives to productivity, I have concluded we no longer need the drastic negative enforcement of poverty. The United States is sufficiently wealthy, and technology is sufficiently advanced, that we can survive quite nicely with the incentive to do better. We no longer need the incentive to survive.

Another fundamental difference lies in the varying concepts of why people are poor and whether those who are poor should bear the brunt of their own behavior. Everyone seems to accept there are at least a few who are poor "through no fault of their own." However, a gulf exists between those who feel others (perhaps most) deserve to be poor and, therefore, should have no claim on the resources of the rest of society, and those who feel justice dictates we as a society should show concern for *all* poor people.

In an effort to establish my own position on this issue, I investigated the literature on justice, particularly as it applies to economic justice. It appears that the solution to the issue of justice depends on the conclusions of a more elemental debate. People's attitudes toward justice depend on their fundamental view of human nature. The particular view centers on the concept of *determinism*. That concept is therefore the subject of a full chapter. Points made in that chapter are vital to the development of one's view of justice (both economic and other types), which, in turn, forms a basis for my recommended social policy.

WHO ARE YOU?

My intended audience includes policy makers, to be sure, but more important, educated citizens who are ready, willing, and able to consider some dramatic new ideas.[12] It is my intent that this book be read, not only by college students but also by everyone interested in finding a better way of dealing with the problem of inadequate income.

I firmly believe the arguments in this book can appeal to both liberals and conservatives. Naturally, some of the arguments will be more or less easily accepted by one of the groups. The conclusion that a guaranteed adequate income is preferable to our current welfare system may seem, at first glance, a strictly liberal notion. I assure you, it is not. It is a concept that lends itself to consensus—there are strong arguments for it from a liberal perspective, but it has equally compelling appeal to conservatives. Each side must avoid the tendency to reject it out-of-hand because it is supported by the other.

Those readers who disagree with me on very fundamental issues may not profit from reading this book. Others will gain some insights, and perhaps ultimately agree with my conclusions. You will probably be among the latter group if you:

• Feel there is a poverty problem. It surprises me to discover that some in our society are so insulated from the problems of poverty that they hardly think it exists.[13] The authors of the book *The Challenges of Humanistic Economics* demonstrate this point by relating the comments of a well-to-do person visiting, for the first time, a family in poverty. When he discovers the family has to walk some distance to get water, he indicates that when someone told him these people had no water, he thought they meant no *drinking* water. He could not conceive that they had no water piped into their house. The significant point is not the fact that the people had no running water; rather, that the visitor could not even conceive of a family in the United States having *no* running water. This was also epitomized by a friend of mine who commented, during a discussion of these problems, "Why don't they [those with no incomes] just sell their assets?" The fact that there are many people without any assets seemed to this person unlikely.

• Don't believe that God meant some people to be poor. Some believe that the poor are that way because God meant for them to be, basing their conclusion on, for example, the Biblical lines "The Lord maketh poor and maketh rich"[14] or "For ye have the poor always with you."[15] For those who take these to mean that only God is in charge of who is poor and that God intends us to always have poor people, neither my discussion of why people are poor nor my means to remedy the situation will have any impact.

• Agree that government should play some role in redistributing income. A supportable case can be made for the position that government should not extend beyond providing for the common defense and protecting us from each other. This is a view held by many Libertarians, and is a position on which reasonable people could reasonably disagree.[16] In my own Libertarian period, I held these views. I personally have concluded, however, that government welfare activity is justifiable, in that it protects us from the vagaries of the economic sphere. Government activity in a democracy is essentially the majority of us getting together and agreeing that some things need to be done, and we are willing to help see that they get done (by paying taxes).[17] Those who are open to that view will have an interest in my arguments about the *types* of government programs we need to deal with the problems of poverty.

• Believe we can make changes without making matters worse. Another of my friends (yes, I still have friends, in spite of my unconventional views) rejected my proposal almost before hearing it. His position was that any attempts to bring change will result in a worsened situation. Of course, it should be noted that this friend is doing quite well under the system that currently exists. Nonetheless, if you are among those who believe that "This is the way we do it and, therefore, this must be the way we *should* keep on doing it," then none of my arguments proposing change will matter to you. A related concern that additional laws make it harder to enforce the already saturated statutes certainly has merit. However, my proposal will eliminate many more laws than it introduces.

• Agree that "survival of the fittest" should no longer be the law of the land. A reasonable case can be made that, since society progresses through adaptation of the species, any programs which aid the weaker among us only slow that progress. If we conclude that those in poverty are less well adapted to participate in our economic system, then, so the argument would go, we should not institute programs which enhance their survival chances. Since I hope not too many people take this position, I'll not spend much time arguing against it. Perhaps just this one point. In order for natural selection to have any impact, procreation must be inhibited for those less well adapted. I fail to see how failure in our economic system will have this effect.

• Recognize that "the market" does not make an optimum income allocation. As a business professor I know a lot of people who have almost a mystical reverence for the market. They seem to feel Adam Smith's "invisible hand" really does guide our economic lives. As a result, incomes are always apportioned as they should be. These zealots believe that *any* attempt to interfere in this "plan" will only result in suboptimization. If you are among this group, you will not be interested in ways the government can counter the shortcomings of the market. However, if you believe, as I do, that in general the unfettered market is probably the best way to allocate incomes, but that it results in numerous inequities, you will be interested in my plan to *reduce* the amount of governmental impact on the market.

HOW CAN I CONVINCE YOU?

Let me note, up front, that I do not intend to dazzle you with facts. Facts are beneficial. I'm all for collecting and disseminating them. However, as we've seen frequently, the various interpretations of those facts can leave one aswirl. For example:

• Did the twelve years of Republican administration result in more or less poverty? You can find support for either position. It depends on whom you ask and how they measure.
• Does the United States have more people in poverty than other nations? It depends on how you define poverty.
• Do government programs result in more or less poverty?[18]
• How much of the welfare dollar is actually going to help the poor?
• Did the distribution of income shift in the 1980s in favor of the well-to-do?
• Would a guaranteed income lead to a reduction in work?[19]

The "facts" related to all these questions can lead you either way. I know—I've been convinced in both directions many times. You'll see some facts in this book, but they do not provide the essence of my argument.

Nor will I attack the motivations of those who come to different conclusions. Rather, I provide a reasoned argument for your consideration. We waste too much time trying to convince the body politic that the omnipresent "they" are not to be believed. All too often, this is accompanied by *ad hominem* references, including impugning the motives of the supporters of the other side.[20] My intent is not to provide one side with ammunition to prove "the idiots" to be wrong. It is rather to provide a basis for people of goodwill to concur on a program for dramatic improvement in the way we view the problems of poverty, and in the ways we deal with them through government.

When we reason, we build on one assumption or conclusion and show how it logically leads to another. I will identify a set of assumptions on which most can agree. As I noted earlier in this Introduction, there will be some whose personal set of assumptions is so different from mine that we can never agree on the conclusions. If you are still reading this book, you are probably not in that group.

The guaranteed adequate income makes sense to me. Come along while I take you on an intellectual trip to see why that is so.

Notes

1. This concept most commonly has been referred to as a guaranteed *annual* income, or GAI. While I will continue to refer to it as GAI, I prefer the term guaranteed *adequate* income. My two reasons for this are: (1) The benefits should be provided much more frequently than annually, and (2) The level of the benefit should be just "adequate." Some readers may be familiar with "negative income tax" proposals; these are one form of a GAI.

2. Robert Theobald, ed., *The Guaranteed Income*, p. 104.

3. The primary limitation is the inability of a private insurance mechanism to guarantee security of income when the loss of that income is the result of major market forces. These major economic changes cause losses to too many insureds at one time. However, in the absence of this guarantee of minimum income, all the security provided by insurance is moot.

4. Ibid., p. 186 (emphasis added).

5. Milton Friedman, *Capitalism and Freedom*, p. 191.

6. Ibid., p. 192.

7. Barbara Branden, in a biography titled *The Passion of Ayn Rand*, quotes Rand as saying, "My philosophy, in essence, is the concept of man as a heroic being, with his own happiness as the moral purpose of his life, with productive achievement as his noblest activity, and reason as his only absolute," p. 52.

8. OK. I know we really are *forcing* some of us to share. In a democracy, the majority often compels some individuals to do things they would rather not do.

However, we have already generally accepted the idea of some sharing; my goal is to make that sharing a more rational process.

9. Daniel Moynihan, *The Politics of a Guaranteed Income.*

10. I am not, however, totally opposed to *any* socialist enterprises. I recognize the contribution our socialist public education system has made; I appreciate the benefits of the socialist Social Security insurance system; I'm not one who knocks the semisocialist postal system; and I feel a socialist health delivery system may be the only real solution to our health-care crisis.

11. Of course, if by your definition the present system is communist, then the label also applies to the GAI.

12. The idea of a guaranteed income is not new. What is new is the set of arguments I make on its behalf.

13. They probably have not read *The Other America.*

14. I Samuel 2:7, King James Version.

15. Matthew 26:11, King James Version.

16. If you adopt it, you must, of course, decry government activity in education, fire fighting, provision of water, building of roads, et al.

17. Of course, with majority rule, there is no requirement that we *all* agree. The negative aspect is that we end up with most of us telling all of us what we will do. However, there is something quite beneficial to a system which requires everyone to kick in because it removes the "I'm not going to help unless others are helping also" psychology. It is also true that our views do not get directly implemented, going first through our elected representatives; I continue to believe, however, the views of the majority are eventually implemented.

18. For a compelling case that public assistance programs have actually caused more poverty, see Charles Murray (no relation), *Losing Ground.* Note that many of the problems with our current welfare programs as pointed out by Charles Murray would be alleviated by the guaranteed income recommended in this book.

19. Elsewhere in this book I will discuss the results of an experiment on this issue. For now I simply note that the implications of the results of that experiment are as much related to the perspective of the person interpreting them as they are to the facts themselves.

20. Currently, a very popular radio talk show host epitomizes this tendency. It took me a while to realize the reason he galls me is not that I occasionally disagree with his logic or positions. It is rather that he is so divisive. His appeal is to a combative instinct in his listeners—an instinct that *requires* they feel the other side is nefariously motivated and/or stupid.

1

Life Is Not Fair, But People Can Be

This chapter is about justice. We Americans certainly believe in justice. We grow up reciting:

> I pledge allegiance to the Flag of the United States of America and to the Republic for which it stands, one nation under God, indivisible, with liberty and justice for all.

As youngsters, we did not give a lot of thought to what we meant when we said "and justice for all." As adults, we may have some vague notion. It's time to get at the essence of that notion. The primary issue in this chapter will be whether we wish to include economic issues in our concept of justice.

ECONOMIC JUSTICE — SHOULD IT BE A GOAL?

When we say "and justice for all" in our Pledge of Allegiance, we do not necessarily include any notions of income or wealth. Should they be included? For guidance we might look to our other important documents. We find in the Preamble to the Constitution of the United States of America:

> We, the People of the United States, in Order to form a more perfect union, establish Justice, insure domestic Tranquility, provide for the common defence, promote the general Welfare. . . .

Here justice and the "general welfare" appear to be two different issues. Even in the Bill of Rights (the first ten amendments to our Constitution), there is no specific mention of economic rights .[1]
According to the Declaration of Independence:

> We hold these truths to be self-evident, that all men are created equal, that they are endowed by their Creator with certain unalienable Rights, that among these are Life, Liberty, and the pursuit of Happiness. That to secure these rights, Governments are instituted among Men. . . .

Assuming for the time being that to be just is to grant ''men'' their ''unalienable Rights,'' there is no direct indication here that our founders meant to include any economic rights.[2]

The United States has, however, indicated some recognition of economic rights when it signed the Universal Declaration of Human Rights (adopted by the United Nations in 1948). It includes the following:

> Everyone has the right to a standard of living adequate for the health and well-being of himself and his family. . . .

Finally, our leaders have, on occasion, expressed a belief in economic rights:

> At a news conference after her congressional appearance [following a trip to South America] she [Rosalyn Carter] was asked if she found a feeling that America should achieve full human rights itself before applying pressure for them in other countries. ''I was asked about human rights here,'' she replied, ''and I told them that Jimmy [then President Carter] was committed to it and that he believed human rights did not mean just freedom from political oppression but also freedom from hunger, social and economic rights.'' [3]

> Secretary of State Cyrus Vance has defined what the [Carter] administration means by human rights: ''First, there is the right to be free from government violation of the integrity of the person. . . . Second, there is the right to the fulfillment of such vital needs as food, shelter, health care, and education. Third, there is the right to enjoy civil and political liberties.'' [4]

It is true these views were not often expressed throughout the years of the Reagan or Bush administrations, nor yet during Clinton's term. Nonetheless, there is evidence at least one segment of the body politic holds them.[5] Note, however, that the conclusion reached in this book (a recommendation for a guaranteed adequate income) does not require us to base it on a ''right.''

Other Rights Require Economic Rights

Even if we, in the United States, do not directly recognize the rights of citizens to any measure of wealth or income,[6] certainly the rights to life and the pursuit of happiness require some minimum level of economic well-being, at least in today's society.[7]

One cannot live without the ability to purchase food. On this point it might be well to pause and contemplate a difference in the conditions faced by the average person, at the time the Constitution was written, from those faced today. At that time, many of the necessities of life were available for the taking. All that was required was that one make an effort. To say people had a right to sustenance would have been superfluous because, unless the person were physically incapable or physically restrained, food could generally be obtained (by hunting, fishing, gathering, or farming). Shelter could be obtained by felling trees or piling up sod or using animal skins. The point is that it was *assumed* that all had the rights to obtain these goods. Only as resources have become tied up—either by private interests or by the public at large through the government—has the notion of economic rights become important.

Today, this is no longer a reasonable assumption. There is very little land which is not either privately owned or publicly committed to a particular use.[8] One reason homelessness is such a problem, for those of us with homes, is the homeless have no place to go to get out of the way. Today we must think in terms of a right to a place to live; two hundred years ago that was not a concern.[9] Even such a vital necessity as water is no longer free for the finding. It is extremely difficult to find potable water today without paying for it.

The "pursuit of happiness" also requires some economic wherewithal. Now don't jump to the conclusion that I am talking about any *guarantee* of happiness—I know we can never provide enough to accomplish this. I refer simply to the acknowledged right to *pursue* it. Some degree of economic well-being, as well as security, is necessary to create the conditions under which one can *pursue* happiness.

There are also economic implications of the right to a fair trial and the right to vote.[10] Without nourishment it is difficult to exercise either of these rights.[11] The right granted in the Eighth Amendment ("excessive bail shall not be required") is impossible to operationalize in cases where the defendant is indigent.

Rights Are Not a Necessary Basis for Economic Justice

A case can be made, as shown above, for providing economic rights in order to make other rights meaningful. I do not choose to rely on these arguments, however. Even though I believe they have merit, they leave too much room for reasonable disagreement. "Nobody owes me [or you] a living" is an often-heard response to any suggestion of a right to an income. It is simply not necessary to try to establish the existence of economic rights in order to make the case that justice requires everyone be provided with some level of income.

RELEVANCE OF DETERMINISM

Determinism provides a basis for this discussion of justice. This concept is developed more fully in a later chapter. For now, I would like simply to point out treating a person more or less favorably, based on *who one is,* is inconsistent with a determinist view. Even differential rewards and penalties, based on *what one does,* are difficult to justify. Since we are products of our inheritance and our upbringing, our accomplishments (or shortcomings) are also products of those factors. The credit (or blame) does not belong to us. Of course, once we start thinking this way we run into an "infinite regress." Giving our parents credit (or blame) implies that their parents should get the credit or blame for their actions, and so on back. There really is no place for the buck to stop. This raises one of those conflicts between what we should believe and what we want to believe. It is only natural that we want to place the blame on, or give the credit to, someone. One scholar, Jennifer Trusted, speaks to this issue, noting "it [determinism] carries implications which conflict with our instinctive beliefs about people (including ourselves)."[12] My later discussion of determinism is an attempt to counter these "instinctive beliefs." Readers who need more information on this issue might turn to that chapter before proceeding. For others, I simply note at this point that a concept of justice based in determinism does not have room for placing blame.

I cannot quarrel with Trusted's conclusion that we have an inclination to hold ourselves and others responsible. I argue, however, that her conclusions are based on circular reasoning. According to her view, we should adopt a concept which *allows* us to hold people responsible because we feel it is *necessary* to hold people responsible. While it may be true we all have a need to hold others responsible, this need can be explained in ways which are consistent with determinism (without the circularity problem). One reasonable explanation is that we developed this attitude during the eons in which we knew very little about what makes people tick. (We did not know until recently, for example, that a chemical imbalance in the brain could account for some psychotic behavior.) Whenever we can't explain the behavior of others, or ourselves, it makes sense to simply blame the person. However, the greater our ability to explain, the narrower the realm in which it is necessary to blame. Thus, this need to hold others responsible is really a psychological anachronism, having served us well in the millennia before we had explanations.

The second explanation is that we have learned as social animals that it is *necessary* to hold others responsible (and to expect that we ourselves will be held responsible) in order to develop a functioning society with rules of behavior. Trusted implies we should give precedence to our instinctive beliefs when these conflict with the scientific explanation. I am arguing the opposite—we must strive to overcome these instinctive views in light of the determinist evidence. This is an important point with respect to the arguments I make for justice.

When it comes to *economic* justice, a determinist view severely limits the occasions on which we can justify (or claim as just) any wealth differentials. First, however, let us consider whether economic issues should even be considered in a discussion of justice.

CONCEPTS OF JUSTICE

The focus of this book is on economic justice. We can approach that issue by first discussing the various concepts of justice in general. I'll take as a given that when citizens of the United States say "with . . . justice for all" in pledging allegiance to the flag, they are not only saying that their country *does* provide justice for all but that it *should* do so. From this starting point, we are led to the following questions:

What does one mean when one says "and justice for all"?
What *should* one mean when making this statement?

These questions are both very difficult, if not impossible, to answer. Since people hold a wide range of views about what is "just," we cannot know, without considerable inquiry, what any one person means. Given this range of views, it would be presumptuous of me to tell you what you should believe. What I propose to do in the following section is to work through the various concepts to which the name "justice" can be applied. I then point out what I believe is the only concept which is consistent with a deterministic viewpoint.[13] Your part in the following discussion will be implied from the many discussions I have had with others on this subject.

You: "When I say justice, I mean everybody getting what they deserve."
Me: "That is reasonable, but it requires you to describe what you mean by deserve."

Deserving as a Basis for Justice

Under what circumstances would you say someone "deserves" something? It seems there are many possible answers to this question, and most of them are quite defensible. Some of them are, however, less useful than others. For example:

You: "I think everyone deserves the same treatment."

The problem with this is it's essentially the same description one might use for a right. Wouldn't you be inclined to say:

"Everyone has a right to the same treatment"?

We can give the word "deserve" a meaning different from "has a right" if we use it only for situations different from those which apply equally to everyone; thus "deserving" is best used when a particular characteristic of the person is the basis of our assessment of that person.[14]

For similar reasons, the following response is not very useful:

"If someone is in need, they deserve to be helped."

Perhaps you hold the view that it is *just* for people to get what they need. That itself is a point on which reasonable people might reasonably disagree. However, it adds nothing to the discussion if you inject the concept of "deserving" into that line of reasoning.

When Does One "Deserve?"

The answer to this question must include a description of either the person or of a specific behavior of that person.

Can One Person Be More Deserving than Another?

No! Here is the primary basis for my guaranteed adequate income proposal.[15] An implication of the determinist thesis is "None of us is better than any others of us." I realize there are those among my readers who will never be convinced this is the case.[16] Perhaps for you, it conflicts with firmly held religious beliefs.

Religious Beliefs About Deserving People. If, for example, you believe God will send some people to heaven and some to hell, you probably feel that God believes certain people are good and some bad. Since that is the case you probably believe you should view people the same way. Since you know your religious views better than I, it may be presumptuous of me to try to convince you otherwise. Please allow me, however, to make a couple of points to at least give you a basis for reconsideration.

Is it not true that God's determination of whether you are good or bad is made only at one point in time? That point, at least in the Christian religion, is on the judgment day.[17] Until that time, even the worst of sinners is deemed eligible for salvation.[18] I conclude, therefore, that mere mortals ought not to make this judgment at all, and certainly not at a time prior to when God is deemed to make it.[19]

The other point relates to the concept of original sin. It is a widely held belief among Christians that Adam and Eve's disobedience in the Garden of Eden branded all humans as sinners. From that view, one might decide that none of us is "deserving" or "worthy." This is not a view to which I subscribe; however, I feel that one who holds it can still accept the recommendations of this book. This view says nothing about how we are different, one from another. Therefore, there is no suggestion that some of us are better or more deserving or more worthy than others. My arguments for treating everyone the same is not damaged by the belief that all of us are bad.[20]

Determinist Perspective on Deserving People. The following statements are incompatible with determinism:

"That person deserves to be punished."
"That person deserves a comfortable lifestyle."

The determinism view is that who we are is a function of factors outside our control. Therefore, it is not acceptable (as noted in the chapter on determinism) to credit someone with being a good person or to deride them as being a bad person. Therefore, we should reorient our thinking and speaking as follows:

Inconsistent with Determinism	Consistent with Determinism
He is to be admired.	His accomplishments are to be admired
He is a reprehensible person.	That was a reprehensible act.
She is a good girl.	She has done many good things.
Ruth is a better person than Bob.	Ruth has done more kind things than has Bob.

The preferable statements refer to actions of the person. If we accept a determinist outlook, we realize none of us can take credit for who we are, and others should therefore not give us that credit. Nor is it logically permissible to demean other people. None of us is more worthy than any of the others of us.[21]

I've discussed this point with others enough times to recognize that my readers are mentally besieging me with "but's" at this point:

• *But* shouldn't we punish people?
• *But* shouldn't some people earn more money than others?
• *But* shouldn't we react differently to some people's actions than to others?

My answers are:

• Yes
• Yes
• Yes

Can One Action Be More Deserving than Another?

Yes. While continuing to emphasize the point that we should not regard one *person* as better than another, I nonetheless can take the position that we can, should, and even must regard some actions as better than others. The underlying basis for this differential response is social necessity. It is necessary for us as a society to reward favored behavior and to punish unacceptable behavior in order to promote our interests.

What Are ''Our Interests''? There are three interpretations of this phrase: self-interest, species, and society. The first of our interests is *self-interest*. As individuals, we react to the behavior of others on the basis of how it affects us. By expressing thanks, by repaying kindnesses, and by compensating services, we let others know we appreciate that behavior. By so doing, we encourage that person and others to engage in the same type of behavior. When those actions make us feel better or enhance the quality of our lives, we benefit.

In one sense, all behavior is motivated by self-interest.[22] Even those who act out of ostensibly altruistic motives do so because it makes them feel good. The difference between a person who gives a handout to a panhandler and one who does not is not that one is acting out of self-interest and the other is not. It may simply be that it makes the former feel good, but does not have the same effect on the latter. Even the most dedicated missionary derives a psychic satisfaction out of helping or redeeming others. How many times have we heard someone say:

"I really don't like trying to help others, but I do it anyhow."

I'll venture to say "Never!" Having presented the case that people act basically out of self-interest (and that it's OK for them to do so), I hasten to affirm some such behavior is more desirable than other. Each of us wants to encourage other people to engage in actions supportive of our own interests. Thus, owners of businesses reward hard work because it increases profits for the firm and the owners' well-being. Parents reward obedience because it makes the parents' lives more pleasant, and because well-behaved children will be better received by others, and that will reflect well on the parents.[23]

The second interest is *species* interest. I have read well-reasoned presentations of the case that everything we do is designed to promote the continuation of our species. The presenters claim this is true not only of humans but of all living creatures. One school of thought even holds that we are driven by our genes—that they are the only perpetual life, and we are merely vehicles to accommodate their propagation.[24] To the extent this is true, we are each inclined to reward behavior in others that works to the betterment of the species.[25]

The final, and perhaps most palatable, version of "our interest" is that we reward behavior which enhances our *society*. How broadly the notion of "our society" is interpreted is not critical at this point. My own position is that it incorporates all the world's people, but for now a view that it includes only one's own school or neighborhood or state or country still allows us to make the point.

"So what *is* your point?" you ask. Here it is: rewarding certain types of behavior and punishing others is not inconsistent with a determinist view. It is simply a recognition that it is *necessary* to react in these ways in order to promote the well-being of *society* (or ourselves or our species). We can hold true to the belief that no person is better than another, while having a basis for reacting differently to things people *do*.

Once we adopt the conclusion that "People don't deserve; actions do," we have a much more useful framework for deciding which actions deserve what kinds of responses. It is essential at this point that readers recognize the fundamental difference within the following pairs of statements:

You are a bad child because you hit your mother.
Hitting your brother was a bad thing to do.

Murderers deserve the death penalty.
Murder deserves the death penalty.

That student deserves an A.
The work that student did deserves an A.

That ball player deserves to earn $6.2 million a year.
Consistently great performance should be compensated with $6.2 million a year.

Bill deserves to earn more than Jill.
The work Bill does deserves greater pay than the work Jill does.

Ralph, who refuses to work, deserves to starve.
Refusal to work should be penalized with starvation.

To the extent we wish to use the notion of "deserving" to justify differential rewards and punishments, it must be applied to the *action* and not to the *person*. However, as can be seen from the above examples, it is often awkward to describe behavior as deserving. The better option is to base justice on something other than "deserving."[26] However, for those who insist on retaining this basis for rewards and punishments, I offer the following analysis, which is organized following David Miller's version of the principles of economic desert.[27]

Principles of Economic Desert

According to Miller, there are three principles which can be used to justify differential rewards, using the notion of deserts. They are contribution, effort and compensation.

Contribution

According to this principle a person's reward depends on the value of the contribution made to social welfare, in one's work activity. This principle can be based on one of three arguments:

Utilitarian Arguments. According to this view, there is more for all when people are encouraged to develop skills. The problem is that the correct action is to reward only for those skills which wouldn't have been obtained without the incentive (e.g., many would seek education even without economic incentives).[28]

Locke's Claim. The seventeenth-century English philosopher John Locke claimed that each man has a *right* to the product of his labor. However, this is based on a hypothetical state of nature which cannot be shifted to a real society.

Commutative Argument. Those who provide more product *to* society should receive more *from* society. However, this contention rests on the assumption of the right to the product of one's labor; a premise which Miller has shown to be faulty.

In addition to the problems noted within each of these three contentions, there are problems in applying this principle. The size of the contribution may be dictated by extraneous factors, and individual contributions may have no meaning in cooperative situations. Therefore, efforts to base desert on contribution will prove unsuccessful.

Effort

The principle is usually expressed that if two people work equally hard and for an equally long time, they deserve equal remuneration, even if one, because of superior ability, produces more. This conclusion depends on the more basic claim that persons' deserts depend on their voluntary actions. To apply the "effort" principle, effort and voluntarily acquired abilities need to be separated from innate abilities and abilities which are implanted by other people. However, even the willingness to exert effort is one of those "abilities implanted by other people." Is it not true some people are taught by their parents to work hard, whereas others are not?

Why should one who happened to be raised by parents who instilled a work ethic be more "deserving" than one whose parents did not impart that ethic? A reward system based on deserving, based on effort, is not just, and it is impossible to apply.

Compensation

An individual incurs a "cost" when his or her work is unpleasant, and, therefore, the individual should be compensated to the extent of that unpleasantness. In other words, one deserves more when one gives up more. This is the most defensible basis for justice founded on deserving. The major caveat is that it must be applied only in those cases where everyone is deemed to be equally capable of giving up something. The only factor I am able to suggest which meets this criterion is time. Assuming for the present that one's leisure is a positive good, willingness to forgo that leisure in order to provide a service is deserving of compensation.[29]

Another candidate for "equally available good which can be traded for compensation" is comfort. To the extent one is willing to forgo comfort to, for example, go out into the hot sun or brave the chill or accept a boss's abuse or strain muscles, that action "deserves" compensation. Application of this principle is impeded, however, by the absence of a common starting point of comfort. A fair assessment requires that everyone give up the same level of comfort. In reality, there is a tremendous difference in the comfort one has to "trade."[30] Also required is some assessment of the discomfort associated with a particular labor. This assessment is rendered nearly impossible by the recognition that one person's drudge is another's joy.

One hypothetical example of the application of this principle was described by B. F. Skinner in *Walden II*.[31] In his community, rewards were equally distributed, based upon how onerous the work was. Those who engaged in the more unpleasant jobs were not required to spend as many hours at work for their contribution to the community. This represented the inverse of the theory behind our actual compensation in a capitalist society. According to the "differential wage" theory, the market allocates more per hour to those who perform more onerous or dangerous tasks. Is this theory borne out by observation? We'll look closer at that issue in the chapter dealing with the market. Suffice it to say at this point that Skinner's community probably would do as good a job of "compensating justly" as the market does presently.

My conclusion is that the use of "deserving" as a basis for justice must be severely circumscribed. To provide yet another perspective on this issue, I now draw on the views of two authors who have quite contrasting theories of justice.

RAWLS AND NOZICK—CONTRASTING VIEWS OF JUSTICE

From the many writers who have pursued the elusive concept of justice, I have elected to present these two.[32] I do so because they provide a sharp contrast between a view I find particularly appealing (Rawls) and one I feel has widespread support (Nozick).[33]

Justice as Perceived by John Rawls

Have you heard of the "the natural lottery" or "veil of ignorance"? These are names for two of the enlightened concepts introduced by John Rawls.[34] An understanding of these two provides a significant insight into his views.

The Natural Lottery

Is it not clear that some people are born into more favorable circumstances than others? Do these circumstances not include a wide range of factors? Would not these factors include:

- Intelligence
- Family wealth
- Stability of family
- The country in which one was born
- Interest of parents in providing education
- Physical prowess
- Natural beauty
- Family values

Even if one believes people can overcome any obstacles, one must still recognize that some "draw" greater obstacles to overcome than others. Compounding the issue is the observation that the ability to overcome obstacles is also part of the "draw." Why do some succeed and others fail? As discussed more fully in the determinism chapter, this ability to overcome obstacles is simply another factor determined by our inheritance and upbringing (in this case I would emphasize the latter; parents admonitions to "keep trying," as well as early successes, make a great deal of difference). Keep in mind that Rawls's "natural lottery" includes not only our innate abilities but also the situation into which we are born, including the parents and teachers with whom we are blessed or cursed.

The importance of this concept is revealed when Rawls discusses the notion of "liberal equality," which is:

a sort of fair meritocracy in which social and economic inequalities are mitigated by equality of opportunity and the attempt to provide everyone with an equal start.[35]

This notion is flawed, however, because it:

permits the distribution of wealth and income to be determined by the natural distribution of abilities and talents. Within the limits allowed by the background arrangements, distributive shares are decided by the outcome of the natural lottery, and the outcome is arbitrary from a moral perspective. There is no more reason to permit the distribution of income and wealth to be settled by the distribution of natural assets than by historical and social fortune.[36]

Allow me to digress from and expand upon this point. What do we mean when we say that "all men are created equal?" Many people implicitly adopt the idyllic view that every person has some greater abilities in some areas which offset their weaknesses in others. According to this view, then, everyone has an equal chance to enjoy life and to succeed in our free economic system. This position is held most strongly by those who have themselves succeeded—"I did it; why can't they?" It is also propped up by the myth of Horatio Alger—"One lad from an impoverished background succeeded handsomely; why can't everyone?" These views ignore the point that Horatio Alger was notable not because he represented the norm but because he was an *exception*. Granted, some people do overcome enormous obstacles; but for every one who does, many more are defeated by these obstacles.

The proper version, then, of "created equal" is "of equal worth." Each human is to be regarded as equally entitled to the blessings of life. Not only are we regarded as equal "in the eyes of God," we also to be deemed equally worthy by society. Whoa! Don't go beyond what I am saying here. I have *not* said that society should or must guarantee equality. I have only contended that any deviations from equality are not defensible on the grounds that some people are more worthy than others. (Later in this chapter, I consider and reject the idea of egalitarianism.)

The Veil of Ignorance

It is probably impossible for any of us to objectively arrive at a concept of justice. Each of us brings to the discussion too much baggage. We know where we already fit into the economic scheme, and we have a pretty good idea how the implementation of any notion of justice might affect that position. Recognizing this, Rawls hypothesizes a determination made from behind a "veil of ignorance."

Behind this veil, parties know neither their individual, natural abilities nor their position in society. By implication, then, they would not know what their position would be once the agreed-upon concept of justice were implemented.

According to Derek Phillips, there is a flaw in Rawls's argument here. In his zeal to place everyone in what he calls the "original position" behind this veil, Rawls strips them not only of their social status but also of all characteristics which distinguish them one from another. Phillips points out that this makes it impossible for them to have different viewpoints about the choice of principles to guide the just society.

> If . . . agents are deprived of all knowledge of their own specific identity, what is the nature of the "beings" who are supposed to think about social justice?[37]

Phillips has a point. Nonetheless, I continue to believe Rawls's concept provides us with a valuable insight in our attempt to find justice. While arriving at our conclusions, our goal must be to unfetter ourselves as much as possible from our personal circumstances.

Justice as Perceived by Robert Nozick

Do you have an intuitive notion that justice is served when those who have something are allowed to keep it? If so, Robert Nozick might be your choice for favorite theoretician.[38] His views are popular with those who wish to justify their present status.[39] He does this by focusing on the processes through which distribution comes about.

According to Nozick, one's holdings (or status) are "just" if the ways in which they came about were just. This "justice in holdings" says:

1. A person who acquires a holding in accordance with the principle of justice in acquisition is entitled to that holding.
2. A person who acquires a holding in accordance with the principle of justice in transfer, is entitled to the holding.
3. No one is entitled to a holding except by (repeated) applications of 1 and 2.[40]

If I obtained property properly then it is just that I have it, irrespective of how much I have relative to other people or of how little others have. The pattern of distribution is not of concern to Nozick. He points out, quite rightly I believe, that attempts to modify this pattern involve interferences in people's lives. I agree that it is desirable to minimize this interference. However, I am troubled by the difficulty in determining the extent to which property was initially justly acquired so that it could be justly transferred.[41,42] This point was succinctly made in the poem *The People, Yes* by Carl Sandburg:

"Get off this estate"
"What for?"
"Because it's mine"
"Where did you get it?"
"From my father"
"Where did he get it?"
"From his father"
"And where did he get it?"
"He fought for it"
"Well, I'll fight you for it."[43]

From Nozick's perspective, the only role of government in the distribution of wealth is to rectify unjust acquisitions. He makes a point on which reasonable people can reasonably disagree. On one hand, attempts to modify the distribution of income by use of the government mechanism, even in a democratic society, are fraught with difficulties. Some readers may take the position, perhaps even going beyond Nozick, that government should *never* be the means of addressing economic inequality. I recognize there is merit to this position. My responses, however, are twofold:

• As a democratic society, we have decided to take *some* governmental action against inadequate income.[44] A major theme of this book is that, given we have decided to take some action, the guaranteed adequate income makes much more sense than our present system.
• An argument for some minimum level of income for all, even those who have been unable to "justly acquire" any property, is necessary in order to enable everyone to enjoy the other benefits promised to them in the Constitution.

I next present a view of justice which is appealing to a great number of people, most notably many economists.

THE UTILITARIAN VIEW OF JUSTICE

The essence of utilitarianism is: *Actions or programs can be justified only if they increase the total wealth of all those involved.*

This notion formed a theoretical foundation for what became known during the 1980s as the "trickle-down theory." Proponents of this theory claimed that the first goal was to maximize production and thus wealth. Having accomplished this goal, we would see that even those on the lower rungs of the economic ladder benefited.

As in so many of these issues, there is merit to this argument. Even the poorest 10 percent of the population in the United States is relatively well off (in a historical and cross-cultural perspective) because the aggregate wealth in the United States is so great. Nonetheless, those who agree that increasing the wealth of the country as a whole is generally beneficial to all members of society may reasonably take issue with the implication that *any* efforts by government to meddle with the distribution of wealth will reduce the total wealth. My own position on this was affected to a great extent by an effect of the economic policies of the early 1980s.

My Neighbor and I, and the Trickle-Down Theory

In the 1980s, I lived next door to an extremely hardworking man. For much of his life, he worked two jobs, often returning from the night job only a few hours before he was due at his daytime construction job. This effort (coupled with his wife's income, also earned from hard work) yielded him a nice home, a nice car, and other amenities. Enter the new administration in the early 1980s and the (very real) need to control inflation in order to increase total wealth. The resulting economic policies knocked the bottom out of the construction industry. While I, a professor at a large state university, continued to draw my comfortable salary, my neighbor did his part to increase the total utility of the country—he became unemployed. Because of his pride, he was reluctant to even draw the unemployment compensation to which he was entitled. Once his ''contribution'' to the country became sufficiently great (that is, his unemployment lasted long enough), he did finally accept this benefit.

Why him and not me? That is a question to which the utilitarians have no answer. The ''justice'' of my neighbor's unemployment is an issue which cannot be accounted for by this theory. Utilitarianism provides no basis for decisions dealing with the *distribution* of incomes or wealth.

JUSTICE AS AN EMOTIONAL RESPONSE

Central to my discussion thus far, and to the writings of the cited authors, is a desire to make rational a concept of justice. An alternative basis for justice is provided by Robert Soloman. In his book *A Passion for Justice*,[45] he suggests we would be better served to allow our emotions to dictate the proper concept of justice. To wit:

> How we feel about justice obviously depends, in part, on how we see ourselves and our roles in the world. John Rawls may apply the liberal principles of justice to a selfless situation of rational deliberation, but I think that conservative critics are much closer to the mark when they argue (ad hominem) that liberalism is first of all a keen sense of personal guilt about one's own privileged place in the world. [46]

My interpretation of the central thesis from Soloman is: *Man should not seek justice, but rather be just.* In his own words:

The idea to be defended here is that justice is basically not an ideal state or a scheme for the way of the world or a perfect government system, but rather the way that one *lives*, the way that one *feels* [emphasis in the original].[47]

In his preface, Soloman describes how so many of us rationalize our not acting justly on the grounds that no system of applying justice is without fault. He thus appeals to our emotions, rather than to reason, as a basis for acting justly as individuals.

Among the emotions which Soloman states can, should, and do affect our notions of justice is resentment. He describes how resentment, often thought of as a pejorative term, can be the foundation for a system of justice. The essence is a generalization of observed injustices and a desire to correct them.

Resentment lies at the heart of democracy. . . . It is the will to power, not as mere reaction but as a keen sense of injustice, which is, in turn, the foundation of our sense of justice.[48]

It is hard even to imagine what justice would be without resentment.[49]

In his defense of resentment as a basis for justice, Soloman appears to conflict with those commentators who decry the "jealousy of liberals." According to this latter view, liberals are driven by a resentment of the fact that some people have a lot of money. The implication is that they, as individuals, feel personally aggrieved by this disparity. Soloman appears to be telling us that this is a perfectly noble basis for justice if, and only if, it is generalized to a larger group (to which the resenter may or may not belong).

Vengeance is another of the emotions Soloman defends as a basis for justice. His position relates well to my comments below, on criminal justice.

CRIMINAL JUSTICE

Although the subject of this book is economic justice, there are some significant parallels to concepts of criminal justice.[50] The determinist perspective leads to a clear conclusion regarding punishment. Criminals, like the rest of us, are products of their past. Their actions are determined by their heritage and their nurture. Granted they, like the rest of us,[51] make a choice when they commit the forbidden act. That choice, however, is a function of factors which determine their behavior. Is punishment, then, a viable alternative for those of us who accept this view?

The conclusion I offer is that we punish because we *must* punish. We recognize that society cannot function in the absence of official sanctions against certain behavior.

However, those of us who accept the determinist view are required—and this is a critical point—to punish with sympathy and empathy.[52] We must be prepared to say to the person who has violated society's norms:

"I am sorry that your life has been such that you were led to this behavior. However, in order to preserve a society as I conceive it, it is necessary to punish you for that behavior."

This may even apply to capital punishment. We must say *and mean it*: "May God have mercy on your soul."[53]

Punishment, from a determinist perspective, serves three purposes: First, the individual who has a propensity for anti-social behavior will be deterred to the extent he or she is incarcerated or executed. Second, it has an educational effect. It is much more visible than the written law which forms its basis. As a society, we clearly demonstrate what we find unacceptable. We also thus inform each other of what will happen if we commit a crime.[54]

Our system of punishment, from a determinist perspective, should not be labeled "criminal justice." A more appropriate term would be "necessary punishment."

Robert Soloman points out the third sense in which punishment is necessary. He quotes from the United States Supreme Court decision in the case of *Gregg vs. Georgia* (1976).

When people begin to believe that organized society is unwilling or unable to impose upon criminal offenders the punishment they "deserve," then there are sown the seeds of anarchy—of self-help, vigilante justice, and lynch law.[55]

Soloman introduces this quote during his defense of the emotion of vengeance as a motivating factor in justice. Although the desire for vengeance is a common emotional reaction, we would be better served to eliminate it as a driving force. Nonetheless, the contention that, as long as individuals harbor vengeance society must preempt their actions, I recognize as soundly reasoned.

The Irrationality of the Insanity Defense

One particularly troubling aspect of our criminal justice system, from a determinist perspective, is the insanity defense. While some may be found "innocent by reason of insanity," others are deemed "guilty by reason of inability to prove insanity." Everyone's behavior is caused by something; the idea of treating some differently because we can identify the cause, and the cause we identify is labeled and included in a lexicon of mental illnesses, is irrational.[56] We must punish for the act; we ought not to punish for who one is.[57]

In summary, punishment of anti-social behavior is, from a determinist vantage, founded only on necessity. We should take no pleasure in the meting out of punishment, but rather feel compassion for those whose lives have led them to create misery for others and themselves.

RECTIFYING LIFE'S INJUSTICES

As a committed determinist, I continue to believe and argue that no one deserves to get more from life than anyone else. I recognize that the way things work out, some people do get a better deal than do others. As the chapter title says, "Life is not fair." I contend, however, that "people can be (fair, just)." Acting either individually through our private associations or democratically through government, we can, and should, act to rectify life's injustices. Whether our actions are based upon the tenets of a religious faith or our emotions, or are the consequence of reasoned thought, is not particularly important. For those who already are driven by faith or emotion to correct what they perceive as economic injustices, my task is to suggest how and to what extent this might be done. For others, the goal has been to present conclusions from a reasoned argument why they should be so driven, and then to recommend this implementation of these conclusions in the economic realm.

The first issue in implementation is outcomes vs. opportunities.

Resources vs. Results

Do we agree at this point that no one deserves more (income, wealth, happiness, whatever) than anyone else, and that by life's natural unfairness, some get more than others, and that we (as individuals or as a society) should and can do something to offset this injustice? If so, what exactly is it we should try to do? The first quesion with which we need to deal is whether to try to make a change at the starting line or at the finish line.

Earlier in the chapter, I discussed briefly the contention/belief that "all men are created equal." I dismissed the notion[58] that this is taken to mean we all have equal ability to succeed (in jobs, in relationships, in sports, in life). Given this disparity, in what John Rawls termed the "natural lottery," should our goal be to minimize these differences? Should we *desire* that everyone have an equal chance? Of course. Should we *try to give* everyone an "equal chance"? I say no.

Although the equal-chance goal is perhaps the most intuitively appealing, it is impossible to implement. Perhaps our most sweeping attempt in this respect, in the United States, is public school education. But whereas we like to think of this as a great equalizer, it is nothing of the sort. When those who have greater natural learning ability are given the same education as those with less, the more able will still come out on top.[59] Only when we provide greater service to the less well endowed

do our efforts close the gap.[60] In addition, even the attempt to provide
e*qual* treatment is made more difficult by the natural tendency of
teachers to provide more help to the quicker (or more eager) learners.
This same point can be made even more strongly with respect to
athletics. How much effort do we put into helping the slow runners
become as fast as the already speedy, compared to the help we give the
naturally gifted to improve?

The above points are compounded by our current propensity to fund
the educational system at the local level. Starting from a well-established
tendency of those in poverty to do less well in school, we add to their
woes a less well-funded school system—a classic example of "the rich
(bright) get richer (better educated) and poor (less bright) get poorer (less
well educated)."

Not only do we currently do little to equalize opportunities, it may be
that any attempts to do so are destined to fail.[61] There is simply no way
in which transferable assets (e.g., money) can adequately compensate for
the value of nontransferable assets (e.g., intelligence). Head Start
programs are a classic example of this effort.

> Much of the support for Head Start is based on the belief that it levels the
> playing field for poor kids, as Bush put it in his 1988 campaign, "an equal
> place at the starting line."[62]

While there has been admittedly some success from these efforts,
there is also evidence that the gains no longer exist three or four years
after youngsters leave the programs.

> But now, a new long-term study suggests underprivileged youngsters need a
> much bigger boost if they are going to finish the race.[63]

As appealing as it might be to argue for a system in which we give
everyone an equal chance and then say, "The devil take the hindmost,"
this is simply not feasible. It is probably not even practical or desirable to
implement many programs which are designed to make some correction
in perceived imbalances. I argue, therefore, that our efforts must be
directed at rectifying the injustice of results.

Egalitarianism—Neither Possible nor Preferred

Having opted for a results-oriented program, I am compelled to describe
the type of results I envision. First, for comparison, I present the extreme
income distribution goal which is commonly referred to as
e*galitarianism*. This is the view that humankind should strive to equalize
conditions for all its members. The development and merits of this
position are well documented by Henry Phelps Brown.[64] Brown
distinguishes three applications of this doctrine:

• Of treatment: We must react to any one individual the same as we would to another engaged in the same behavior. Thus our criminal laws should treat each individual alike, and our system of compensation should award the same benefit for a given job no matter who performs the job.

• Of opportunity: We should develop mechanisms to ensure that each individual has an equal opportunity to succeed economically. Although some believe that this actually exists in the United States, we have argued that it is far from being realized.[65]

• Of consideration: This may be the version that comes to most minds when egalitarianism is mentioned. It suggests that everyone should end up with the same amount.

Brown suggests a number of impulses which lead some to advocate egalitarianism:

> Our spontaneous sympathy for our fellow men, the solidarity of the species; and the recognition that, in transfers from the rich to the poor, the rich lose less than the poor gain. These can be added to the ascetic impulse . . . ; those who themselves exercise self-restraint prefer arrangements in which moderation is enforced equally on all.[66]

As indicated earlier, I do not argue for an egalitarian outcome.[67] Although the dictates of justice demand such a distribution of resources, this is neither possible nor desirable.

Why Egalitarian Distribution Is Not Possible

Theoretically, it would be possible to equalize incomes in the United States. This could be accomplished through strict controls on income and/or with a tax policy designed to redistribute incomes. This would seem to be the epitome of economic justice. However, even this drastic step would leave us far short of any ultimate goal of comparable lifestyles.

Equal incomes would fail to provide equal lifestyles because of differential abilities to utilize the incomes. First, people are endowed with different levels of wealth. A prime example is ownership of a home, or even of land. For a given level of income, those who own property will be able to accomplish much more. Second, we are all endowed with different levels of ability. This will manifest itself in our sense of how to spend the money wisely.[68] This could be reflected in trades we make with others, with the swift taking advantage of the slower.[69] Finally, assuming we allow people to take risks with their income, some will by chance be rewarded and others not. Any egalitarian plan is destined to be thwarted by near-instant redistribution.

Why Egalitarian Distribution Is Not Desirable

The primary defense of unequal distributions of income and wealth is that they serve as incentives for people to be productive. In today's society, they appear to be the *primary* incentives. Indeed, it has long been thus:

> Inequality of property, in the degree in which it exists in most countries of Europe, abstractly considered, is an evil; but it is an evil which flows from those rules concerning the acquisition and disposal of property, by which men are incited to industry, and by which the object of their industry is rendered secure and valuable.[70]

The most commonly expressed, intuitive objection to equal distribution is the elimination of incentive. It is generally conceded that we are driven by economic motives to work and thus produce. We should note that it is at least theoretically possible that this motivation could be replaced with one based on altruism or a sense of accomplishment or service to a higher power. Nonetheless, I am not willing to argue that as a practical matter this possibility should form a basis for our decision making.[71]

Should those who want less be given the same amount as those who want more? Consider the ascetic. Having chosen a life of self-denial, would this person be appreciative if we said "Here, take the same amount everyone else has"? I think not. Granted, this person could give away immediately what we had imposed upon him or her, but what would be the point? True, there are very few of those around anymore, but there are different degrees of acquisitiveness. Given this unequal desire for material wealth, equal treatment might be taken to imply the unequal distribution of goods.

Another reason for preferring an unequal distribution of wealth is the good that can arise from the accumulation of resources by one person. The ability to commission works of art, sponsor new enterprises, and endow charitable activities are a few of the beneficial uses of accumulated wealth. It appears also to be the source of vicarious enjoyment for many of lesser wealth; witness the popularity of television shows like "Lifestyles of the Rich and Famous." In a later chapter, I'll discuss some of the negative consequences of large accumulations.[72] The reader must decide whether the scale should be tipped in favor of such accumulations. For now, the purpose is simply to note that there are some advantages.

A final argument I wish to make against distributing wealth equally is the inordinate emphasis on material well-being that is implied by such a distribution. It is ironic that many of those who would favor equal distribution are themselves opposed to measuring a person's worth by his or her economic status. Yet to emphasize the degree of distribution is to imply an importance. At this stage in the development of mankind, our emphasis as a society should be on reducing the importance of material goods. I am trusting the reader to remember that I continue to insist upon some adequate level of material well-being for everyone. It is only the redistribution, above this level, which I argue against.   Food for everyone, yes. Jewelry for everyone, no.

SOMETHING FOR EVERYONE, BUT MORE FOR SOME— JUSTICE AND REALITY RECONCILED

It is necessary, and may even be desirable, to allow disparities in wealth. It is neither necessary nor desirable to require that some go without an adequate income. My conclusion is that, in the economic sphere, a just society is one in which *all* citizens are accorded the economic resources necessary to provide them opportunities—opportunity to enjoy liberty, opportunity to improve their economic well-being, opportunity to live free of the fear of starvation.

Notes

1. The New York State Constitution has a provision requiring aid, care, and support of the needy. This is not, however, necessarily based on a right.

2. Since this is the reference in the document, I repeat it here. I am not, however, among those who feel that "men" means "men and women." Gender-neutral language is not just "politically correct," it is socially considerate and grammatically accurate.

3. As cited by Gilbert Cranberg in "Should Economic Rights Be Guaranteed by Law?," *Des Moines Register*, October 30, 1977, p. 2B.

4. Ibid.

5. To the extent our concept of rights is based on a Judeo-Christian heritage, we can take note of Biblical admonitions. For example, "Defend the poor and fatherless: do justice to the afflicted and needy," Psalm 82:3. In Jeremiah 5, where the sins of Judah are described, the civil leaders are criticized for, among other things, "the right of the needy do they not judge." Jeremiah 5:28, King James Version.

6. The whole area of what constitutes a right is itself very complex. David Miller discusses these complexities in *Social Justice*, especially the distinction between legal and moral rights and positive and ideal rights.

7. cf. Derek L. Phillips, *Toward a Just Social Order*, ''Unless people have adequate food, clothing, shelter, and health care, they cannot meaningfully exercise their right to freedom,'' p. 115.

8. John Locke bases his defense of private property on the right of those who clear a piece of land to own that land. ''This *Labour* being the unquestionable Property of the Labourer, no Man but he can have a right to what that is once joined to, at least where there is enough, and as good left in common for others.'' *(First and Second) Treatise on Government: an Essay Concerning the True, Original, Extent and End of Civil Government* (1690), in P. Laslett (ed.), *John Locke, Two Treatises of Government*, 2nd ed. (Cambridge, 1967), p. v, 27. As quoted in Henry Phelps Brown, *Egalitarianism and the Generation of Inequality*. Brown goes on to note ''but how did Locke cope with its application to Europe, where every inch was already appropriated? His only defence was to observe that the problem would never have arisen but for the invention of money,'' p. 61.

9. Poverty was a problem, but homelessness per se was not the issue.

10. The ability of a defendant to obtain justice is unavoidably related to that person's economic status. ''It works like this. On the one side is the indigent defendant represented by an overloaded public defender, or a lawyer appointed from the private bar and paid minimally by the courts. The public defender usually has very little time, resources or support staff to protect the rights of the client.'' Ray Cornell, ''What Is Price of Justice for America's Poor?'' *Des Moines Register*, September 21, 1992, p. 15A.

11. According to the 1993 United Nations Human Development Report, ''For millions of people all over the world, the daily struggle for survival absorbs so much of their time and energy that, even if they live in democratic countries, genuine political participation is, for all practical purposes, a luxury.'' As quoted in ''The Standard-of-Living Gap,'' *Des Moines Register*, May 16, 1993, p. 5C.

12. Jennifer Trusted, *Free Will and Responsibility,* p. 166.

13. Readers who cannot accept the deterministic view may well arrive at a different conclusion. Nonetheless, the process will still be useful to them.

14. For this point, and for much of the discussion of rights, I am indebted to David Miller, *Social Justice.*

15. To me, this is the most compelling basis. Nonetheless, those who don't share this view could still support the GAI, based on a religious/humanitarian position or on the economic efficiency/reduction of government interference argument.

16. One of the characters in Edward Bellamy's novel *Looking Backward: 2000-1887,* remarking on attitudes in the nineteenth century, likens society to a coach pulled by "toilers at the rope" with others riding comfortably on top. He says there were two reasons this was accepted. First, a belief it could not be changed, and second, "a singular hallucination which those on top of the coach generally shared that they were not exactly like their brothers and sisters who pulled at the rope, but of finer clay, in some way belonging to a higher order of being who might justly expect to be drawn," p. 13.

17. There are a variety of notions as to when this occurs—it could be when one dies, or at Armageddon, or after purgatory. In any case, it is at one point in time.

18. Once again, views differ on how this is achieved. For some, it requires a very specific act, including saying particular words.

19. Jesus said "Judge not, that ye be not judged." Matthew 7:1, King James Version.

20. This might be a good point at which to note that I claim no status as a religious scholar. My observations are based on a Methodist upbringing, close associations with many Catholics, and numerous discussions with those of other persuasions. I prefer to base my discussion on a lay interpretation of religious belief because it is the laity to whom I must appeal if I hope to bring about a guaranteed adequate income through the political process.

21. Naturally, this view must be extended not only to our fellow citizens in the United States, but also to people in other countries. That this is not a widely held sentiment was evident during the debate over the North American Free Trade Agreement. Much of the opposition was founded on the implicit assumption that those of us in the United States were somehow more deserving of the jobs and income that could be affected by this treaty. Some commentators were even explicit on this point, suggesting that Mexicans don't deserve the standard of living we have because their values are not as desirable as ours.

22. I make a distinction between "self-interest" and "selfishness." According to my dictionary, "selfish" is: "Caring only or chiefly for self; regarding one's own interests chiefly or solely; proceeding from love of self; influenced in actions solely by a view to private advantage." Thus one can be self-serving (making oneself feel good) without being selfish. Most would agree we are being selfish when we say to ourselves "To heck with them, I'm doing what I want." Ayn Rand makes a compelling argument for an innate but desirable selfishness in her novels.

23. Yes, our love for our children also dictates we want them to be well treated for their own sakes. But doesn't that also make us feel better?

24. This definitely falls into the category of those claims which we don't want to believe; however, let us not reject it out of hand for that reason.

25. Some would conclude this suggests rewarding cooperative behavior; others conclude that competitive behavior is best for the advancement of the species. It is not necessary for me to address this debate—whichever way, my point holds.

26. This view is supported by Henry Sidgwick: ''The only tenable Determinist interpretation of Desert is, in my opinion, the Utilitarian: according to which, when a man is said to deserve reward for any services to society, the meaning is that it is expedient to reward him, in order that he and others may be induced to render similar services by the expectation of similar rewards.'' *The Methods of Ethics,* p. 284.

27. Miller, *Social Justice*, pp. 103-113.

28. My own observation is that, in today's society, the use of rewards to encourage education has had a perverse effect on the acquisition of learning. Too many students miss the education in their efforts to get the monetary rewards. We end up rewarding degrees, not education.

29. Complicating even this criterion is the fact that, for many, productive work is preferable to leisure.

30. This leads to a perverse result when we ask, ''Should one whose life is basically miserable, and thus gives up little when going to work, be compensated *less* for the effort?''

31. B. F. Skinner, *Walden II*.

32. My goal is to provide the reader with a taste of these views. Since the authors require entire books to fully present the concepts, I cannot expect to provide a full description.

33. I am indebted to Phillips, *Toward a Just Social Order*, for a clear presentation of these theories, as well as insightful commentary. Phillips also provides an in-depth discussion of the views of Habermas and Gewirth, and concludes that the latter's theory is the most attractive. I was not convinced.

34. The primary source usually cited for Rawls's views is *A Theory of Justice*.

35. Phillips, *Toward a Just Social Order*, p. 59.

36. Rawls, *A Theory of Justice*, p. 25, as cited by Phillips, *Toward a Just Social Order*, p. 59.

37. Phillips, *Toward a Just Social Order*, p. 63.

38. A primary source of Nozick's views is *Anarchy, State, and Utopia*.

39. This might include those economic conservatives whose goal is to conserve what they have.

40. Nozick, *Anarchy, State, and Utopia,* p. 151, as cited in Phillips, *Toward a Just Social Order*, p. 69.

41. Phillips is also troubled: "Nozick's entitlement theory has the serious shortcoming of not adequately addressing the question of what constitutes an *originally just* holding." Phillips, *Toward a Just Social Order*, p. 72.

42. The Catholic Church has codified its view on this issue. In the revised catechism, they note: "Any manner of taking and unjustly holding the property of another, even if it does not specifically contradict civil law, is contrary to the Seventh Commandment [Thou shalt not steal]." As quoted in the *Des Moines Register*, November 17, 1992, p. 8A.

43. *The Complete Poems of Carl Sandburg,* pp. 483-484. This exchange is a part of verse 37 of the epic poem. This poem is also reproduced as a preface to the novel *Trespass*, by Fletcher Knebel. In this story, a group of African Americans are intent upon setting up a black nation in a number of southern states. They plan to hold wealthy landowners hostage until their demands are met. The black revolutionaries argue the justice of their position similarly to Sandburg.

44. I refuse to refer to "the government" as something separate from the people because I continue to believe our government ultimately responds to the views of the people. Therefore, I say "we" when referring to governmental actions.

45. Robert C. Soloman, *A Passion for Justice.*

46. Ibid., p. 256.

47. Ibid., p. 15.

48. Ibid., p. 270.

49. Ibid., p. 272.

50. A difference is also important. When it comes to criminal justice, the status quo from birth is acceptable—i.e., continued freedom for those who do not violate the law. In the economic sphere, the status quo may not be acceptable, to the extent we agree affirmative action is necessary to rectify the situation for those who have zero resources. As noted elsewhere, this was not as great a problem when bountiful, natural resources were available to all as a birthright. This latter point is recognized in the recent revision of the Catechism of the Catholic Church: "The church's once-sacrosanct stance on private property has been modified to state that the Earth is the heritage of all mankind." As reported in the *Des Moines Register*, November 17, 1992, p. 8A.

51. As a frequent speeder, once-upon-a-time underage drinker, and single-occasion user of marijuana (I didn't inhale—really! Maybe that's why I never used it again?) I am admittedly being disingenuous when I refer to criminals as "they."

52. "There but for the grace of God go I."

53. My point is not so much that we need to invoke the idea of God as it is to demonstrate that genuine compassion is in order.

54. I'm sure there is some deterrent effect. I'm not sure how strong it is. Convicted murderer David Lawson, interviewed on the NBC Television *Today Show*, May 10, 1994, while awaiting execution, made the case that punishment does not deter because criminals do not think they are going to get caught.

55. Soloman, *A Passion For Justice*, pp. 284-285.

56. David Lawson (see footnote above) also discussed his clinical depression, suffered most of his life. In his case, this was not sufficient grounds to benefit from the insanity defense.

57. Relevant to this point is a comment made by reporter Diane Sawyer on ABC's *Prime Time Live*, July 17, 1996. In a story about prison inmates in Louisiana, she asked "Are we to judge people by the worst thing they ever did?"

58. Talk show host Rush Limbaugh dismisses the entire idea: "Equality is a totally flawed premise. It's not possible," January 3, 1994. Some years earlier, Jeremy Bentham expressed a similar view: "The establishment of equality is a chimera: the only thing which can be done is to diminish inequality," quoted in J. Bowring (ed.), *Works of Jeremy Bentham*, Vol. 1 (London, 1843), and cited in Brown, *Egalitarianism and the Generation of Inequality*, p. 159.

59. By "more able" I mean not only those with greater natural intelligence but also those with greater natural motivation, longer attention spans, better physical health, *ad infinitum*.

60. This type of effort is seen in our special education programs. Is it reasonable to expect that we would apply this same logic to provide greater attention to those who are just somewhat less intelligent? I doubt it.

61. John Roemer demonstrates this point in his paper "Equality of Talent." He describes two methods of attempting to achieve an "equality of resources." The first, an "equal-division mechanism" may make worse off the people whose position we had hoped to improve. The second method is an insurance mechanism, proposed by Ronald Dworkin (cf., "What is Equality? Part 2: Equality of Resources," *Philosophy and Public Affairs* 10: 283-345). Roemer suggests, quite rightly I believe, that Dworkin's attempt to develop a mechanism

which is "ambition-sensitive" but not "endowment-sensitive" fails on the grounds that ambition is a part of one's endowments.

62. "A Head Start Does Not Last," *Newsweek*, January 27, 1992, pp. 44-45.

63. Professor J. S. Fuerst of Chicago Loyola University School of Social Work studied kids who attended six special, publicly funded schools for 2 years of preschool and 2-7 years in an intensive elementary-school program. "In 1974, when he first looked at reading—and math—test scores of center graduates, Fuerst found that they outranked their neighborhood peers and even exceed national norms. . . . A decade later . . . he found that many of those early gains had been lost. Only 62 percent graduated from high school. That was better than the 49 percent graduation rate among a control group . . . but well under the national average," ibid.

64. Brown, *Egalitarianism and the Generation of Inequality*.

65. Reporting a study of inequality in various countries, Henry Phelps Brown states: "The confidently held belief that the United States had attained a social equality unknown in Europe and has stood out in particular as the land of opportunity, was seen to be unfounded. But there is no question of the self-image of the American people," Ibid., p. 243. And later: "[Americans] have their own egalitarianism already. It is realized in an equality of manners that proclaims the absence of class distinctions, and through a belief in equality of opportunity which, whatever the facts, encourages young people to set out with hope and vigor," p. 245.

66. Ibid., p. 48.

67. Brown notes that even Karl Marx was not an egalitarian. "His [Marx] basic objection to capitalism is that of Shelley—it denies mankind self-realization. The aim of change is not to make people equal, but to set their spirits free to realize their humanity," ibid., p. 208.

68. Of course, it is also reflected in a differential ability to make more money, but if that additional income is also controlled, this will make no difference.

69. David Hume expressed this succinctly: "Render possessions ever so equal, man's different degrees of art, care and industry will immediately break that equality," *Essays, Moral, Political and Literary*, T. H. Green and T. H. Grose (eds.), 2 vols. London, 1875, as cited in Brown, *Egalitarianism and the Generation of Inequality*, p. 107.

70. W. Paley, *The Principles of Moral and Political Philosophy*, London (1785), III, pt. 1, ch. II, as quoted in Brown, ibid., p. 111.

71. The point is made similarly by Arthur Okun, "Abstracting from the costs and consequences, I would prefer more equality of income to less and would like complete equality of income best of all. . . . In pursuing such a goal, society would forego any opportunity to use material rewards as incentives to production. And that would lead to inefficiencies that would be harmful to the welfare of the majority. . . . Insofar as inequality does serve to promote efficiency. . . . I can accept some measure of it as a practicality." As cited by John Cobbs in "Egalitarianism: Threat to a Free Market," *Business Week*, December 1, 1975, p. 84. Cobbs referred to Okun's book (*Equality and Efficiency, The Big Tradeoff*) as "the coolest and most objective appraisal of the egalitarians yet to appear."

72. Management consultant Michael Vance made an interesting point in this regard in a lecture to the annual meeting of the Society of Chartered Property and Casualty Underwriters (October 27, 1993), "When you get too many resources, you get arrogant, which makes you indifferent."

2

Are You Worthy?

Current U.S. Welfare Programs

We now know what a just economic distribution should look like and realize there are some practical limitations on making it totally just. The task in this chapter is to evaluate our current public assistance programs to determine how well they achieve the goal of justice.[1]

The main point of the evaluation is that the philosophy behind our present programs is quite different from the dictates of justice developed thus far in this book. The primary evidence of this is the "categorical" nature of these programs. They attempt to segregate those who are deemed to be "worthy" of benefits from those who are not.[2] At the base of this approach is a belief that certain people who are in poverty are deserving of public assistance and others are not. Since we have argued previously that the notion of "deserving" cannot form the foundation for a just system, the current philosophy is flawed.

In discussing our present public assistance programs my emphasis is on the significant characteristics, with minimal attention to details. The significant characteristics are those subject to criticism from the vantage point of the requirements of justice as established earlier in this book. As indicated in the Introduction, I won't attempt to prove any points through the use of facts. Details change frequently, as evidenced by the recent "welfare reform" legislation; the underlying philosophy and the implied attitudes toward the poor, as revealed by the major provisions, are the relevant targets.

CURRENT PUBLIC ASSISTANCE PROGRAMS IN THE UNITED STATES

These programs will be presented under three headings. The first group is the "categorical" programs. In order to receive benefits from one of these programs, the individual must show that his or her poverty is a function of certain allowable personal characteristics. The second group is those which provide "in-kind" benefits where those in need are given assistance in the form we, as a society, have determined is best for them. Rather than simply providing cash to alleviate their poverty, we provide food, housing, or medical care. While this type of benefit is not necessarily contrary to the dictates of justice, it is subject to criticism on other grounds. The third group is those which "leak" benefits to those who are not in poverty. While ostensibly designed to alleviate poverty, they aid many who are far from being poor.

The Categorical Public Assistance Programs

Supplemental Security Income (SSI)

To be deemed worthy of benefits under this program, one must be aged, blind, or disabled. This federal system has replaced programs previously run at the state level. It provides a monthly income to those who qualify.

Each of the three eligibility categories under this program requires standards for determining who is entitled to benefits. Benefits are available under the "aged" category for those who are over a certain age.[3] We[4] have chosen an age over which poor people are deemed worthy of our assistance. Presumably this is because we don't feel it's necessary for them to seek employment. The arbitrary nature of this limitation is evident when one considers there are many people over this age who are capable of, and interested in, working, while many under this age cannot find employment.

To qualify for benefits to the blind, one's vision impairment must exceed some level. Not only is this eligibility level itself arbitrary, but so is the whole idea of stipulating one type of disability. This is undoubtedly a result of the sympathy blindness elicits from the general public. One must ask, however, why not deafness or quadriplegia, or a host of other disabling afflictions?[5]

The disability portion of this program suffers not only from the infliction of the categorical requirement but also from the tremendous bureaucratic burden of determining just who meets the requirement. Whereas it is relatively easy to determine age and vision ability, other types of disability are very difficult to assess. Rules must be written and ad hoc decisions made in individual cases. Appeals must be handled, ultimately with a drain on the judicial system. Since the determination is a medical one, there are unavoidably cases of persons qualifying who, because of a strong will to work and/or because of a demand for their talents, could be gainfully employed. Others, who for one reason or another, cannot work but who are unable to prove they are disabled, are excluded from benefits. Still others are granted benefits for "disabilities" such as drug addiction, which many find an objectionable basis for government assistance.[6]

The problem of making determinations in this area is further compounded by the increasing recognition of mental disabilities. These limitations run the gamut from those whose overall mental ability is that of a young child to those whose chronic depression prevents them from holding down a job. It could include those whose fear of being out in public manifests itself as a diagnosable psychosis. Many would be reluctant to provide special benefits to someone afraid to go to work, but if a person can prove that fear meets certain medical requirements, he or she could be deemed eligible. Even children who have mental and behavioral impairments which impede their ability to function in an "age-appropriate manner" can be eligible.[7]

It is important to recall at this point the essence of this discussion. It is not to criticize certain categories. It is rather to point out the injustice of "categorizing" in general. Public assistance benefits should be a function of one's income, not of income *plus* some arbitrary category.

The Aid to Families with Dependent Children (AFDC) Program

In kicking this program around, I will have lots of company. It bears the brunt of the criticisms of our "welfare" programs.[8] Unfortunately, the common criticism is of the beneficiaries rather than the provisions of the program. Welfare recipients are commonly criticized for their perceived propensity to take advantage of the system. This does not go unnoticed by the recipients themselves. According to one former welfare mother:

> We were ensnared in the ugliest system for responding to people in dire need that could be imagined. It was beyond belief, a bottomless pit of cruelty. Recipients were treated like untouchables in the newspapers, by all the politicians who opened their mouths about us, by every institution we came into contact with.[9]

"They" are often discussed as though they were a distinct culture of people whose values are very different from those held by "us."

Are "they" different?

I am somewhat reluctant to address this issue here because the discussion can become very lengthy. Nonetheless, we must at least recognize the culture vs. situation debate. The essence of the controversy is this: Do those in poverty represent a distinct subculture with ingrained characteristics differentiating them from those of us who are not so afflicted? One's answer to this question will explain, to a great extent, the position he or she will take on programs designed to alleviate poverty.

This is one of those issues on which reasonable people can reasonably disagree.[10] Over the years, I have read many compelling arguments on both sides.[11] On balance, I side with the "situationalists." I agree with George Orwell when he said:

[Many have the] idea there is some mysterious, fundamental difference between rich and poor, as though they were two different races . . . . But in reality there is no such difference. The mass of the rich and the poor are differentiated by their incomes and nothing else, and the average millionaire is only the average dishwasher dressed in a new suit. Change places, and handy dandy, which is the justice, which is the thief?[12]

Teresa Funiciello, herself a former welfare recipient and one who has worked with a multitude of the poor, says:

When their personal conditions, like quality child care, are right and they are asked to learn and do something that gives them pride, poor women will jump at the opportunity like anybody else.[13]

Similar views were expressed by Bill Leonard and Jane Schorer regarding welfare recipients in Iowa:

A common misconception holds that welfare is a way of life for some people, that generation after generation chooses welfare over working. . . . The misconceptions come from ignorance. Few Iowans know welfare recipients personally. . . . In any company, in any system—maybe in any family—there are those who don't want to carry their share of the load. But mostly, it seems, there are people who got caught off guard.[14]

I side with Ernest Hemingway in the reputed and much-quoted exchange between him and F. Scott Fitzgerald. As reported by Michael Harrington, they said:

Fitzgerald: "The rich are different."

Hemingway: "Yes, they have money."[15]

In fairness, I should note Harrington sides with Fitzgerald. According to Harrington:

Fitzgerald had much the better of the exchange. He understood that being rich was not a simple fact, like a large bank account, but a way of looking at reality, a series of attitudes, a special type of life. If this is true of the rich, it is ten times truer of the poor.[16]

Harrington also makes a strong case and deserves credibility. I don't quarrel with his observations, but rather with the implications. I agree that being in poverty has a significant effect on a person's behavior and outlook. This is undoubtedly an experience which helps "determine" who a person is. The point to be made is that any of "us" who found ourselves in this position would likely develop similar characteristics.[17]

By the same token, and here is the crux, removing this condition will create a climate in which "they" will behave very much like "us." The length of time it takes for one to adjust will be a function of the length of time spent in the previous condition. Nonetheless, to the extent the poor are different, it is only temporary and, to a great extent, a consequence of, rather than a cause of, poverty.[18]

It is thus the system, rather than those in need, which should be criticized. Funiciello refers to it as a

> crude and irrational system of income distribution, usually capricious and often downright cruel.[19]

Who Should Qualify for This Program?

The AFDC program provides a classic example of how good intentions can go awry (or the Law of Unintended Consequences). The original idea was that poor single-parents of young children needed and deserved help. Since this parent was needed in the home to care for the child(ren), society should not demand that she obtain employment in order to survive.[20] In addition, the children themselves could not be expected to work.

It is the eligibility criterion in AFDC which has been blamed for the crisis not only in our welfare system but to some extent in society in general. It is partly on this point that Charles Murray has built a strong case against our current welfare system.[21] He begins his criticism by presenting facts showing the number of people in poverty increasing, at the same time significantly more money was being spent to eliminate it. In his opinion, the nature of the program is such that it is destined to swell the ranks of those receiving benefits.[22] He describes how a rational decision maker who is poor and has children would choose to not marry and receive AFDC benefits rather than get married and go to work.

The original notion has been tweaked by the federal policy makers over time. Realizing that payments made to only single-parent households has led to the breakup of many families, Congress decided to permit the states to provide some benefits to two-parent families. Some states elected to do this, but, of course, the requirements for qualifying are quite stringent. There must be an acceptable reason why one of the family members is not working.

A reduction of the breadth of the program was attempted by some states in the late 1950s, when efforts were made to ban illegitimate children from benefits.[23]

A belief that mothers could and perhaps should be working outside the home has led in the past to the development of programs to assist and even compel participation in the work force. It was also incorporated in the federal law in the welfare reform legislation of 1996. Mothers who have no children under the age of six will be limited to two years on AFDC, after which they will be required to work outside the home.

The Work (Dis) Incentives

In order to qualify for AFDC, one must have earnings and wealth below stipulated levels. Once one establishes eligibility on this criterion, recipients must continue to comply with income and wealth restrictions. In the early years of this program, the recipients' employment earnings were used to offset the benefits on a dollar-for-dollar basis. The rationale was that if they were earning some money, they did not need as much from the AFDC program. As might be expected, this created a substantial work disincentive, as it was the equivalent of a 100 percent tax on wages. In order to create an incentive for employment, the program was changed to allow recipients to keep some of their earnings. Under the "30-and-a-third-rule," the first $30 in monthly earnings and one-third of the remainder is exempt from this offset requirement. While this is an improvement, it should be noted that the 67 percent "tax" is still quite stiff.[24,25]

Perhaps the most significant disincentive for going to work is the possibility of losing eligibility for AFDC benefits entirely, and thus losing Medicaid benefits.[26]

The wealth limitation also poses a problem. Should recipients try to save some money out of earnings, they might exceed the allowable level of property. This makes it difficult for one to develop some economic security, or to accumulate property which would make life easier and allow them to become independent of welfare. For example, programs generally limit the value of one's car.

Welfare Reform

Over the past decade, a number of states have passed some form of welfare reform legislation. In 1996, the federal government enacted significant welfare reform legislation. I present the essence of and reactions to these bills.

State Legislation

Iowa's Reform. The 1993 legislature enacted a plan to allow welfare families who have employment to keep much more of their earnings without losing their state benefits. In exchange, most recipients were required to sign written contracts agreeing to steps toward achieving financial self-sufficiency. In these agreements, recipients promise to take specific actions to find and keep jobs. The contract specifies a termination date for the receipt of state benefits. Failure to live up to the terms of the agreement results in reduction or elimination of benefits.

The only exceptions to the requirement are those already working, the disabled, and mothers with a child younger than six months old.

Under the program, a three-member family can earn nearly $17,000 a year before losing welfare payments and Medicaid coverage. Under the old system, state support would end when earnings reached about $9,000. In addition, the amount of assets a recipient can have without losing benefits is increased. For example, the plan increases to $3,000 from $1,500 the value of a car that may be owned by a recipient. The state has also decided to promote family stability by making it easier for two-parent families to qualify for welfare.

The hope is that the work incentives built into the new plan will result in more welfare recipients finding jobs, leading to a reduction in caseload and thus lowered costs. There is concern, however, that by subsidizing low-wage employment, the plan will dramatically increase the number of people on welfare.[27] There is also criticism that a lack of funding for a sufficient number of caseworkers will destine the program for failure.[28] The greatest cause for concern, however, has to be the absence of jobs. According to one observer:

> It's a loser. The one thing that tells us to a virtual certainty that this program will not work is that there are no jobs.[29]

An overall critical assessment of the program was given by a Des Moines poverty lawyer who said that by requiring the work contracts:

> The state takes the . . . benevolent role of protector and partner of (welfare) recipients while at the same time retaining power to terminate benefits when it sees fit.[30]

The Wisconsin Experiment. End welfare by 1999—this is the grand goal set by the Wisconsin legislature. Labeled ''Work, Not Welfare,'' the plan is to replace welfare with plans connecting people to work. As a step in that direction, the state is conducting an experiment with 1,000 test cases. These recipients have been put on a two-year time limit for their welfare benefits. In exchange, the state is making efforts to find them work.[31] In testimony before the Senate Welfare Reform Committee, State Senator Antonio Riley noted:

> The current system is so flawed, that reform is impossible. It must be scrapped and replaced with programs connecting people to work.[32]

Criticism of this plan was succinctly stated by Ruth Conniff:

> Politicians are acting as if by doing away with welfare they can outlaw poverty. . . . The poor will still be with us in 1999. . . . It is easier to attack the poor than it is to do something about poverty.[33]

The Vermont Plan. As of July 1, 1994, Vermont put time limits of thirty months on welfare benefits. After that, parents with children under thirteen years of age must work one-half time. If no jobs are available, jobs will be created.[34]

For those who refuse work, benefits will not be terminated (because of concern for the welfare of the children). However, their financial matters will be taken over by the state. Payments will be made directly to vendors for housing, food, and utilities, with a goal of reducing to a minimum the disposable cash available to the family.

Vermont has added incentives for obtaining work. They will subsidize child care, allow the recipient to keep more of the earned income, retain Medicaid for up to thirty-six months, and accumulate assets in excess of those traditionally allowed for AFDC qualification. The state does not expect to save money (at least in the short run) with this reform. The primary goal is to foster a culture of working, rather than welfare. According to Governor Dean:

> Nobody owes anybody a living. What we owe them is a standard of decency. Welfare fosters a culture of poverty.[35]

In order to study the effects of this plan, Vermont has established two demonstration programs: one with a thirty-month time limit and one with no time limits. These will be compared with the experience of a control group operating under the current system.

The New Jersey Reform. New Jersey provides an example of the states which have attempted to reduce the number of children on welfare by capping the benefits for additional children. Since August of 1993, women on welfare who have another child are denied additional cash assistance. While an early study found there were positive effects of this law, a later, more extensive study determined there was "no reduction in the birthrate of welfare mothers attributable to the family cap."[36]

The Federal Welfare Reform Legislation of 1996

Ironically, on the eve of publication of this book, Congress passed a bill which reflects attitudes diametrically opposed to those espoused in this book and which incorporates provisions going in the opposite direction of what is proposed herein. This is propitious in the sense that it justifies the subtitle of this book, "Welfare Reform for the 21st Century." I am aware that a paradigm shift in public thinking about welfare and welfare recipients is necessary in order for my proposals to bear fruit. My prediction is that the current legislation will verify the contention of those of us who feel that it is the wrong approach, and speed the acceptance of the alternative.

The legislation was prompted by a feeling among many legislators, and indeed by many citizens, that something was dramatically wrong with welfare. There was even a view frequently expressed that the current system was *causing* poverty, primarily by encouraging illegitimate births. An insightful reaction to this line of thinking was provided by Professor Frances Fox Piven in a *New York Times* editorial.[37] Professor Piven compares today's line of reasoning to that which prevailed in early nineteenth-century England. At that time many argued that giving the poor even meager quantities of bread harmed the poor themselves. This attitude led to the development of the workhouse, which was eventually replaced with the modern system of social assistance. Today, according to Piven, a similar attitude prevails—that welfare is responsible for the moral problems in society:

> Never mind low wages and irregular work; never mind the spreading social disorganization to which they lead; never mind changes in family and sexual norms occurring among all classes and in all Western countries. The solution is to slash welfare.[38]

Professor Piven goes on to note:

> Other facts also argue against the welfare-causes-illegitimacy argument. Most obvious, welfare benefits set by the states have declined sharply since 1975, while the out-of-wedlock birthrate has risen nationwide. In addition, there is no discernible relationship between the widely varying levels of benefits provided by the states and the out-of-wedlock birth rates in the states.[39]

Herewith, the essential elements of the legislation.

Block Grants to the States. Reflecting the view that "Washington doesn't have all the answers," and a general desire on the part of most Republicans to turn over more power to the states, this provision sends to the states lump sums of tax money to be administered at the state's discretion (within constraints imposed in the legislation).

A significant implication of this provision is that the long-standing federal guarantee of a minimum income to poor children will end.[40]

Work Requirements. Among the constraints imposed by the federal government is a requirement that states find ways to move welfare recipients into work.[41] Failure to accomplish this with a sufficient percentage of recipients can result in loss of some of the federal funding. A particularly controversial aspect of this provision is that it applies even to mothers of young children (except those age five and less) and even if they cannot find adequate daycare facilities. (An earlier version of the bill had limited the application of this provision to mothers with children over eleven.)

In a speech before the Senate during debate on this bill, Senator Christopher Dodd (Dem, Conn.) provided an interesting perspective on this provision. He noted that there are currently 270 million Americans, of whom 13 million receive AFDC benefits. Of these, 9 million are under the age of 18 (80% of those are under the age of 12 and 50% are under the age of 6). Two million of the adults are unemployable. Thus, according to Senator Dodd, the goal is to put 1 million of the remaining 2 million adults to work, while putting the 9 million children in jeopardy.[42]

Senator Dianne Feinstein (Dem, Calif.) also noted that more than one-half of welfare recipients lack a high school education and two-thirds live in central cities from whence jobs have fled. Partly for these reasons no state in six years has been able to move 50 percent of welfare recipients into jobs.[43]

Some of the concerns of those on welfare were presented in a *New York Times* article, where it was noted that at least one single mom

> suspected that the ''work'' legislators were promising would end up being one more government myth about how, with enough effort and hope, things turn out for the best.[44]

Lifetime Welfare Limits. This provision reflects an increasingly prevalent view that welfare benefits were becoming a ''way of life.''[45] Recipients will be limited to a total of five years of benefits (although the states are allowed to lower this limit). States are, however, allowed to make ''hardship'' exceptions for up to 15 percent of families.

Lifestyle Restrictions on Teenage Mothers. States are permitted to make payments to unmarried teenage parents only if a mother under the age of eighteen stays in school and lives with an adult. This provision reflects a view that women are getting pregnant for the purpose of obtaining welfare benefits and thus being enabled to leave home. The implied goal is a reduction in teenage pregnancies.[46]

Food Stamp Limitations. Able-bodied adults who are not raising children will be allowed to receive food stamps only for three months in any three-year period (unless they are unemployed, in which case another three months will be added). In addition, illegal immigrants no longer are eligible.

Although there were numerous other provisions in this bill, those listed above are the ones most relevant to the issues being raised in this book.

The "Elimination" Proposal

A reform option which has also received significant attention is the proposal by Charles Murray to do away with welfare programs entirely and replace them with nothing.[47] While I agree with the logic behind his argument for doing away with the present system, I disagree with his assumption that poor people will be able to get jobs or rely on private or family aid. I believe the government has a role to play; it should be an entirely different role than is now being played.

Unemployment Compensation

This program was first established as part of the Social Security Act of 1935. Although a federal law, it gave the states the option to set up their own program if they wished. If their programs meet the minimum standards established by the federal law, they receive most of the Federal Unemployment Tax Act (FUTA) revenues collected in their state.[48] To be deemed worthy of benefits under this program, recipients must pass three primary, categorical requirements. They must be unemployed, they must have "paid their dues," and they cannot be unemployed too long.

The Unemployment Requirement

To be eligible for unemployment compensation benefits one must, as would be expected, be unemployed. In addition, however, the unemployment must be "involuntary." Benefits are generally restricted to those who are unemployed "through no fault of their own." This makes sense in an insurance-type program. We don't want people to be able to simply choose unemployment—that is, to quit work—in order to receive benefits.

On the other hand, states now provide compensation in numerous instances where the person was not laid off, but rather made a decision to leave employment. These exceptions to the general rule have led to very complex regulations and considerable litigation. Benefits may be available when one quits "for good cause attributable to the employer" or "for compelling personal reasons."

Quitting May Be OK. As this program aged, it has become apparent there are many people who, although not technically laid off, are "worthy" of benefits. For one reason or another, their quitting is deemed to be justified. One rationale for this is that the work conditions were intolerable. Examples include situations where there was a physical threat to the person's health, and where the employer was harassing the employee. There have also been cases where the employee was asked to do something which conflicted with her or his moral values.[49]

The other general case of "quitting is O.K." arises when an employee feels compelled to tend to some personal business for a period of time and then returns to find no work available. For example, a family member may be seriously ill or a doctor may have prescribed the employee or a family member to spend time in a warmer climate. If, for these reasons, the employee quits for a period of time, returns, and seeks the old job back, and is told that no work is available—at that point, the former employee may become eligible for unemployment compensation benefits.

I have only described the bare bones of these rules here. The specifics and court cases applying them are voluminous. My purpose is neither to make the reader conversant with the rules nor to evaluate the merits of the specific rules. It is rather to point out the morass into which one falls when trying to actualize a categorical program such as this. Another example of rule modifications arises when someone is fired.

Being Fired for Cause May Be OK. As might be expected, benefits will often be denied when an employee is fired for good cause—for example, if one has been consistently late or if one steals from the employer. To allow benefits in these circumstances would be to condone the behavior and/or to allow the employees to ostensibly quit (by forcing the employer to fire them). However, most states allow at least partial benefits to be paid even in some misconduct situations. While it is true that benefits are denied entirely in cases of "gross misconduct" (e.g., stealing), for some of the lesser offenses (e.g., chronic lateness) there may be only a waiting period during which no benefits are paid. After that, the still-unemployed may collect. Again, whether these are good or bad rules is not the issue here. I simply decry the complexity and arbitrariness of the rules, and note that they necessarily arise from efforts to limit benefits to "worthy" people.

The Work Requirement

Because this is an insurance program, premiums must be paid for the coverage. The premiums (or taxes) are paid by employers as a percentage of salaries. In order to qualify for benefits, one must have been employed for a minimum period of time, and thus have had taxes paid on one's behalf. The primary impact of this rule is that those who have never been employed are not eligible for benefits. They are not deemed "worthy" by this system—this, in spite of the fact that one who has never been able to find a job or has been employed for less than the required time period is probably at least as much in need as someone who has been employed for a period of time.

The amount of the tax is a function of the recent experience of the employer. Those employers who have had a greater number of former employees drawing benefits will pay higher taxes. One of the effects of this experience rating is that employers have a stake in whether benefits are provided. This helps contribute to the substantial amount of litigation between employees and employers over whether a person is entitled to benefits.

The Benefit Limitation

Benefits are commonly payable for only twenty-six weeks. In periods of high unemployment, extended benefits may be available for a longer period. From the standpoint of the individual, it does not make sense to set the benefits as a function of the overall unemployment level. Granted, it may be harder for many to find jobs under those circumstances. Nonetheless, the individual who has been unsuccessful in job hunting in a period of low unemployment needs the benefits just as much as someone whose lack of success occurred during a period of high unemployment.

These categorical requirements mean one must be deemed "deserving" of benefits in order to get public assistance. This is not a just system.

The Earned-Income Tax Credit

For those persons employed in low-wage jobs this provides a supplement to their earnings. By filing Federal Schedule EIC along with the Form 1040 income tax form, a qualifying individual can receive a once-a-year check. The amount of the check is a percentage of the person's earnings.[50]

This is a popular program in that it aids the esteemed working poor. However, it is still a categorical program in that only employed persons can apply. In addition,

> it is sufficiently complex that hundreds of thousands of people who are eligible for it now do not apply, while many others who are not supposed to receive the credit do claim it, often without triggering an audit.[51]

I turn next to a criticism of those programs which provide benefits in forms other than cash.

The In-Kind Public Assistance Programs

A widely held belief is benefits should not be paid to poor people in cash, but rather in the form of goods which the poor need. Contributing to this conclusion is the belief "they" will not spend cash wisely—that they will waste it on booze or gambling or cars. At the root of this belief is the feeling that the poor are different from the rest of us; while "we" spend our money wisely, "they" would not. As I indicated previously, I do not subscribe to that view. Many do, however, and that has led to food stamps,[52] subsidized housing, Medicaid, school lunches, infant nutrition programs, and more.

The Food Stamp Program

Many are surprised to discover this program is administered by the Department of Agriculture. They are unaware the program was originally passed as a means to help farmers. The feeling was that by stimulating the purchase of food, we would increase demand and thus prices. Wasn't it nice that, at the same time, we would also help other poor people? This program has grown to the point where it benefits more people than any of our other public assistance programs.

Who Is Eligible?

Benefits are available not only to the unemployed but also to many working poor. The number of stamps one can receive is a function of income and family size.

What Is Food? Complexity is introduced into this program not only by the eligibility requirements but also by the need to determine just what constitutes food. One cannot simply take these stamps to a grocery store and pay the bill. Among the items which cannot be bought with these stamps are cleaning supplies, paper products, cigarettes, and alcohol. I suspect most would agree that at least some of these are reasonable limitations. We should take note, however, of the extent to which we (through government) substitute our judgment for that of the person doing the purchasing. If the individual's most pressing need is for soap, and he or she has no cash, the person is precluded from purchasing this.

The other side of this issue creates the most controversy. There are almost no limitations on the types of food which can be purchased. Everyone knows of someone (or knows someone who knows someone) who was in line behind a welfare person using food stamps, and observed him or her purchasing frozen dinners or steaks or lobster or some such. It is not surprising that many are aggrieved by this observation, particularly when they themselves do not feel they can afford such luxuries. I contend, however, this is simply evidence of the difficulty running any program which attempts to limit the way resources are used. We do not stipulate the portion of a person's *earned* income to be spent for food nor criticize that person's choice of food. Why do we feel we should do so with poor people?[53] Are we to deny them the benefit of convenience or the enjoyment of their favorite food?[54]

Alternative Food Programs

There are a number of other ways in which we attempt to provide the poor with food. Soup kitchens, surplus commodities programs, and food banks are a few. I agree with Funiciello when she says:

Establishing institutionalized begging sites was never a solution. Poor people lacked the normal means of access: money. Anything other than that would become a means of further separating the haves and the have-nots.[55]

Food banks, where donated food is collected and distributed to needy recipients, are a noble idea. However, they have problems. Much of the donated "food" is not. It consists of snacks, candy, and nonfood items in many cases.[56] The tax deduction allowed businesses for these donations is questionable. Usually the product is being donated because it cannot be sold. If it can't be sold, it has no value. Yet the donor values it for the purposes of a tax deduction.

The school lunch program, administered by the Department of Agriculture, is another source of subsidized meals. This is supplemented with a Summer Food Service Program for Children. In the latter, sponsors may operate feeding sites in geographical areas in which at least half of the children live in low-income households or at sites where half of the children participating are from low-income families. The latter program has been criticized because of its failure to reach a high percentage of the target population.[57]

Subsidized Housing

There have been, over the years, a variety of methods for providing housing assistance through government. At one end of this spectrum are the council houses in Scotland. These apartment buildings are built and owned by the local government. A below-market rent is charged to the occupants. This constitutes a classic example of socialism.[58] The government entity must become involved in the business of constructing and managing residences. In the United States, we are more inclined to leave the construction and managing to private business, but to subsidize the rent through government.

The cost of administering these programs is significant. Not only must eligibility rules be determined and administered so also must the housing itself be evaluated for suitability.

Another form of in-kind payment, used in some states, is the "two-party rent check." This may be used by a welfare department to ensure the payment goes to the landlord. The endorsement of both the recipient and the landlord is required before the check can be cashed.[59]

Finally, there are the government-run shelters. According to Funiciello, it was not unusual for $1,000 to be spent weekly in New York City in the late 1980s to shelter a poor family.[60] She suggests most families would find it possible to live in a private home on that amount. Instead of giving people the wherewithal to find housing, we, through our representatives, decide for them where they will live.

Medicare and Medicaid

The two major federal programs assisting in the cost of medical care are often confused. *Medicare* is the insurance-type program, primarily for those over age 65. It is not "means tested"—that is, the benefits are not contingent upon the wealth or income level of the recipient. It is therefore more properly regarded as a social insurance program than as public assistance.[61] Benefits are funded with specially designated taxes. Eligibility rules are, of necessity, arbitrary. Why age 65? As is the case with old-age benefits under Social Security, it is more a historical accident than a logical decision. Many are not aware these benefits have been extended to two nonelderly groups—those who have received Social Security Disability benefits for more than two years, and those suffering from final-stage kidney failure. Again, there are good arguments for making these specific extensions, but the choice to include these groups and not others is arbitrary.

Anyone who has had the "opportunity" to deal with the Medicare program will know how complex it has become. Much of this complexity is a result of efforts to reduce the overall cost, which has skyrocketed over the last two decades. It is not my purpose here to delineate the specific problems within this program. I simply wish to emphasize that we, as a country, have made two significant choices in passing it. The first is to provide in-kind benefits rather than simply cash which could be used to purchase coverage, and the second is to provide the coverage in the public sector rather than relying on private enterprise.

The *Medicaid* program is the "welfare" aspect of our health care. In order to receive these benefits, one must be sufficiently poor. This means neither wealth nor income can exceed stipulated levels. If one qualifies, a wide range of benefits becomes available.

It is not uncommon for a person to receive both Medicare and Medicaid benefits (if she or he is elderly and poor). Anyone who wishes a Kafkaesque experience with the government might try helping an elderly, poor person decipher his or her eligibility for benefits. I have had this experience personally. After teaching the provisions of these programs for more than twenty years, I was still stumped when I tried to deal with the regulations and the bureaucracy. In so saying, I am not intent upon criticizing those who made the regulations nor those who administer them. They are generally well-meaning, intelligent people. They simply must deal with the difficulty engendered by attempts to provide categorical benefits through the government.[62]

One of the greatest shortcomings of the Medicaid program is its connection to AFDC. Persons attempting to work their way off the welfare roles are hampered by the potential for loss of this coverage. Many have no medical benefits available to take its place. One controversial aspect of the recent welfare reform legislation is a provision that states must continue Medicaid benefits for one year for those who lose eligibility because of the new standards. However, this has no impact on those who lose coverage because of previous rules (e.g., income becomes too high).

General Relief

In most states, there are state or county programs which act as a last resort for those with no recourse in the broader-based assistance programs. These programs generally provide assistance on an ad hoc basis to those who can plead their cases compellingly. Assistance may be provided on a temporary basis for specific needs such as rent, utilities, and/or transportation.[63]

These programs are a help, but they suffer from major defects. The first is that they are very expensive to administer. Each grant of aid must be preceded by a discussion with a caseworker. They are demeaning to the recipients, who are essentially required to beg for the assistance. Finally, they provide no security. One can never be sure the benefits will be available.[64]

The Public Assistance Programs Aiding the Non-Poor

We support a number of government programs, ostensibly because they provide some relief to poorer segments of our population. However, because of the nature of these programs, we unavoidably "leak" much of the benefit to the non-poor. I make no claim to catalog all such programs here. Rather I mention a few which provide a sample of the problem. These are farm price supports, disaster relief payments, Social Security benefits, and certain provisions of our tax codes.

Farm Price Supports and Commodity Subsidies

Although these benefits are not generally considered a component of the public assistance programs, at least part of their purpose is to help maintain a minimum standard of living for farmers. It is reasonable to question, in the first place, why we provide support to this one segment of our economy. It may be we are concerned with maintaining the supply of food or in preserving a way of life. Neither of these arguments makes as much sense today as it once might have. The advent of the corporate farm has changed the structure of farm life and food production. Because of this, we also now find the benefit of our farm support programs going, to a great extent, to large corporations rather than to the family farmer with whom we are more sympathetic.[65]

Years ago, economist Milton Friedman made a compelling case against these benefits:

Insofar as they can be justified at all on grounds other than the political fact that rural areas are over-represented in the electoral college and Congress, it must be on the belief that farmers on the average have low incomes. Even if this be accepted as fact, farm price supports do not accomplish the intended purpose of helping the farmers who need help.[66]

Friedman goes on to point out:

The consumer has paid twice, once in taxes for farm benefit payments, again by paying a higher price for food; the farmer has been saddled with onerous restrictions and detailed centralized control; the nation has been saddled with a spreading bureaucracy.[67]

Another writer made the case this way:

Propping up corn, wheat, cotton and other major commodity prices tends to benefit the large-scale, richer farm businesses more than the smaller, "family farm" style of farming. . . . Yet all the farm organizations, conservative and liberal, preaching family-farm doctrine, campaign for higher price supports. They don't want "welfare" and want to earn their incomes in the market. What they're doing, though, is providing welfare for the rich and penalizing the poor.[68]

Disaster Relief Payments

It is doubtful we would ever create a government program designed to help just wealthy people. However, disaster relief programs certainly favor *wealthier* people, since they benefit only those with property. Disaster relief payments are generally not means-tested, even though our primary goal must surely be to aid the more unfortunate members of society. Two aspects of these payments particularly intrigue me. The first is the great sympathy—perhaps because of greater empathy —we have for those who have lost material goods. We seem more concerned with those who have had something and lost it than we do with those who never had anything in the first place. The second is the ease with which we refer to "federal disaster relief funds" as though the federal government had an independent source of money. When the state of Iowa experienced a flood in 1993, the governor was quick to point out how much federal money we were able to obtain. How many people stopped to realize this was money paid in taxes by citizens of Arizona, Utah, and all the other states (including Iowa, of course)?

This program could also have been listed under the "categorical" heading. Benefits are available only to those whose personal disaster was part of a larger disaster. This results in an arbitrary determination of eligibility.[69] Why should one whose home was destroyed by a flood only receive benefits when many other homes were also destroyed? It would seem more logical to decide just the opposite—if only a few homes are destroyed, we can afford to provide benefits, but when many are destroyed we have to say, "Sorry, that would be too costly."[70]

A disaster which deprives one of property should be regarded as no worse than the disastrous results of the "natural lottery" which plague some people for their entire lives. We should be just as concerned with rectifying the latter as the former.

Social Security Benefits

Is Social Security a "public assistance" program? There are good reasons to answer no. It was originally conceived as an insurance program. People would pay premiums (in the form of Federal Insurance Contribution Act (FICA) taxes) during their working years and receive benefits only if they suffered an insured loss (retiring after age 65 was regarded as a loss, as were permanent disability and surviving an insured person). Since benefits are payable without regard to the income or wealth of the recipient, it is not "welfare." There are many negative reactions to this aspect of the program. The idea of a millionaire receiving Social Security benefits seems ludicrous to some. There are, however, at least two good reasons why it should be so. First, most recipients want to feel that the benefits are something they earned rather than some form of handout. To limit these benefits to those below a certain income would add an element of handout to them. To understand the second point, consider two persons who worked the same number of years at the same income. Under the current system, they are entitled to the same Social Security retirement benefits. Suppose person A had been very frugal during the working years and had saved a substantial amount of money. Person B was a wastrel and arrived at retirement with nothing saved. Would it seem fair to pay person A a lower level of retirement income under Social Security because he or she had income from savings? Probably not.

There are, however, some aspects of the program which give it a welfare flavor. First, although benefits are a percentage of income earned while working, the calculation is weighted in favor of low-income earners. They receive a benefit which is a higher percentage of their average wages than do higher-income recipients.[71] Second, past recipients have, on average, received much more back from the system than they put in. This occurred primarily because of legislated increases in benefits. Milton Friedman has pointed out how this amounts to a redistribution from the working persons (some of whom may be poor) to the retired persons (some of whom may be wealthy).[72] Finally, in recent years, income taxes have been imposed upon up to 85 percent of the Social Security benefits of high-income recipients.[73]

Income Tax Provisions

At first glance, our income tax system seems designed to transfer income from rich to poor. After all, isn't it a ''progressive'' tax? Aren't taxes a higher percentage of higher incomes than they are of lower incomes? This is true, but there are some aspects of the code which work in the other direction. First, we should note the highest tax bracket has been reduced considerably in recent years.[74] We still allow certain deductions which inure unequally to the benefit of higher-income people. Chief among these is interest on home mortgages. This benefit is available only to those who can afford to buy a house in the first place. An obscene aspect of this provision allows this interest to be deducted even on very large homes. Certainly an intent of this provision must have been to encourage home ownership. To allow it to be used to facilitate the purchase of very expensive homes is a travesty.

The ability to deduct the cost of health insurance is available only to those who have jobs where their employers have set up group insurance plans.[75] Owners of businesses and the self-employed are able to take advantage of certain business deductions not available to others. A prime example is business lunches. No laborers are able to deduct the cost of their food. Another of the obscene deductions is golf course fees. Anyone who can show he or she conducted business during a round of golf is able to deduct the cost of that round.[76] Finally, there is the whole area of tax shelters. Funiciello points out that horse purchasing, owning, breeding, and even putting out to pasture have been used as one of the many forms of tax shelters.[77]

NEGATIVE ASPECTS OF CURRENT U.S. PUBLIC ASSISTANCE PROGRAMS

There are two major themes to my argument for a guaranteed adequate income. The first is it makes good sense from the standpoint of a balance between justice and necessity. The second, addressed primarily in this chapter, is that our present system for aiding the poor has numerous shortcomings. These faults are not, as many would prefer to believe, the result of ignorant decisions. They are, rather, a necessary result of the nature of the system. Among them, I have chosen to discuss gaps, leakage to the non-poor, costs of administration, demeaning of recipients, intrusion in people's lives, undesirable incentives, and finally, overlaps in programs.

Gaps in Present Programs

Because of their categorical nature, our present programs omit some people. Granted, there are some ad hoc benefits available under certain circumstances to those in dire straits. However, there is no program providing secure income to other than those qualifying under one of the headings previously discussed. Examples of those not benefited include the long-term unemployed, those who have never been employed, married couples with children in states where AFDC benefits are not available to them, married couples or single people with no children, disabled persons who are unable to prove their disability is sufficiently severe, and elderly retired persons who are not old enough for the SSI or OASI benefits.

These omissions are the result of a general philosophy which dictates that we make sure the "unworthy" do not get benefits. Personally, I prefer a system in which everybody is covered, even if some "undeserving" do get benefits, to a system in which some are left out in order to make sure the "undeserving" get no benefits. Each individual's attitude toward the proposal in this book will hinge to a great extent on where she or he stands on this dichotomy.

Leakage to the Non-Poor

Because our public assistance is not simply a function of income, we end up providing benefits to some people who are not in need. Some unemployed managers, for example, could get by quite nicely without unemployment benefits. However, because these come through an insurance-type program, they can receive them. Many elderly do not need their Social Security benefits, but they receive them. We have already noted how farm price supports benefit other than poor farmers.

Costs and Complexity of Administration

Herein lies an enigma for the political conservative. By my observation, many who would label themselves conservatives would take the following positions. First, they are likely to argue that benefits should not be paid to people who won't work. In other words, only those people who are "deserving" should get benefits. Second, they want to limit the amount of government activity. They base this desire at least in part on the inherent inefficiencies of government. Without the incentives generated by the competitive system and the profit motive, they argue, government is hopelessly inefficient. They may also point to the intrusion into people's lives and privacy, necessitated by government activities.

The irony is the desire to limit public assistance benefits to only those persons deemed worthy creates the need for a huge government bureaucracy to administer the program. Not only must rules be written to establish the "worthy" categories, but people must be hired to interpret and enforce these rules. Since those who are running this enterprise have no one with whom to compete, there is no incentive to stay "lean and mean."[78]

These costs are rising at a rapid rate:

> The cost of running welfare programs is rising more than twice as fast as the number of people on the rolls, according to federal investigators who blame an overly complex and bloated bureaucracy. . . .The investigators say the system must be changed or administrative costs will continue their "accelerated growth and remain burdensome and costly to audit."[79]

A recent government report says the federal government spends $6 billion to $8 billion a year helping states deliver food stamps, Medicaid, and AFDC benefits. Not only is the cost high, but the inability to determine the actual amount within less than $2 billion is astounding.[80]

The complexity of the program also works a hardship on the recipients. Funiciello suggests to those of us who have never experienced this process:

> Think of the worst experience you have ever had with a clerk in some government service job—motor vehicles, hospital, whatever—and add the life-threatening condition of impending starvation or homelessness to the waiting line, multiply the anxiety by an exponent of ten, and you have some idea of what it's like in a welfare center.[81]

After describing the seventeen-page application form, Funiciello notes:

> That's another thing about the welfare—the regulations are so complicated no two people working there would come to the same conclusions.[82]

Similar views were expressed by an Iowa observer:

> There are endless . . . examples of the government setting the rules and then making them virtually impossible to live with. The poor are tied to welfare programs like puppets on strings, and bureaucrats who twist the dials that manipulate their lives have snarled the red tape in knots that defy solution.[83]

The most popular "reforms" to our present welfare system—the workfare-type programs—will only make the costs and complexity of administration worse.

Demeaning of the Poor

Is it desirable to separate out poor persons in terms of their economic status? Some might argue that it is, in that it gives "them" one more incentive to change their status. I don't agree. It is unnecessary to further damage one's self-esteem when it is already bruised by the feeling of being poor in a society which esteems wealth.

Have you ever been to the office which administers public assistance benefits? I can't speak for all offices in the country, but on the basis of my limited experience and what I've read, I'm convinced it must be ego-bruising just to make the trip to the welfare office.[84] The process of filling out the application adds to this. The applications are sufficiently complex to cause one to question one's own intelligence. They ask many questions about one's private life, and require one to acknowledge one's financial defeat in extensive detail.

Once benefits are granted, one must again identify oneself as a poor person. This occurs when purchasing food with food stamps, using a Medicaid card to obtain medical care, or renting in subsidized housing.[85] It may also occur when the identifiable cash assistance checks are delivered by the postal service. School children receiving subsidized lunches may also be so distinguished.

Intrusion in People's Lives

How do we know that a mother receiving AFDC benefits does not have a man living with her who should be providing some support? Well, we could just ask her. Since we are likely to not trust the answer, however, we must hire and assign someone to check up on her. This can be accomplished with visits, talking with neighbors, or reviewing various records.[86] All of this involves government intrusion into the recipient's life. Similar activities must be undertaken with regard to recipients of disability benefits.

Undesirable Incentives

Imagine, in this era when there is so much concern about population growth, a program which encourages people to have children. Not very logical, right? But of course that is what the AFDC program does. Let's be very careful with this discussion, however. It is all too easy to point the finger at the beneficiaries of this program, suggesting that their immoral behavior is at the root of the problem.[87] I believe nothing of the sort. The fault lies in a system which rewards the behavior. Many of us faced with the same choices would choose the same course of action. Remember that having a baby is quite a natural thing to do. People resist doing so because of constraints. A powerful constraint is finances. However, when we have a system that provides money *only* if one has a baby, the incentives are inverted. It is this characteristic of the program which was one of the prime motivators for the 1996 welfare reform. The reformers have elected to simply tinker with the program, however, leaving intact the basic premise that benefits must be limited to poor people with children. They fail to recognize that it is that basic premise which is at the heart of the problem.

There is another myth with which we should deal at this point—that is, the belief in the prevalence of large families among those on welfare. While it is true that there is great incentive to have one baby in order to become eligible for AFDC, the benefits accruing from having additional children are not that great.

Overlaps in the Programs

Once a person becomes eligible for public assistance, there is an wide array of programs for which he or she may qualify. I have mentioned some in this chapter. There are too many to discuss them all. Among the major benefits available are the monthly grant under AFDC, food stamps, Medicaid, subsidized housing, subsidized school lunches, job training, and emergency relief. It is very difficult to determine the total value of all the benefits for which one person might qualify.[88]

Because of these overlaps we are providing a total package of benefits in excess of what an employed person earning the minimum wage is receiving. Representative Kay Baily Hutchison (Rep, Texas), speaking before congress during the welfare reform debate, said that in forty states welfare pays more than an $8 an hour job, and in nine of those states it is more than the average first year's salary of a teacher.[89] A significant advantage of a guaranteed adequate income plan will be the fact that it will be the sole source of assistance benefits. We will thus be able to ensure that an unemployed person does not receive more income than an employed person.

SUMMARY

At this point in history, the United States is a sufficiently wealthy country to support a system of benefits to its less fortunate citizens. The citizens of the United States are sufficiently compassionate to wish to provide such benefits. Many benefits are currently in place. The problem is, the system we now have does not make sense. It is founded on a notion that the poor are somehow different from the rest of us. Partly for this reason, it distinguishes between worthy and unworthy poor and determines for the poor how their income will be spent (in most cases through in-kind benefits). It is a terribly cumbersome system to administer, and therefore requires a considerable government bureaucracy. It also requires considerable government intrusion in people's lives.

I agree with Charles Murray and those members of Congress who voted for welfare reform—this system needs to be scrapped. Where our paths diverge, however, is with the replacement. Where Murray would rely on private charity and the hope all could find jobs, and Congress relies on the states and hopes that changed incentives will reduce the problem of poverty, I will recommend a guaranteed adequate income. This proposal is described in subsequent chapters.

Notes

1. Many readers probably refer to these as "welfare" programs. At some point in the not too distant past, it became conventional wisdom that this was a demeaning term. I'm not sure why. I'll use both terms.

2. Of note is the fact that we do not limit the use of public facilities to "worthy" people. Even bums and loafers can use parks, libraries, roads, etc.

3. The fact that this age is presently 62, while interesting, is not particularly significant for our purposes.

4. Here again I use the political "we." Although the decision was actually made by legislators and details are honed out by bureaucrats, I believe, in this democracy, it is fair to conclude that it reflects our will.

5. As will be discussed elsewhere, the very fact that this affliction elicits so much sympathy makes it a very good candidate for private charity to supplement a guaranteed adequate public income.

6. "Disability Benefits Are Used for Drugs," *Des Moines Register*, February 6, 1994, p. 2A.

7. "Study: SSI Money for Kids Unchecked," *Des Moines Register*, October 14, 1994, p. 5A.

8. There are still some who are willing to set the record straight when the criticism is exaggerated, however. "Whatever its impact on illegitimacy, ADC is not the major drain on taxpayer resources that it's thought to be, and the welfare Cadillac is nonsense, popular political myth notwithstanding. . . . The average annual welfare payment per Iowan living in a nursing home on Medicaid comes to more than $14,000; to an SSI recipient, $5,362; to an ADC recipient, around $1,500." Editorial "Does Welfare Worsen the Poverty It's Meant to Cure?" *Des Moines Register,* January 2, 1994, p. 1C.

9. Theresa Funiciello, *Tyranny of Kindness*, pp. 35-36.

10. In some cases, it is done without thinking. "It was not uncommon for white liberals who would mull over every thought for racist content to revile poor people with impunity." Funiciello, ibid., p. 67.

11. As an example of contrasting views, here are the views of some Dear Ann Landers writers: "Most welfare mothers aren't interested in going anywhere. They want to stay home and enjoy the lazy life," and "You're sure to be swamped with letters saying welfare mothers are lazy scum, and some of them are, but I'm a decent woman who would have been totally sunk without that check. It saved my life, and I am certain many others are in the same spot I was in 10 years ago," and "I've been following your readers' comments about people on welfare. You know who I mean—the trash who crank out one kid

after another, those freeloaders who sponge off hard-working people like me,'' and from a mother of a four-year-old: ''There is no family member I would trust to watch my son. . . . I've been trying to find work I can do at home. . . . When my son goes to kindergarten I will take any kind of job I can find and get off your back, Mr. Taxpayer. Until then, I'm just hanging on and thankful that welfare has made it possible for me to raise my child.'' Ann Landers' summary, with which I agree, ''Granted, some folks do abuse welfare and should be tracked down and rooted out. But the majority of welfare recipients are decent people who are in desperate need of government assistance and mighty glad to have it.'' Ann Landers columns, *Des Moines Register*, September 3, 1991, p. 2T, and November 11, 1991, p. 2T.

12. George Orwell, *Down and Out in Paris and London*, p. 88. This book is a chronicle of Orwell's life among the poor. Hence, when he continues, ''Everyone who has mixed on equal terms with the poor knows this quite well,'' he deserves credibility.

13. Funiciello, *Tyranny of Kindness*, p. 101.

14. ''Real Life on Welfare,'' *Des Moines Register*, March 27, 1988, p. 1C.

15. Michael Harrington, *The Other America*, p. 17.

16. Ibid. As examples of differences, Harrington mentions the condition of their teeth, the way in which they love, their attitudes toward the police, and their family structure.

17. One example of this is cited by Charles Murray in *Losing Ground.* ''The short time frame people use for making decisions has been a central feature of the 'culture of poverty' discussion [for some time]. In such discussions, however, the source of the foreshortened time horizon has generally been seen in cultural or mental attributes. It is hard to understand why the logical reason for shortsightedness—that the poor person hasn't the luxury of thinking about far-distant events—has received so little attention,'' footnote 1 to chap. 12. And in general, ''surprisingly little has been made of the distinction between the behaviors that make sense when one is poor and the behaviors that make sense when one is not poor,'' p. 156.

18. The perception of a culture of welfare dependency appears to be overblown. ''Links between parents and children's economic circumstances do exist. However, long term dependency as a child does not cause long term dependency as an adult.'' Quoted from the Panel Study of Income Dynamics by Martha Hill and Michael Ponza in Funiciello, *Tyranny of Kindness,* p. 59. Funiciello states: ''The most frequent precipitator of welfare receipt is a change in family composition, such as divorce, separation, or the birth of a child.''

19. Ibid., p. 9.

20. Originally it was expected that this program would benefit mothers and their children. Today, it could provide benefits to a single father and children also.

21. Murray, *Losing Ground*. He continues to argue this case. "Restoring economic penalties [for illegitimacy] translates into the first and central policy prescription: to end all economic support for single mothers. The AFDC payment goes to zero. Single mothers are not eligible for subsidized housing or for food stamps." "White Illegitimacy Epidemic," *Des Moines Register*, January 2, 1994, p. 2C. (Reprinted from the *Wall Street Journal*.) Note that Charles Murray and I share the goal of eliminating AFDC. After that point we diverge. He would replace the program with *nothing*—save the possibility of help from family and friends. As described later in this book, I would provide an adequate income through government, but would not require motherhood as an eligibility criterion.

22. Although there is a strong incentive to give birth in order to get on the AFDC roles, the perception of large welfare families is mostly a myth. In a study done in Iowa in 1988, it was found only 20 percent of AFDC recipients had more than two children. "Welfare Pays More than Low Wage Jobs," *Des Moines Register*, November 16, 1988, p. 7M.

23. "Louisiana actually reached the point of dropping twenty-three thousand illegitimate children from its AFDC rolls, eventually rescinding the order only after the Eisenhower administration threatened to cut off federal funds." Murray, *Losing Ground*, p. 19.

24. Although some might object to referring to this provision as a tax, it definitely has the same impact on the worker as a tax. For every dollar one earns, 67 cents must be paid (back) to the government.

25. According to Murray, *Losing Ground*, this change actually increased the cost of the program. By his reckoning, making the program more "generous" attracted some people who otherwise might have chosen work over welfare.

26. In a 1988 study in Iowa, it was determined that a welfare mother would need a job paying about $9 an hour just to break even. "Welfare Pays More," *Des Moines Register*, p. 1M.

27. "Expert: Welfare Caseload May Rise," *Des Moines Register*, January 6, 1994, p. 6M.

28. "Critics: Lack of Money Will Doom Iowa's Attempt at Welfare Reform," *Des Moines Register*, December 30, 1993, p. 2M.

29. Mike Maddigan, a human services income maintenance worker, quoted in "Iowa Welfare Reform Plan Already Hits Snags," *Des Moines Register*, May 16, 1993, p. 1B.

30. Comments of Martin Ozga, deputy director of the Legal Services Corp. of Iowa, in a letter to the U.S. Department of Health and Human Services. "Attorney Attacks Welfare Contracts," *Des Moines Register*, May 15, 1993, p. 1M.

31. One interesting aspect is that the experiment is being limited to parts of the state where jobs are generally available. The state apparently wishes to test it first under the most favorable circumstances; thus, they deliberately exclude the city of Milwaukee.

32. In his January 18, 1994, testimony, aired on C-SPAN, Mr. Riley described himself as a former welfare recipient. He recounted how his family had been embarrassed and suffered damaged pride from receiving welfare. His parents faced the dilemma of staying on welfare or going to work earning less than what welfare paid.

33. Ruth Conniff, "War on Welfare in Wisconsin," *Des Moines Sunday Register*, December 19, 1993, p. 3C.

34. An interesting sidelight to this is that Vermont's public employees labor union has been granted "sign-off power" on these jobs. That is, they must agree to the jobs being made available. Their concern is to see that these created jobs not replace regular paid jobs.

35. Expressed before Senate Welfare Reform Committee, January 18, 1994. (Aired on C-SPAN.)

36. Michael Kramer, "The Myth About Welfare Moms," *Time*, July 3, 1995, p. 21. The study cited was done at Rutgers University.

37. Frances Fox Piven, "From Workhouse to Workfare," *New York Times National Edition*, August 1, 1996, p. A17.

38. Ibid.

39. Ibid.

40. There is considerable concern that the bill will shift significant costs to states and even to cities. Mayor Rudolph Giuliani, of New York City, said that "by 2002, the bill could add as much as $720 million in new costs" to the city's budget. *New York Times National Edition*, August 1, 1996, p. A11.

41. Representing the optimistic view of this provision of the bill, Senator John Warner (Rep, Va.), in a speech during debate on the bill, said this bill should be called the "Helping Hand Bill." Speech aired live on C-SPAN 2, August 2, 1996. Speaker of the House Newt Gingrich noted: "I believe this bill

will dramatically help young Americans to have a chance to rise and to do better. I think that by establishing the work experience and by creating the natural expectation that people will be busy working is a very big step.'' *New York Times National Edition*, August 1, 1996, p. A11.

42. Speech aired live on C-SPAN 2, August 2, 1996. Sen. Dodd also noted that the Congressional Budget Office has estimated that the bill is $12 billion short on funds needed to meet the work requirement.

43. Speech aired live on C-SPAN 2, August 2, 1996.

44. ''People on Welfare, Too, Find a Lot to Criticize,'' *New York Times National Edition*, August 1, 1996, p. A9.

45. An expression of this view was provided by Senator Richard Shelby (Rep, Ala.) in a speech during debate on the bill. ''The current welfare system is a death sentence,'' and ''Welfare destroys the natural incentive to become self-sufficient.'' Speech aired live on C-SPAN 2, August 2, 1996. Also, Representative John R. Kasich (Rep, Ohio) noted: ''People are not entitled to anything but opportunity. You can't be on welfare for generations.'' ''Clinton Says He Will Sign Welfare Bill,'' *New York Times National Edition*, August 1, 1996, p. A8.

46. Some had favored a provision which would cut off benefits for the welfare recipients who had another child while on welfare. This was not included in the bill.

47. Murray, *Losing Ground*.

48. The federal government keeps a small percentage to fund administrative and research costs, as well as some extended benefits.

49. Two examples of such cases in Iowa were an employee being asked to do shoddy work and an employee being required to ''cook the books.''

50. Under the Clinton reform proposal, this has been raised from $2.50 for each $10 in earnings, to $4.00 for each $10 for the first $8,500 they earn working.

51. ''Tax Credit Plan Pays the Poverty-Stricken,'' *Des Moines Register*, July 26, 1993, p. 5A.

52. One wonders why we do not have clothing stamps and transportation stamps.

53. The common answer to this question, ''Because the poor person didn't earn it,'' is only a halfway ''why.'' Why should this matter? Is it because, if we are funding the benefits with our taxes, we feel *entitled* to say how they are spent? Even if we are so entitled, why should we exercise that entitlement?

54. Is it not supercilious of us to substitute our judgment for that of the shopper? Consider the following exchange in an Ann Landers column. She had published a letter from a grocery store clerk who criticized a woman who used food stamps to buy a $17 birthday cake and a $32 bag of shrimp. Replies included: "I did buy a big bag of shrimp with food stamps. . . . The shrimp casserole I made was for our wedding anniversary dinner, and it lasted three days. Perhaps the grocery clerk who criticized the woman would have a different view of life after walking a mile in my shoes," and "I'm the woman who bought that $17 cake and paid for it with food stamps. I thought the checkout woman would burn a hole through me with her eyes. What she didn't know (and I would never tell her) is that the cake was for my little girl's birthday. It will be her last. She has bone cancer and will probably be gone within six months. Let this be a lesson to those who sit in judgment of others without knowing all the facts." "Food-Stamp Users Reply to Attack," *Des Moines Register,* May 31, 1993, p. 2T.

55. Funiciello, *Tyranny of Kindness,* p. 127.

56. Ibid., p. 134, provides a graph showing the breakdown of food types donated to the Second Harvest program in New York City. More than 25 percent of the donations were nonfood items or snack foods. Through volunteer work at a food bank in Iowa, I can attest this is not an isolated experience.

57. "Meals Program for Poor Children Fails to Reach Them, Group Charges," *Des Moines Register,* August 7, 1992, p. 7A. An explanation for the lower participation may well be the stigma associated with going to the "feeding sites." This same stigma has been reduced in the case of school lunches, but at one time, it was severe. President Nixon, in his arguments for his Family Assistance Plan, cited the demeaning of schoolchildren who had to go into a separate room to eat their subsidized lunches.

58. There is a wide variety of meanings given to this term. I use it in its more classic sense of government ownership of the means of production. Others use it to refer to all forms of government assistance or income redistribution plans.

59. Funiciello, *Tyranny of Kindness,* suggests that this is often used more for the protection of landlords than for recipients. She reports one case where a recipient was forced into this option where there was no heat, no hot water, and no electricity in her apartment.

60. Ibid., p. 162.

61. Here is socialism in action. This is a government-run insurance enterprise. There are good reasons why this enterprise is better run by government (e.g., ability to make coverage compulsory and to provide universal

coverage) than by private enterprise. Nonetheless, it is subject to the same criticism as all socialized endeavors (e.g., no incentive to efficiency).

62. I have no doubt government-run medical care would be much simpler. While socialized medicine would be subject to the inefficiency dilemma, it would at least be effective (in that it would cover everybody without the need to prove eligibility). While I am not advocating it here, I do hope that readers will not dismiss it out of hand on the grounds it is socialism. We have lived for years in this country with a socialized education system.

63. Some states make cash benefits available, but this is tenuous. In 1991, Michigan cut off benefits to 81,000 recipients--those who were not disabled and didn't have children. "Michigan Poor Try to Cope After State Slashes Welfare," *Des Moines Register*, October 7, 1991, p. 2A.

64. For example, in the Polk County, Iowa, program "about two of every three clients walk away . . . with their problems solved, at least temporarily." "Last Chance for the Desperate," *Des Moines Register*, September 14, 1991, p. 1T.

65. "The top 2 percent of farmers get as many tax dollars as the bottom 69 percent. Forty percent of the total goes to farmers with a net income of at least $100,000 and a net worth of $750,000 or more." Paul Faeth, "Let's Get Farmers Off the Federal Dole," *Des Moines Register*, June 30, 1995, p. 15A.

66. Milton Friedman, *Capitalism and Freedom*, p. 181.

67. Ibid., p. 82.

68. Lauren Soth, "Economic Policy Lacks Equity," *Des Moines Register*, March 4, 1991, p. 10A.

69. Funiciello demonstrates this arbitrary nature when she describes an effort in New York State to capitalize on a provision in the state welfare rules. "Buried within the reams of technical drivel was a provision for special grants to family members on AFDC in the event their clothes had been destroyed by 'flood, fire or other like catastrophe.' *Catastrophe* was the key. President Carter had recently declared inflation a catastrophe." Funiciello, *Tyranny of Kindness*, p. 95. I personally experienced another example of how out of hand these payments have become. I serve on the board of a nonprofit youth drug rehabilitation facility. Out of the blue we received a grant to provide services to youth who had been affected by our recent flood. I still don't know why these kids should be any more entitled to assistance than kids who had not been in a flood.

70. From the viewpoint of maintenance of the social fabric, there is a need to rectify large disasters more than small ones. Nonetheless, from the viewpoint of the individual, there is still little justice in the present system.

71. At one time, this was exacerbated by the existence of a minimum benefit which was available to those who had met the minimum work-years requirement. This has been eliminated.

72. Friedman, *Capitalism and Freedom*. There are, by the way, also some aspects of the program which involve a redistribution from poor to rich. Chief among these is the payroll tax which, because of its applicability only to a limited wage base, amounts to a regressive tax. Friedman concludes: "The only argument I have ever come across to justify the redistribution involved in OASI [Old Age and Survivors Insurance, i.e., Social Security] is one that I regard as thoroughly immoral despite its wide use. This argument is that OASI redistribution on the average helps low-income people more than high-income people despite a large arbitrary element; that it would be better to do this redistribution more efficiently; but that the community will not vote for the redistribution directly though it will vote for it as part of a social security package. In essence, what this argument says is that the community can be fooled into voting for a measure that it opposes by presenting that measure in a false guise," pp. 184-185.

73. Although proposals have been made to "means test" Social Security as a way of cutting the deficit, Treasury Secretary Lloyd Bentsen had indicated the administration had no plans to do so. Said Bentsen: "I believe in the principle that if you pay into Social Security, you get something back, that we don't get it into a welfare mode." "No Plans to Curb Benefits," *Des Moines Register*, December 20, 1993, p. 1A.

74. This decrease from around 50 percent to around 33 percent was "needed," some said, to reduce the disincentive inherent in such high taxes. Although I will argue later in this book for a flat tax in the lower range, I find the "incentive" argument questionable. Many people engaged in high income occupations enjoy their work. It is often comfortable, pleasant, challenging, and rewarding. What amazes me is that we retain the 66 percent-plus tax rate on AFDC recipients, expecting them to seek employment. This in spite of the fact the work available to them is often uncomfortable, unpleasant, nonchallenging, and not rewarding.

75. Or who set up flexible spending accounts into which pre-tax income can be placed to be used for allowable health-care deductions.

76. As a consultant and an avid golfer, I would be able to take advantage of this deduction, but I refuse to do so. I admitted to some moral fallibility earlier in this book, but I do have my limits.

77. Funiciello, *Tyranny of Kindness*, p. 112.

78. I am not arguing the position that government is unavoidably inefficient. It is rather my purpose to point out the dilemma faced by those who do believe this, but also believe in limiting income benefits to those deemed worthy of them.

79. "Report: Welfare Cost Out of Hand," *Des Moines Register*, January 3, 1994, p. 1.

80. Ibid.

81. Funiciello, *Tyranny of Kindness*, p. 24. Funiciello's experience is with the New York system. I have personally observed an office in Iowa, and would not be inclined to refute her conclusion.

82. Ibid., p. 33. Again, my own experience with a Medicaid application for a relative in Iowa confirms this. By the way, "the welfare" is the phrase used by Funiciello and her acquaintances to refer to the system.

83. Bill Leonard, "The Cost of Getting Off Welfare," *Des Moines Register*, March 28, 1988, p. 8A.

84. "To prevent those who were not in serious need from committing welfare fraud, those who *were* had to be tormented. Since welfare recipients are perceived to be the dregs of society, there is no need to treat them humanely." Funiciello, *Tyranny of Kindness*, p. 56.

85. At a hearing before President Clinton's welfare reform task force, welfare mothers gave their views. They referred to welfare as "degrading, humiliating, and dehumanizing." "Panel Hears Pleas of Women on Welfare," *Des Moines Register*, August 12, 1993, p. 2A.

86. According to one recipient, "I am required to do what I am told, present myself when ordered, and drop everything when my caseworker calls." Ibid.

87. Some people suggest that a higher birth rate among the poor is an indication of a lower level of morality. Before one accepts this myth, however, he or she should recognize that: (1) poorer people have less access to birth control; (2) they have fewer options for abortion; and (3) they have less opportunity to legitimize a pregnancy after the fact by getting married.

88. Some have suggested figures in the $20,000 plus per year range. This creates a philosophical debate because figures in this range include a substantial value for Medicaid benefits. On the one hand, it is correctly argued the average

welfare recipient uses medical services worth a substantial amount. However, this is only of benefit to one who actually is ill and uses the services.

89. Speech carried on C-SPAN, August 1, 1996.

3

The Market

Who Gets What, Why, and Whether

Capitalism — awesome or awful? I say neither. It may well be the best system around, but it is far from a perfect operation. Having taught in colleges of business administration for over a quarter-century, I am well aware of the reverential awe in which this system is held by many of my colleagues. It's enough to put me in mind of a popular song, the last line of which might be paraphrased "and you don't mess around with the market."

In this chapter, I argue for a reasoned view of capitalism and its attendant market. In this book, the terms "the market system" and "capitalism" will be used interchangeably. One author points out, however, that they should not. According to Robert Heilbroner, the market system is only one component of capitalism.[1]

While it's desirable to acknowledge the blessings of the market, we must also acknowledge its blemishes. It has been suggested that one of the blemishes of capitalism is the view of human nature it presupposes. In *Looking Backward: 2000-1887*, Edward Bellamy has a speaker give the following report to people in the year 2000 on the views of those in 1887:

> It was the sincere belief of even the best of men at that epoch [1887] that the only stable elements in human nature, on which a social system could be safely founded, were its worst propensities.[The speaker was referring to greed and self-seeking.][2]

Chief among the faults, and the focus of this book, is the lousy job the market (or capitalism) does of allocating wealth. The results are far from just.

ALTERNATIVES TO THE MARKET

Who decided the United States should be a capitalist country? There are some who seem to feel God is responsible—since he likes us best, he gave us this wonderful economic system. I don't think so! Face it—it's a historical accident. This was the system operating in Europe, primarily in Great Britain, at the time this country was founded. It has been argued that this system got its impetus from the capture of a hoard of gold from the Spanish armada by Sir Francis Drake. This accumulated wealth provided the basis for investments and development, and capitalism has flourished since. Transplanted to a country with enormous natural resources, including arable land available for the taking (by force, of course), it was bound to succeed. Oh yes, we shouldn't forget the people, most of whom were imbued with the Calvinist doctrine of "work as a virtue."

Nobody or no group of people *chose* capitalism. It just happened. Over the centuries, economists and others have developed arguments in support of it. Partly for this reason, and partly because the countries in which it has existed have been so successful, it is accepted (yes, even revered).

It may seem to some readers, perhaps after glancing at the conclusions of this book, that the author is anticapitalism. *Au contraire!* The guaranteed adequate income proposal is designed to enhance, not replace, the market. In the balance of this chapter, I look at the virtues and shortcomings of this system. I also show how a guaranteed adequate income can help this system flourish. First, however, a few comments on some alternative systems.

Command Economies

A "command economy," according to Heilbroner, is an economy organized by people, and is distinguished from "tradition" and "market" economies.[3] Those in power make decisions designed to allocate resources. One such economic system is socialism. Under this political/economic scheme, business is run through, and by, the government. The theory is that, by so doing, the people—through their government—can provide economic security to all.

Current evidence suggests that this approach is not completely effective and is certainly not efficient. A word of caution, however: let us not jump on the bandwagon of those who claim socialism has been "proven" a failure. For anyone with a smattering of training in the scientific method, it is obvious that the sample size is too small to draw such a conclusion. In addition, the "trials" were quite different.

For example, the primary socialist attempt was in the Soviet Union. The new system was barely in place when the country became engaged in a war, partly on its own soil. Thereafter, it endured a period under a despot whose political style ravaged the country. This was followed by another war, again fought to a great extent on Soviet soil, which decimated the population. There was a long period of cold war, requiring major military expenses from a country which was not yet fully economically developed. The problems were compounded by the klieg light of international communications, which reflected negatively on the relative status of the country. To emphasize, I am not saying socialism is good; I am only arguing it has not been proven bad.

Lest we bask too warmly in the glow of our capitalism, we should take note of another Heilbroner comment:

> The widening gulf between rich and poor nations is undoubtedly not just a measure of the superior performance of the capitalist world, but also an indication of its exploitative powers.[4]

To adherents of the capitalist religion, this may sound like heresy. Let's be clear—I have no intention of arguing the case for socialism. Rather, I am intent on keeping the record in perspective. Capitalism may be better, but it's not perfect. Socialism may not be as desirable, but it is not without merit. I side with the columnist Donald Kaul, who wrote:

> Generally speaking, socialism doesn't scare me. . . . You go up to most Americans and say "socialism" real loud, they run away with their hands over their ears, shouting "He said the 'S' word, he said the 'S' word." My motto is "Socialism, schmocialism: so long as it works." [5]

Tradition Economies

These economies are characterized by informal, unwritten rules. Included in these rules are stipulations about who is entitled to what. Certain members of society may be deemed entitled to a share in the wealth, without regard to whether they had personally produced anything. This could describe the economies of native Americans prior to the capitalist conquest.

Welfare Economies

I'll use this term to refer to hybrid systems—those which are basically market oriented, but in which government plays a significant role in reallocating resources. Some have argued this more accurately describes most of the countries in Europe, and perhaps even the United States. In these economies, government not only redistributes incomes, it also provides many of the services which are needed to enhance the "welfare" of the people.

THE VIRTUES OF THE MARKET

There are a great number of benefits society derives from the existence of a market-based economic system. My proposal for a guaranteed adequate income is designed to build on and enhance these positive elements.

Enhances Freedom

"Nobody's going to tell *me* where I have to work or what business I can go into!" Such a statement might reflect one of the attitudes of ardent defenders of the market system. With an unfettered economy, people are free to start whatever business they wish, work for whomever they wish (as long as they can get the job), and hire whomever they wish. These freedoms work hand in hand with the political freedoms associated with a democracy.

This point is eloquently made by Heilbroner:

> No noncapitalist country has attained the levels of political, civil, religious, and intellectual freedom found in all advanced capitalisms. To make the case differently, the state of explicit political liberty we loosely call "democracy" has so far appeared only in nations in which capitalism is the mode of economic organization. What is important, however, is the argument behind this connection. It is certainly not that the pursuit of capital breeds a liberty-loving frame of mind. It is rather that the presence of an economy within a polity gives an inestimable aid to freedom by permitting political dissidents to make their livings without interdiction by an all-powerful regime.[6]

Provides Opportunity

What one does is, at least theoretically, the only thing that matters to "the market." It is not concerned with who you are or who your parents were. In this sense, everyone is provided with an opportunity to succeed economically.[7]

Encourages Growth

The evidence suggests that capitalist economies produce a rapid rate of growth.[8] Why should this be so?

Rewards for Innovation

Growth is driven by innovation.[9] Innovation is encouraged by rewards for innovating. The market system provides those rewards.

Promotes Capital Accumulation

Growth is enhanced by taking advantage of economies of scale and scope. Bigger enterprises can often more efficiently produce and distribute goods. In order for enterprises to get larger, they need invested capital. Under capitalism, such investments are rewarded, therefore they are likely to be made.

Allocates Better than Committees

Growth is an important aspect of a successful economy.[10] So is allocation. There are two aspects of allocation. First, there is the directing of resources to those areas where the need is the greatest. On this, capitalism and the market economy work very well.

> A capitalist system uses differences in wages and profits to make the economic machine operate just as a steam engine uses differences in heat and pressure to make the wheels turn. Wage differentials move workers from the less-productive industries to the more productive. Profit differentials move capital from decaying industries to growing areas.[11]

The second aspect of allocation is the ultimate determination of who ends up with what. Most of us would regard as unsuccessful the fastest growing economy if all of the wealth were concentrated in the hands of one family. There must be some method by which the wealth is distributed.

The classic example of an allocation system based upon edict is the Marxian slogan: "From each according to his ability; to each according to his need."

The first half of this statement relates to the issue of freedom: when people are told how much they must contribute, freedom is reduced. The second half is the point at issue here: allocation will be based on a person's need. There are two major problems with this. The first is that someone or some group must decide what constitutes need. The second is that these criteria must be applied in individual cases.

It is unlikely a just system can be based on need. The only supportable version would be one which concludes that everyone needs the same amount. Any system in which we try to differentiate the needs of different people runs afoul of at least two problems. The first is that there is no universal agreement on the basis for needing. Who *needs* more food? Skinny people? Fat people? Bulemics? Gourmands?

The second problem is the difference in perception between the recipient and the allocator. It is likely each individual has an inflated notion of his or her own needs, relative to the perception of others. Chances are we could never satisfy the needs of most people because the rest of us would not perceive them to be as great as they themselves do.

How well does the market allocate? Not well. But here is a major conclusion of this chapter—even though the market does not allocate well, it allocates at least as well as any other system we know of. Our goal should be to recognize the limitations of the market and offset them without interfering with its basic operation.

What are some of these limitations?

THE SHORTCOMINGS OF THE MARKET

According to Adam Smith, the market acts like an "invisible hand" to allocate goods and wealth. This is a perfectly acceptable simile, unless we assume this hand is attached to a sentient being.[12] Sure, this hand distributes rewards to those who produce or who own capital, and this distribution reflects the value of the contribution to the economy. Because of the hand, people are encouraged to produce that which is needed. Nonetheless, this hand is not guided by "the mind," a benevolent market god who has deemed this distribution to be right or just or fair.[13]

Wealth and Income Distribution Not Just

One of the shortcomings of the hand is it's inability to consider any questions of justice.[14] Since it does not have the benefit of the mind, or the heart, or perhaps the soul, it blindly transfers wealth only as it benefits the overall market.[15] The consequences to individuals are of no concern. Consider the following examples of current income distribution:

> Chief executives at the nations' 200 largest companies had median income [in 1992] of $2.7 million, including stock options—143 times the average worker's pay of $18,925, according to compensation expert Graef Crystal; that compares with 35 times the average worker's pay in the mid-1970s. Average pay for institutional securities brokers is now $271,000, up 139% since 1981, says the Securities Industry Association. A survey by American Lawyer magazine puts the average yearly profit for a partner at one of the 100 top-grossing law firms at $406,000. An average schoolteacher, meanwhile, earned $35,334 in 1992-93, while a college faculty member made $46,270, according to union data. Median income for social workers in 1992, says the Labor Department, was $25,428.
>
> "In 1970, you just didn't find two people of roughly equal education where one made 20 times what the other made," says Steven Davis, a professor at University of Chicago's Graduate Business School who studies compensation. "The real acceleration in pay for certain professions . . . has left us with a situation where the relative penalties for going into some of the lower paying, so-called high-commitment professions has gone way up."[16]

And then there are the "working stiffs." According to Barbara Ehrenreich:

> Conditions in the low-wage end of the work force are beginning to look like what Friedrich Engels found in 19th century Manchester and described as immiserization. . . . Nationwide the fraction of the work force earning wages that are inadequate to lift a family out of poverty rose from 25.7% in 1979 to 31.5% in 1987.[17]

Unfair Advantages of Some People over Others

Since the market encourages production, it compensates more highly those who produce more. This is necessary, and in a macro sense also desirable. It is not, however, *just*. As we argued previously, people have differing levels of ability to produce. This differentiation can be attributed to genetics, environment, God—it doesn't matter. Some simply reach the productive period in their lives with much greater ability to succeed economically. This greater ability is not something for which they deserve credit, nor something for which they should be rewarded. Nonetheless, the market rewards them more highly, and necessarily gives a lower reward to those who are unable to produce as much.

Does this mean some people are better than others? No way! I'm sure my mother would have said "Everybody can contribute in his or her own way." And indeed everybody can. The problem is, for some, "their way" is not valued by the market.

Effects of Discrimination

Compounding this problem is the existence of discrimination. It is nice to think the market does not discriminate. People are theoretically valued for their ability to contribute, nothing more and nothing less. Unfortunately, discrimination does exist. Henry Phelps Brown suggests it exists both "*within* the market and *before* the market."[18] Discrimination within the market occurs when preconceived notions about the value of the input from certain groups influences wage decisions. Discrimination before the market occurs when there is, for example, unequal schooling.[19] It is nigh impossible to determine which of these effects is operating in any given case, but it seems clear to me that one or the other is.

Women. Consider the relative treatment of women. In 1992, women in general earned about 71 cents for every dollar paid to men.[20] There are a number of reasons for this. Women have traditionally worked in lower paying occupations.[21] (Or is it that occupations where there are a significant number of women are traditionally low paid?) Also, since the number of women entering the work force has been increasing, more of them are closer to entry-level positions. Part of the cause could be the fact that women have historically not received (or sought?) as many years of education.[22]   It is also possible that they are discriminated against:

> A National Academy of Sciences study shows that women may earn less than men because they have less seniority, stay in the labor force less consistently and tend to work in jobs with lower intrinsic value. But the study also shows that half of the wage gap is due to discrimination.[23]

This view is reinforced by facts such as the following:

> The average female manager—corporate vice president or higher— earned . . . about 57% of her male counterparts' earnings [in 1992].[24]

Blacks. A Census Bureau study conducted in 1989 and 1990 showed that college-educated white men earn nearly one-third a year more than black men with similar backgrounds.[25] The extent to which this is a result of discrimination *before* the market or *within* the market is not clear. A Labor Department report said:

> Much of the bias was unintentional, caused by such practices as word-of-mouth recruiting, lack of access to management development and training and the failure of executives to foster advancement of minorities and women.[26]

Three other factors which influenced this result were:

• Jobs sought by college-educated blacks have moved from the cities, where they live, to the suburbs, where there are fewer blacks. (According to Ronald Walters, political science chairman at Howard University.)
• College-educated blacks are more likely to work in service industries, where salaries are lower. (According to Claudette Bennett, author of the Census Bureau report.)
• College-educated blacks are relative newcomers to the labor market and so have less time than whites to earn promotion and higher pay. (According to Taynia Mann, a research demographer at the Population Reference Bureau, a Washington research group.)[27]

Less Attractive People. Less attractive people provide another example of discrimination:

> Attractive people with MBAs can earn $10,000 a year more than their equally qualified—but plainer—counterparts.[28]

A common theme permeating all of these differences is that it is not *people* who are discriminating, but rather the market. That is, to a great extent the discriminatory incomes are a consequence not so much of ill-intentioned people as of the unfortunate workings of the market place. Of course, some of these market factors are a product of past injustices, which may well be attributed to ill-intentioned people.[29]

Onerous Jobs Not Highly Compensated

Have you heard of the differential wage theory? According to this theory, work which is more difficult or more dangerous will be more highly compensated. There is sound intuition behind this argument. The more onerous the job, the fewer the people willing to do it. The lower the supply of labor, the higher the price of that labor.

When workers compensation laws were first being debated in this country (starting around 1910), opponents used the differential wage theory to argue that the new laws were not needed. Granted, they said, a lot of workers are getting injured in factories, in mines, and so on. However, they are already compensated for their injuries. How? Because their wages include a hidden bonus which is their compensation for taking the risk of injury. The more dangerous the job, the greater the bonus. Since they were already being paid for taking this risk, they should bear the consequences.

Makes sense, doesn't it? The only problem is, facts don't seem to support it. It doesn't take too much personal observation to note the relative level of wages in dangerous and/or onerous jobs. They don't seem to be highly compensated. Granted, the analysis is difficult. It can still be argued that for any given level of contribution, a more dangerous job or a more onerous job will pay more. If this is the case, the market does work.[30] I'll grant for now that may be the case. But here's the rub. The ability of some people to contribute limits them to jobs which are more dangerous or more onerous. Since there are so many people like this, the price of their labor is reduced.

Questionable Allocation Among Occupations

If you believe whatever the market does it must be right, then this section will be of no interest to you. However, my own feeling is the invisible hand places its blessings in some unseemly ways.

> Life isn't always fair, and who gets what seems like a case in point. How is it that a college football coach gets more than a college professor, that hotshot Wall Street brokers make far more than noted scientists, or that company controllers, who watch the money, tend to be paid more than the senior engineers, who are responsible for making it?[31]

The Case of Athletes

> It all started with Babe Ruth—when, in 1932, the Sultan of Swat signed for $80,000 and was asked how he felt about getting more money than the

President of the United States. Replied the Babe, "I had a better year than he did."[32]

This flippant remark satisfies a lot of people, particularly those who have faith in the rightness of the market. Upon reflection, however, one must contemplate whether there isn't a glitch in the market when those who have the pleasure of playing games for a living also reap such large financial rewards.[33]

The Case of CEOs

Theoretically, corporations provide income to their chief executive officers commensurate with the contribution they make to the wealth of the firm. In the finance literature, there are numerous articles explaining why this is so. Even if it is so, we still might question the justice of such a compensation criterion. The wealth of the firm will be affected by many factors other than the ability of the CEO, including changing demand for particular products. In addition, there are some who say the theory isn't even accurate:

> In a *USA Today* survey of 243 deans and top administrators of graduate and undergraduate schools, 82 percent say public outrage over chief executive officer pay is justified.[34]

While the deans did not feel government should get involved in determining the pay, they did feel that CEOs should not be able to sit on the boards which determine their compensation. On the other hand, some of the high-paid CEOs are founders of their own companies. In addition, much of their compensation comes from stock options.[35]

Steven Ross, in a book titled *In Search of Excess,* pointed out examples of executive over (and under) compensation. One pair of executives he suggested were paid about 35 times what they were worth.[36]

The Case of Physicians

Do physicians make too much money?[37] Many of us probably believe they deserve to be paid well. They invest a lot of time, money, and energy in their training. They have very important duties. Many of their jobs are quite stressful. Nonetheless, many Americans feel that some doctors, particularly specialists, are overpaid. Physicians in general are a very highly paid segment of our economy. It is interesting to note that in other countries, where medical care is run by the government, this is not so. Does the market do a better job of determining these earnings than bureaucrats do? Although I continue to argue that the market in general makes these allocations better than planners, I do have a reservation, particularly in the case of the health-care sector. I'm just not sure consumers of medical care can effectively play their assigned roles. Those roles require them to choose the best product at the lowest price in order to induce innovation and efficiency. Since the initial selection of "the best" physician is so difficult, and since subsequent medical care is determined to such a great extent by that physician, the consumer is a weak ally to the market.

Current Income Distribution

If there were an invisible mind accompanying the invisible hand, do you suppose it would create an income distribution resembling that which exists in the United States today? Can there be a good argument for the tremendous disparities in income? The only arguments I hear are:

"That's the way the market allocated, so it must be right."
"People who want to change it are suffering from poor person's greed or liberal guilt."[38]

Well I don't think it's right, and I'm not being greedy and I don't feel guilty. Nonetheless, I do feel the distribution is a bit skewed. As the audience at the old *Tonight Show* might respond, "How skewed is it?" I promised I wouldn't try to convince you with facts, but in Table 3.1 I present a few of them to give you something to think about in this regard.

Table 3.1

Selected Indicators of Income Distribution

| | All Households | | | Black Households | |
Income Class	Percent of Aggregate Income (1992)	Mean Income (1992) ($)	Percent of Aggregate Income (1967)	Mean Income (1992) ($)	Percent of Aggregate Income (1992)
Everyone		39,020		25,409	
Lowest 20%	3.8	7,328	4.0	3,930	3.1
Highest 20%	46.9	91,494	43.8	63,178	49.7
Top 5%	18.6	45,244	17.5	97,430	19.2

Source: Table B-3, Share of Aggregate Income and Mean Income in 1967 to 1992 Received by Each Fifth and Top 5 Percent of Households, by Race and Hispanic Origin of Householder, U.S. Bureau of the Census, Current Population Reports, Series P60-184, *Money Income of Households, Families and Persons in the United States: 1992* (Washington, D.C.: U.S. Government Printing Office, 1993).

Another view of the distribution is provided by the following: In 1967, the ratio of the average earnings of the highest quintile to the poverty level was 6.06. By 1992 this figure was 8.43. The lowest quintile percentage of the poverty level went from .97 (below the poverty level) to .91. For blacks in 1992, the lowest quintile was .37, and the highest quintile was 5.40. (In 1967, the figures were .50 and 5.40, respectively.)[39]

Does this represent a just or an acceptable distribution of income?[40] Each reader will have her or his own view on this. If you're interested in my view, it's this. The United States could certainly flatten out this distribution without eliminating the incentive to improve one's economic position. Also, I am concerned about the tendency for the distribution to become more skewed.[41] Efforts to change this trend seem justified.

We need to note at this point that there is some dispute in the literature about how income should be measured.[42] The choice of measurement does have an impact on the shape of the distribution.

Robert Rector of the conservative Heritage Foundation called the poverty numbers "largely a myth," saying the Census Bureau's methods fail to account for billions of dollars in non-cash assistance to low-income families.[43]

Rector has a point, as will be demonstrated in the following table. However, I would disagree that the numbers are a myth. They simply reflect varying views as to how the poverty rate should be measured. In addition, it is important to remember that we are focusing here on the market. The unadjusted numbers give a better indication of what the market would do in the absence of government programs

In Table 3.2, I present some of the alternate measures, along with their impact on the distribution.

Readers who are interested in these numbers can find much more detail and explanation in the source report. I'll offer the following interpretations. First, row 2 shows essentially the market distribution, without government intervention. It suggests that the market distribution, as might be expected, is more skewed than the final distribution in the United States. Second, row 5 shows primarily the effect of federal income taxes. It is interesting to note that our progressive taxes have relatively little impact on the distribution. Third, rows 6, 7, and 8 indicate the effect of adding in government transfer payments. Each shows an improvement in the relative status of the lowest 20 percent. Adding in items like Social Security payments (row 6), then payments such as AFDC benefits (row 7), and finally transfers such as food stamps (row 7) increases the percentage share significantly. Is it enough? Since there is no objective measure, we're sure to get considerable debate. Is it too much? I doubt that many would argue that 5.1 percent of "the pie" is too much for the lowest-income 20 percent of the population. In fairness, however, if they (or you) do feel this way, there is again no objective way of proving you wrong. This would have to remain an issue on which reasonable people (I'll give you the benefit of the doubt if you'll allow me the same) can reasonably disagree.

Table 3.2

Impact of Varying Measures of Income on Income Distribution

Definition of Income	Lowest Fifth	Highest Fifth
1. Money income (current measure)	3.8	46.8
2. Def. 1 less government cash transfers	1.0	50.4
3. Def. 2 plus capital gains	0.9	51.3
4. Def. 3 plus capital gains and health insurance supplements, less OASDHI taxes	0.9	51.3
5. Def. 4 less federal income taxes plus the earned income tax credit less state income taxes (small impact from the last two)	1.1	48.6
6. Def. 5 plus nonmeans-tested government cash transfers	3.6	45.1
7. Def. 6 plus the value of Medicare, the value of regular-price school lunches, and means tested government cash transfers (small impact from first two)	4.4	43.9
8. Def. 7 plus the value of Medicaid, plus the value of other means-tested government noncash transfers (largest impact of the three), plus net imputed return on equity in home	5.1	43.3

Source: Table B, Percentage of Aggregate Income Received by Income Quintiles and Index of Income Concentration, by Definition of Income: 1991 and 1992, U.S. Bureau of the Census, Current Population Reports, Series P-60-186RD, *Measuring the Effect of Benefits and Taxes on Income and Poverty: 1992* (Washington, DC: U.S. Government Printing Office, 1993).

Another set of figures that frequently interest policy makers is the poverty rate. This figure is also controversial because there is no universal agreement on just what the poverty line should be. The essence of our current poverty line is some determination of the cost of an adequate diet. This is multiplied by about 3, on the grounds the average family needs to spend about one-third of its income on food. There is some evidence that this percentage today should be less than one-third, but the original multiple persists. There is also disagreement about the types of income which should be included, such as the differences discussed above. Nonetheless, I present in Table 3.3 the current numbers. I regard them as reasonable estimates.

Another interesting statistic: the average amount of money needed to raise the incomes of each poor family above the poverty level was $5,751 in 1992.[44]

Table 3.3

Number of Families Below the Poverty Level and Poverty Rate:
1959-1992

Year	Poverty Rate
1992	11.7
1973	8.8
1959	18.5

Source: Table D, U.S. Bureau of the Census, Current Population Reports, Series P-60-185, *Poverty in the United States: 1992* (Washington, DC: U.S. Government Printing Office, 1993).

Current Wealth Distribution

If the distribution of income is skewed more than seems justified, even more so is wealth. In 1989, the top 1 percent of households in the United States accounted for 37 percent of private net worth and was worth more than the bottom 90 percent.[45] According to Harvard University economic historian Claudia Goldin,

> inequality is at its highest since the great leveling of wages and wealth during the New Deal and World War II.[46]

On an international scale, the picture is even more dramatic. In 1993, the 101 wealthiest people in the world had a total net worth of $455 billion—just less than the gross domestic product of Spain. Led by the Sultan of Brunei with $37 billion, their average net worth was $4.5 billion.[47]

Developments Affecting Wealth Distribution

There are two trends which should give us cause for concern about the future of wealth distribution. These are advances in technology and reduction in available land.

Improvements in Technology

Advancements in technology have certainly been a boon to our economic existence. One of the banes of such advances, however, is the tendency toward concentration of wealth. Consider the possibility of a robot which can do the work of twenty humans. The one person who owns this robot is able to garner all the income from its production, without the need to share it with any of the previously needed twenty humans.

Reduction in Available Land

When it was still possible for ambitious persons to acquire land and work it for a profit, or even for personal use, that land was the means of distributing wealth among more people. Today, there is virtually no new land available. Those who already own what is there have the opportunity to capitalize on that fact.

Requirement for a Pool of Unemployed Labor

In the market system, the price of labor (wages) is a function of supply and demand. If the supply of labor were fully employed, those at the bottom of the pay scale could demand higher wages, knowing there was no one with whom the employer could replace them. This, it is generally agreed, would lead to an unacceptable level of inflation. The conventional wisdom among economists is that unemployment must be no less than some percentage in order to prevent this inflationary impact. Just what that level is no one knows for sure. It appears to have increased in recent years, however, and probably lies somewhere between 3 and 6 percent.

Thus, while the federal government policy is ostensibly to reduce unemployment, there looms always the specter of being too successful. We must remember that this ''4 percent'' is not just a figure, but represents real human beings who are not at the moment being compensated by the market.[48]

The actual unemployment rate has in recent years been well above the minimum.[49] For example, from August, 1991 to July, 1992 it fluctuated between 6.8 percent and 7.8 percent.[50]

Some Costs Not Adequately Reflected

In a totally fair system, the costs of all goods would reflect all of the costs which went into producing them. Producers currently, of course, pay wages and the costs of energy and raw materials. The problem is that sometimes the price they must pay does not incorporate certain hidden costs.

Human Costs

Even if we concede that the market values relative contributions correctly, there remain some underlying costs which are not reflected. One such cost has been incorporated to a degree. Some of the trauma to the individual laborer has, since the advent of workers compensation laws, become a part of the price of the product produced by that worker. This occurs because the employer is compelled to pay a stipulated level of benefits to employees who are injured on the job. The cost of these benefits, in the form of either insurance premiums or direct payments to the injured worker, become a cost of doing business. They are then passed on to the consumer in a higher-priced product. Thus, products which are more dangerous to produce become more expensive.

This move has not completely incorporated these costs, however. Only those injuries which can be shown to have been caused by the work will be compensated. The general wear and tear on a person's body or the mental problems caused by continuous stress are generally not compensated.[51] Even the staunch advocate of the market system, Adam Smith,[52] made reference to the effects of subjecting people to mind-numbing routines.[53]

Depletion of Resources

Over the years, producers and users of products have benefited from the taking of things of value while paying little or nothing for them. They have taken these valuable resources from the rest of us. By us, I refer not only to the generation currently living but also to future generations. The list of such free goods starts in farming. How can we ever value the soil which has been lost because of tilling? We need not even introduce the idea of careless farming to recognize that farming itself will inevitably result in depletion of the land. Granted, modern farming techniques have made vast improvements in this respect. However, these improvements have been driven to a great extent by the tremendous soil losses of the past—losses which were never reflected in the price of the product produced by the farmers. In addition to tilling, grazing has also operated to deplete rangelands.[54]

Timber harvest in old-growth forests, open-sea fishing, and mining are other examples of this problem. Granted, in some of these activities the owners must pay "us" something for the use of the resource. For example, mining rights must generally be purchased today. However, in the past there was no such cost imposed. Even today, "we" receive nothing to compensate for the depletion of the ocean's supply of fish nor for the loss of wild creatures which accompanies this activity.

This topic brings to mind an analogy used by a former colleague. It seems one of his children set up a lemonade stand in the front yard. At the end of the day, the child was proud that he had cleared some 25 cents from the operation. My colleague pointed out, however, that the lemons, the ice, the water, the sugar, and even the land were provided free of charge.[55] Today when those who harvest our natural resources are not required to pay an adequate charge for those resources, their profits are similarly inflated.[56]

Pollution

In addition to those enterprises and users which take from the environment without paying an adequate price, there are those who put things into the environment without paying a price for the deterioration of natural resources. Progress has been made in recent years to impose a cost for pollution, but this effort had to be made through government. The private enterprise system, in and of itself, would not have adequately reflected these costs.

Tendency Toward Monopolies

The image of the small entrepreneur competing for customers with other similar businesses is the quintessential idea of private enterprise. In business after business, that vision no longer coincides with reality. Efforts have been made over the years through government to stem this growth, but it is rowing against the tide. The primary effort is the anti-trust laws. These laws are a recognition of the natural tendency in some industries for one firm to become dominant. This occurs when, for example, economies of scale allow the larger firm to sell at lower prices. When that happens, the benefits of competition are lost.

Among the other governmental efforts over the years to stem the growth of dominant firms were the fair trade laws. One aspect of these laws was a stipulation that retailers charge the price set by the manufacturer. This prevented larger outlets from dominating the market by charging lower prices than on which smaller businesses could survive. In the insurance area, there are anti-rebate laws which prevent large insurance agencies from selling at lower commissions, thus "unfairly" competing with small agencies. Even the laws prohibiting advertising by lawyers are at least in part designed to prevent large law firms from dominating the market.

All of these government actions reflect a recognition that unfettered free enterprise cannot be tolerated. It may well be the best economic system, but it has its blemishes, and these must be mitigated by government.

Effects of Mass Society on Income Distribution

The problem of monopolies has plagued the private enterprise system for over a century. A relatively new phenomenon is the ability of a few individuals to "monopolize" certain services. For examples, I point to the entertainment industry, sports,[57] and news broadcasting.

Where once there were traveling troupes or local groups of actors, vaudevillians, and circus performers, we now have television and movie theaters. As a result, one singer or actor is able to satisfy the entertainment needs of millions at one time. Where once there were semi-pro baseball teams, now there are major league teams playing to huge audiences with fans all over the country. Where once there were local news broadcasters handling even the national news (and before that, the town criers), now there are national news anchors. In a later chapter I will focus on the effect of this phenomenon on the availability of jobs. At this point I want to emphasize the tendency to concentrate incomes in a relatively small number of people.

Less Competition Where Less Demand

The travails of those with low incomes are often compounded by the market. The challenge of getting oneself out of poverty is not only one of income but also of expenses. Among the expenditures which are more costly for poor people are groceries, housing (relative to the quality of the accommodations), and interest on loans.

The first two are a consequence of the areas in which low-income people generally live. Because the demand in these areas is relatively low, the eagerness with which stores are opened is also low. Within six blocks of where I live there are two huge supermarkets, as well as three discount stores carrying some groceries. Competition is fierce. The cost of goods for a given level of quality is naturally lower in a situation like this than it is in a central city area or an isolated rural area. This is compounded when merchants in central city areas must charge a premium to cover security costs or those in rural areas have to build in the greater costs of transportation.

Housing costs are often a function of low supply relative to demand. Where space is at a premium, as in central city areas, prices soar. This would be no problem when people have a choice where to live, but because the mobility of the poor is limited, it is a problem.

Higher interest rates are a natural consequence of poverty. (This point may be too obvious to require elaboration, but I didn't want to have a paragraph that was only one short sentence.) Those with few assets and an inadequate credit history pay a higher rate of interest than those with greater resources. These resources in some cases belong to family members of wealthier individuals, who themselves can supply collateral and/or co-signatures on notes. We should add here the point that the inability to get credit at all has negative consequences which compound the plight of the poor. For example, they frequently are constrained to leasing household furnishings, when purchasing would in the long run be so much less expensive.

Income Changes as Demand Changes

"Of course!" say the believers. "That is the beauty of the market system. Resources are automatically reallocated to meet the new demand." And so it is, and so they are. Nonetheless, we must recognize the ugliness of this from the standpoint of justice. Where is the justice in relating one's income to the vagaries of demand? Suppose, for example, the demand for beef drops. The talents of cattle ranchers are consequently less highly valued. An individual rancher can work smarter and harder, and still see a reduction in income. Necessary, yes. Just, no.

Supply-Side Impacts on Low Incomes

Theoretically, the price paid for one's labor is a function of what that labor input is worth. Higher-skilled workers contribute more, so they are paid more. This is partly because there is a greater demand for their talents. The problem is, the wage is also a function of the level of supply of various levels of talent. Since it happens, and probably always will be, that there are a larger number of low-skilled than of high-skilled workers, the price for the input of the low-skilled worker is further depressed. Wages, then, are not only a function of how skilled one is but also of how many other people also have that skill. Sidgwick comments on this thus:

> It does not seem that any individual's social Desert can properly be lessened merely by the increased number or willingness of others rendering the same service.[58]

Sidgwick notes that the shortcomings of the market have led some to propose that value be determined by ''enlightened and competent judges.'' He suggests, however, that:

> This supposes that we have found the rational method of determining value; which, however, is still to seek.[59]

This problem is compounded in our society by the absence of a base income on which to rely. The opportunity for low-skilled workers (or workers with outdated skills) to upgrade their skills is limited by the absence of an income during periods of training.[60]

LONG-RUN PROSPECTS FOR CAPITALISM

According to Heilbroner, there is a widespread consensus among major economists throughout history that the future of capitalism is bleak. Not only does he reference Marx but also Adam Smith, Alfred Marshall, John Maynard Keynes, and Friedrich Hayek, all of whom have some negative things to say about the long-range prospects for this economic system. An underlying theme to all of the concerns is the belief that capitalism requires continued growth in order to survive. Finite limits on resources and threats to the environment are two factors which may limit this growth. Another concern, more relevant to my argument, is rooted in what Heilbroner refers to as ''a widespread sense of disquiet with regard to the moral basis of capitalism.''[61]   Citing text from Adam Smith, he reminds us that capital always has an unequal bargaining position relative to labor. One of the problems is that owners can generally hold out longer in any dispute than can labor. (Of course, unemployment compensation has helped somewhat in this regard, but in most states that benefit cannot be drawn when the unemployment is the result of a strike.) Among the other problems listed by Heilbroner is an unequal distribution of incomes and the required sense of antagonism among the members of a society based upon competition.

Heilbroner discusses a relatively new proposal for a new participatory order, but concludes that this will probably not be achievable until toward the end of the next century.[62] Meanwhile, he suggests:

> Its ideas and ideals would serve us in good purpose while we wrestle with the huge problems of making capitalism work as well as possible as long as possible.[63]

Those interested in the long-term survival of capitalism should look upon my proposal in this book with great favor. One of the major effects would be to improve the bargaining position of labor. With a guaranteed adequate income, they would be able to "hold out" on a more equal footing with owners. In addition, it certainly helps to redress the moral problem of the unequal distribution of incomes.

A primary fault of the market is its unjust treatment of those with little to offer. Government has been active in rectifying this shortcoming also. I argue, however, that many of our current efforts in this regard do undesirable damage to the otherwise beneficial aspects of the market system. That is the subject of the following section.

CURRENT WELFARE INTERFERENCES WITH THE MARKET

Government has a role to play in providing for the welfare of the citizenry. I argue that this role can be most effectively and efficiently played through the provision of a guaranteed adequate income. This would be accomplished through a simple income distribution scheme, which would have a positive impact on the working of the market system. A major benefit would be the concurrent elimination of the present welfare system, with its hodgepodge of programs, many of which have negative consequences for the market.

Minimum Wage Laws

Although these laws have been broadly accepted by the general public, they are anathema to proponents of a free market. These advocates point out, rightly I believe, that a major impact of these laws is to reduce the level of employment. There is evidence that increases in the minimum wage particularly increase teenage unemployment. There are at least two reasons for this. First, some businesses do not exist because of the laws. Those enterprises which could make a profit were labor less expensive than allowed by the laws are prevented from plying their trade because of these laws. Second, many businesses have replaced people with machines in more cases than they otherwise would have, had not these laws existed. Finally, because the laws do not universally apply they act to favor businesses which do not have to comply with them.

Subsidized Housing

In an effort to ensure our welfare dollars go to providing the type of benefit we prefer, we necessarily interfere in the market. In the case of subsidized housing, this occurs in at least two forms. First, the consumption decision of the recipient is altered. Someone whose preference is to spend x percent of her income on clothing and y percent on housing will now spend less than x percent on clothing and more than y percent on housing (when the subsidy is counted, as it should be). It may be that we, as the voting public, wish ''her'' to change her preferences in this way. Even so, we must recognize this interference in the market. Sellers of clothing are doing less business because of this and providers of housing are doing more.

Second, the overall cost of housing, relative to other goods, increases because of the greater relative demand. This is a result directly contrary to our goal of encouraging more spending on housing.

Food Stamps

As indicated in Chapter 2, one of the major purposes of food stamps is to impact the market. By creating a greater demand for food, we increase the price of that food and thus the income of farmers. This is nobly motivated. However, we must recognize that it comes at the expense of some other segment of our economy. If we gave money instead of food stamps, and recipients chose to spend less of this money on food and more, say, on movies, there would be a relative benefit to the movie industry. This would ultimately benefit the grips (whoever they are) and the stunt performers. Who are we to say they are any less deserving than farmers?

Farm Price Supports

As with food stamps, a major impact of this program is to divert resources from one segment of the economy to another. How do we justify this? Perhaps our goal is to support a way of life. If so, why don't we just do this directly. If you want to farm, we will send you $2,000 per year! Done this blatantly, the program would probably not receive much support. In the contorted guise of price supports, it seems more palatable. Is our goal to ensure a steady production of certain commodities? If so, how do we justify inclusion of tobacco farmers in the list of recipients?

A major argument in favor of this program is the desire to reduce poverty among farmers. If that is our goal, the guaranteed adequate income proposal is a much more efficient way of accomplishing it. And it comes without interference in the working of the market.

Selective Income Tax Deductions

Under our present income tax structure we allow each other to keep more of what we earn if we have spent our money in certain ways.[64] For example, if we give money to qualifying charities, that expenditure may be deducted from our income in the process of calculating our income taxes. Even this is a slight impingement upon the market. Since a government agency has the power to decide which charities qualify, it also determines which are going to get more money (since most donors will only give if the gift is deductible).

The ability to deduct interest payments is a prime example of market interference. Presently, we can only deduct interest paid on home mortgages. The effect of this is to encourage us to spend our money on home building or buying, thus favoring that market at the expense of other.[65]

Deductions for medical expenses are also relevant here. In some instances the decision as to which expenses which will be considered medical expenses and which not is arbitrary. The market for the allowable expenses is benefited relative to the others.

Finally, the whole area of business expenses impacts the market. In the first place, we are encouraged to go into business for ourselves because we then have the opportunity to deduct many expenses we could not otherwise. For example, our own meals can be deducted if we are dining out with a business associate. Even a round of golf can be deducted if it has a business purpose.[66]

Progressive Income Taxes

Later in the book I will make an argument for a flat income tax. I will suggest it would be facilitated by the introduction of the guaranteed adequate income. For now, I wish to simply suggest the progressive tax is antimarket. The point can be made by comparing two individuals— let's say they are consultants—who are contemplating taking on one more client. The more successful of the two, who is in a higher tax bracket, will have less incentive to take on the additional work than will the other. The less successful can lower the price of the service and still net the same income after taxes as would the more successful. Hence the effect of generating relatively more business for the less successful consultant.

Public School Education

I personally have no particular quarrels with our socialized public school education. I'm a product of public primary and secondary schools and a public university (an I kin write purty good, huh?). I wish to point out, however, that a main impetus for public education is the inability of some of our citizens to afford private education. Given that we want all to have access, public schools were our only choice. If, on the other hand, all of our citizens had a guaranteed income which was adequate to provide education as well as sustenance, a strong case could be made for private schools. The effects of competition should lead to more innovation and greater efficiency. One caution, however. In order for competition to work effectively, consumers must, in theory, have "perfect knowledge." That is, they must be able to compare products to determine which provides the best quality at the lowest price. Can consumers of education do this? I'm not so sure. I'm even less sure when it comes to the next area.

Publicly Provided Health Care

The health-care segment of our economy certainly has not been socialized to the same extent education has. However, there is considerable activity. This includes social insurance programs and public health clinics, as well as many community-owned hospitals. I have touched on the issue of socialized medicine elsewhere in this book. It makes as much sense as socialized education, but suffers from the same "lack of knowledge" constraint on the part of consumers. At this juncture I wish to make just two points. The first is that public medical care is antimarket, and the second is that the pressure for publicly provided medical care would be a lot less if all citizens had an income adequate to purchase health insurance.

The Kaus Argument

There is another side to this picture. There are those who feel the use of government to provide services should be *expanded* rather than contracted. This case is made quite compellingly in *The End of Equality* by Mickey Kaus.[67] He argues against just the sort of programs that I am advocating. His major thesis is that attempts to equalize incomes will never succeed, and that "money liberals" must give up this pursuit.[68] What he proposes instead is that the public sphere be expanded so as to provide more services on an equal basis for all. Examples would include government-run health care and day-care, as well as the expansion of public parks. In addition, he advocates government intervention to see that certain private institutions remain, or become more, egalitarian.[69]

Kaus's argument is well presented and reasoned. He recognizes the limitations of the market in providing some basic services and envisions a reasonable role for government. I feel, however, that we should limit this role as much as possible in order to maximize the benefits of the market. To do this, however, we need to ensure that all citizens have at least some minimum access to that market.

THE BENEFITS OF THE GAI TO THE MARKET

I'd like to digress for a bit to discuss the purpose of this chapter. Frankly, it is aimed at those who, because of their political philosophy, will tend to dismiss the guaranteed adequate income as a liberal scheme. I genuinely believe, however, that this proposal makes sense not only from the standpoint of justice but also because of its beneficial impact on the private enterprise system. This latter benefit may not be as obvious, but it is there. I intend in this chapter to make those points clear to those readers for whom the defense of capitalism is a primary goal.

The first benefit in this regard is the elimination of the interferences in the market from our current welfare program. Those negative impacts were discussed above. In addition, there are the following benefits.

Eliminates "Bottom-End-Out" Problem

We have previously discussed how the market system virtually demands some be unemployed. To compensate for this, our society has instituted a complex set of social welfare measures designed to alleviate the problems of those who are left out. We have some plans, and a multitude of proposals, for helping people to get into the job force.[70]   My guaranteed adequate income would eliminate all these other programs.

Eliminates Need for Minimum Wage Laws

I have previously discussed the negative impact of these laws. One of the serendipitous effects of the GAI is the elimination of the need for these market-skewing laws. By guaranteeing people a minimum income through the government mechanism, we would eliminate the need to impose restrictions on the private sector. It may be that more jobs would open up, since lower wages could be paid. In addition, more small businesses would be able to make a profit if wages were lower. Whether the lower wages would actually occur, however, is not clear. An effect of the GAI would be to reduce the supply of labor for low-paying jobs, thus causing wages to rise for a given level of demand for labor.

Allows Use of Flat Income Tax

It is commonly accepted that the purpose of the progressive income tax is to impose a higher-percentage tax on wealthier people. It should be noted, however, that a corollary purpose is to avoid imposing too high a tax on low-income people. The GAI, by bringing all citizens up to at least some minimum level, would allow us to impose a higher tax rate on the earnings of those with low incomes. By so doing, we could create a flat tax which would generate sufficient revenue without the need to impose the higher tax rates on higher income earners.

Why would we want to do this? I'll explore this issue in greater depth in a later chapter (incorporating the views of others). For now, I'll simply note two advantages: it would reduce the impact of the progressive tax on the market, and it would allow us to justify eliminating certain deductions which benefit high-income people more than low-income people.

Stimulates Demand

One means of stimulating an economy is to increase demand. One way to increase demand is to put more money into the hands of those who will spend it.[71] The GAI will provide not only an overall stimulus but will also stimulate development in areas currently lacking it. An obvious reason there is so little economic development, particularly at the retail level, in central city areas is that there is insufficient demand. The easiest method of rectifying this is to create a demand. Efforts to solve the problem through the supply side have failed, and will continue to fail.

There is also a shortage of well-maintained, low-rent housing. I argue if the demand were there, the market would create and compete. "Create the demand, and they will build it."

Encourages Mobility

A market system thrives when participants are able to adjust to changes in supply and demand. For example, if the relative demand for labor changes in a particular geographical area, this should be met by a movement of labor to that area. With a guaranteed adequate income providing security, more people will be able to adjust to these changes. A similar point can be made with respect to changes in the relative demand for certain skills. Those who can be assured of an income to tide them over while retooling will have a greater opportunity to obtain these skills.[72]

Where there is presently too great a demand for housing space relative to the supply, as in the central city areas, the GAI will enable movement to areas where there is a greater supply.

SUMMARY

Capitalism, with its attendant market-based economy, is the best system yet devised for accumulating wealth. Its primary shortcoming is the lousy job it does of distributing wealth. It is both necessary and desirable for people in a prosperous country to utilize the government to rectify the unjust distribution. This should be done in a manner which minimizes the adverse effects on the market. Our current welfare system does not meet this criterion. A guaranteed adequate income would.

Notes

1. Robert Heilbroner, *21st Century Capitalism,* pp. 95-96.

2. Edward Bellamy, *Looking Backward: 2000-1887,* p. 282.

3. Heilbroner, *21st Century Capitalism,* pp. 26-29.

4. Ibid., p. 56.

5. "Can Private Sector Outdo Government?" *Cedar Rapids [Iowa] Gazette,* December 1, 1986, p. 2A.

6. Heilbroner, *21st Century Capitalism,* p. 74.

7. In practice, however, some face considerably more impediments than others. I suggested in Chapter 2 that the story of Horatio Alger (the poor boy who strikes it rich) is of such enduring interest because it represents not the norm but the rare exception. Perhaps the fairest opportunity for becoming rich today is the lottery. The probability of success, although slim, may be as high as that of working one's way from poverty to wealth, and one's chances are not a function of natural endowments. As a society, however, we prefer that people try to get rich the old-fashioned way because it encourages the development of talent and ability.

8. Again the caution—we really can't *prove* they grow faster than other economies.

9. Heilbroner issues a cautionary note in this regard: "It is possible—or better perhaps, it is not impossible—that the coming decades will witness a series of massive technological stimuli of the kind that have propelled us forward with irregular regularity over the past two centuries. . . . Alas, the same can be said for a drearier possibility, namely that the future will be dominated by periods of stagnation and decline." Heilbroner, *21st Century Capitalism* , p. 62.

10. It is not likely, however, that we can continue to sustain the level of growth we have seen in western countries in recent centuries. I side with those who believe resource limitations will eventually take their toll. The mystical

faith in the ability of technology to provide infinitesimal growth is, in my view, the result of believing what we want to believe, not what we should believe.

11. John Cobbs, "Egalitarianism: The Corporation as Villain," *Business Week*, December 15, 1975, p. 87. Cobbs's main focus in this work is on decrying trends toward egalitarianism.

12. According to Henry Phelps Brown, we should also be aware that Smith's "invisible hand" was not a proscription against *any* government activity; rather, it was against government trying to favor one enterprise over another and especially against the monopoly associated with government enterprise itself. Henry Phelps Brown, *Egalitarianism and the Generation of Inequality*, p. 169. It is an irony that purported defenders of the market economy engage in just what Smith cautioned against. An example is giving subsidies to firms to encourage them to move from one state to another.

13. As Brown succinctly states "The spirit of humanity works in one way, the market economy in quite another." Ibid., p. 512.

14. Underlying this analysis is the extent to which capitalism has focused attention on money income. "Under capitalism incomes were increasingly monetized. That may have provided unexampled freedoms to the average worker and advanced his income by advancing productive efficiency. But there was a distinct flaw. Monetization labeled every participant by a single, simple number—his money income (or wealth)." Stanley Lebergott, "Income Equality: Some Missing Dimensions," in Hubert J. O'Gorman (ed.), *Surveying Social Life* (Middletown, Conn.: Wesleyan University Press, 1988), p. 394.

15. A committee of the National Conference of Catholic Bishops, in a 1984 pastoral letter, "condemned what it called the 'massive and ugly' failures of the [American economic] system. Among shortcomings that the bishops cited were a 'morally unjustified' current rate of unemployment and 'gross inequalities' of wealth and income." As reported in "Am I My Brother's Keeper?" *Time*, November 26, 1984, p. 80.

16. Ron Suskind, "The Road Taken," *Wall Street Journal*, August 8, 1993, p. 1+. This article is primarily about two brothers who chose different paths. One was a corporate leveraged-buyout specialist, the other trained workers.

17. Barbara Ehrenreich, "Honor to the Working Stiffs," *Time*, September 9, 1991, p. 72.

18. Brown, *Egalitarianism and the Generation of Inequality*, p. 504.

19. Brown also makes the interesting point that those with wealth have a disproportionate impact on the valuation of resources. Since they have more to

spend, their "votes" have more effect on valuation than do the votes of those with less. Ibid., p. 503.

20. "Male-Female Executive Pay Gap Widens," *Des Moines Register*, December 25, 1993, p. 6S, citing an article in *Working Woman*, which referred to census statistics.

21. Citing Bureau of Labor Statistics figures, Nina Totenberg reported the following comparisons: nurses, $18,300 versus pharmacists, $23,000; kindergarten teachers, $20,042 versus mail carriers, $21,000; bank tellers, $9700 versus stockroom clerks, $15,000. "Why Women Earn Less," *Parade Magazine*, June 10, 1984, p. 5.

22. This has certainly changed in recent years. It may be, however, that women are not being as well educated for a given number of years schooling. That case is made in Myra and David Sadker, *Failing at Fairness: How America's Schools Cheat Girls*. See also, by the same authors, "You're Smart, You Can Do It," *USA Weekend* magazine, February 4, 1994, pp. 4-6. "Girls are the only group who begin school scoring ahead and leave behind, a theft occurring so quietly that most people are unaware of its impact."

23. Totenberg, "Why Women Earn Less," p. 5.

24. Ibid., citing a survey by *Working Woman* magazine, which also noted the gap is widening. A study done by Korn-Ferry International reported that over five years women received raises totaling 54 percent while men of equal positions got a 65 percent salary increase.

25. "Census Says Blacks Still Earning Less," *Sioux City [Iowa] Journal*, September 20, 1991, p. A9.

26. Ibid.

27. Ibid.

28. Rick Jost, "Pay Differences Can Get Pretty Ugly," *Des Moines Register*, February 18, 1991, p. 3B, citing a study done at the University of Pittsburgh and reported in *Glamour* magazine. The article also quoted George Daly, then dean of the University of Iowa College of Business Administration: "I must say, I suspect what we've discovered of MBAs is what we've always known to be true of movie stars, janitors, all walks of life. Yes, more-attractive people, like more-intelligent people and more-industrious people, tend to do better than others."

29. I don't mean by this to ignore or fail to deplore the actions of those who still consciously discriminate. However, I feel this is less significant than the influence of these market factors.

30. Football may be one area where the market works well in this regard. The most dangerous position, quarterback, is also the most highly compensated.

However, is this because it's more dangerous or because the quarterback contributes more? I don't know; do you?

31. Bernard Gavzer, "What People Make," *Parade Magazine*, June 10, 1984, p. 4. The article highlighted fifteen people and their incomes, ranging from an insurance businessman at $200,000 to contractor's aide/artist at $5,000, and including an owner of a one-man ad agency ($70,000) and a municipal judge ($57,500).

32. Cleveland Amory, "What the Rich Earn," *Parade Magazine*, June 10, 1984, p. 6.

33. I am aware of the "short career" argument, but am not persuaded. The accumulated value of these earnings early in life more than compensate for this fact. In 1992, Cal Ripken signed for $6.5 million a year for five years with the Baltimore Orioles (at the time, the richest deal in baseball history). He also got a $3 million signing bonus and a $2 million post-playing career contract. "$32.5 Million Contract for Ripken," *Des Moines Register*, August 25, 1992, p. 1S. Assuming he manages to live on $1 million a year during the five years (before taxes, of course), the balance of his income even after taxes could generate at least $1 million dollars a year for the rest of his life.

34. "Business School Deans: Top Exec Pay Out of Line," *Des Moines Register*, April 20, 1992, p. 1. When asked about six specific CEOs "Not one of the six CEOs asked about is 'worth' the pay, the deans say." One of the CEOs, the CEO of Coca-Cola, received $88 million, "apparently the highest ever for a year's labor."

35. In 1993, *Forbes* magazine reported the top CEO incomes for the preceding five years. Including gains on stock options, the highest paid (the CEO of HCA Hospital Corp.) had earned $129 million. As reported in "Stock Options Fatten Wallets of CEOs," *Des Moines Register*, May 10, 1993, p. 1A.

36. "Study: Executives' Worth Fails to Match Their Pay," *Des Moines Register*, October 25, 1991, p. 1.

37. The use of the term *physician* is more apt than doctor; I'm a doctor, but Ph.D.s are usually not criticized for making too much money. Perhaps it's because, as the daughter of another holder of a doctorate said (at a young age), "He's a doctor, but not the kind that does anybody any good."

38. "Liberal guilt" is a term frequently used on talk shows to deride those who favor government programs to aid the poor. I prefer to name the phenomenon "liberal recognition." It stems from a recognition by those more fortunate that they received breaks in life which others did not. Those who

deride this attitude seem more likely to feel they *deserve* to have what they have, and others do not.

39. Table B-8, Average Income-to-Poverty Ratios for Families, by Income Quintile, Race, and Hispanic Origin: 1967 to 1992, U.S. Bureau of the Census, Current Population Reports, Series P60-184, *Money Income of Households, Families and Persons in the United States: 1992* (Washington, D.C.: U.S. Government Printing Office, 1993).

40. Another way of looking at the skewness of incomes is to compare the mean incomes (shown in Table 3.1) with median incomes (see—there is a use for high school math). Where the median income is less than the mean, it suggests that a relatively small number of people are earning a relatively large income. In 1992, the median income for all households was $30,786; for white households $32,368; for black households $18,660; households with Hispanic origin $22,848. Table 1, U.S. Bureau of the Census, Current Population Reports, Series P-60-186RD, *Measuring the Effect of Benefits and Taxes on Income and Poverty: 1992* (Washington, D.C.: U.S. Government Printing Office, 1993).

41. According to Robert Greenstein of the Center on Budget and Policy Priorities, a liberal think tank, "the long-term trend is toward increasing income inequality." "Highest Number in Poverty Since '64," *Des Moines Register*, September 4, 1992, p. 6A.

42. cf. Lebergott, "Income Equality: Some Missing Dimensions." Lebergott suggests we fail to consider *inter alia* such factors as the increase of direct consumption income at the expense of money income; a growing preference for leisure; a growing preference for safer workplaces; and a growing preference for "being a hired hand." He suggests, however, that "proposals to redistribute income, of course, are not endangered by the fragility of [these measures]. But our understanding of what redistributive policies can achieve may be affected," p. 394.

43. "Highest Number in Poverty Since '64," p. 6A.

44. U.S. Bureau of the Census, Current Population Reports, Series P-60-185, *Poverty in the United States: 1992* (Washington, D.C.: U.S. Government Printing Office, 1993), p. viii.

45. According to the government's triennial Survey of Consumer Finances. Reported in "Top 1% Own More than Bottom 90%," *Des Moines Register*, April 21, 1992, p. 4A.

46. Ibid.

47. "Rich Get Richer—But Not Much," *Des Moines Register*, June 10, 1993, p. 7S. The article referred to an article in *Fortune* magazine.

48. Perhaps we should develop an award, such as "Hero of the Market" to at least recognize their contribution.

49. Actually, there is some controversy about what the "actual" unemployment rate is. In order to be counted as unemployed, one must have not worked during the survey period, must have made a positive effort to find a job, and must be currently available to take a job. Thus, for example, disabled people are not counted as unemployed. Neither are those who have become discouraged and quit looking for a job, nor those who are involuntarily only working part-time. Some say this dramatically understates the unemployment rate, particularly for certain groups; cf. "Hispanic Unemployment Called Vastly Understated," *Des Moines Register*, August 8, 1992, p. 3A. The Labor Council for Latin American Advancement claimed the real unemployment rate for Hispanics was 21 percent in mid-1992, not the 11.2 percent reported by the Bureau of Labor Statistics.

50. "Jobless Rate Drops a Bit in July," *Des Moines Register*, August 8, 1992, p. 10S.

51. The trend is toward compensating more such losses. For example, mental injuries are now recognized in some jurisdictions, even in the absence of a physical injury.

52. According to Henry Phelps Brown, Smith recognized the inequalities and injustice stemming from the market system, but felt they had to be accepted because there was no social system at the time to remedy them. Brown, *Egalitarianism and the Generation of Inequality*, p. 106.

53. As noted in Heilbroner, *21st Century Capitalism*, p. 111. Heilbroner adds to the list of market-induced problems the effect on our moral well-being of constant propaganda in the form of advertising.

54. There are even more subtle depletions. Have we not lost something of value as a result of the near extinction of certain species of wild animals because of their impact on farming and ranching?

55. My colleague used this story to point out how government agencies sometimes do not adequately account for the cost of the space they use when they attempt to show how efficient they are. It is equally applicable to my point here.

56. Alternatively, in a competitive market, the benefit inures to those who purchase the product—in the form of lower prices.

57. This could be considered a subcategory of entertainment.

58. Henry Sidgwick, *The Methods of Ethics*, p. 284. Sidgwick also points out that if a person is eager to provide a service, that person will earn less than one who is reluctant to do so—a perverse result.

59. Ibid., p. 289. My own view is that we *ought* to be able to agree everyone is "worth" *at least* some minimum (adequate) amount.

60. Unemployment compensation is available to some—but only to those who are *involuntarily* unemployed and have previously been employed, and then for only a limited time.

61. Heilbroner, *21st Century Capitalism,* p. 131.

62. As proposed by Michael Albert and Robin Hahnel in *Looking Forward: Participatory Economics for the Twenty First Century.*

63. Heilbroner, *21st Century Capitalism,* p. 155.

64. Again, the democratic *we.*

65. I have previously noted the negative welfare implications of this deduction, including the fact that only those who can afford to buy a house can take advantage of the deduction.

66. Even the act of writing this book allows me to deduct some expenses other people cannot deduct.

67. Mickey Kaus, *The End of Equality.*

68. Note, however, that my proposal does not call for equalizing incomes, only for raising the bottom level.

69. He suggests, for example, limiting tax deductions to reduce the impact of corporate boxes at baseball games. Kaus, *The End of Equality*, p. 100.

70. In Chapter 6, I discuss the problems with most proposals for change.

71. I am aware of the potential for a negative consequence of this—inflation. I am also aware of the classic conflict between those who want to stimulate the market through consumption and those who want to do so through savings. I have tried to follow this issue for decades, and frankly I'm not sure which side has the better of this argument. The only thing I'm quite sure about is that no one is justified in being sure about this.

72. This clearly will have less negative impact on the market than the currently popular efforts to impose retraining on people, particularly through government-run programs.

4

Work—Who Needs It?

Work for the night is coming; Work through the sunny noon;
Fill brightest hours with labor; Rest comes sure and soon;
Give every flying minute; Something to keep in store;
Work for the night is coming; When man works no more.[1]

These lines from a popular Protestant hymn provide one example of the zeal with which many of us were taught to regard work.[2] It is something we *should* do, something we *must* do, and even something we should *want* to do.[3] It is also something we want others (particularly our children?) to do. But what is it, and why must we (they) do it?

The answers to these questions are critical to the argument in this book. The most common response I receive when I suggest a guaranteed adequate income is: "But then who would work?" For many, this question is the bete noir[4] of the argument. They seem to suggest the discussion should end there. My smart-aleck response, however, is "So what's your point?" So what if some people choose not to work? Would we face Armageddon?

In this chapter, I consider in greater depth the issue of work. Is it essential to society that we maintain a system that compels people to work in order to survive? Is it essential to individuals themselves that they work? Do we do a disservice to our fellow citizens if we remove part of the incentive to work?[5]

WORK —WHAT IS IT?

It is important to recognize that there is a tremendous range of activities to which we apply the name "work."[6] The nature of work has changed dramatically. Playing ball is now work, and gardening is now leisure. Our attitudes toward work must catch up with reality. Just what are the essential components of work? Just what is it we as a society want people to do in this regard? When our mothers told us "Always do your best work," did they mean strike the golf ball as purely as possible? I don't think so! At least not my mom.

My discussions with students and others have yielded a number of factors which seem to make up the complex notion of work.[7] Among these are:

• Compensation
• Productivity
• Onerousness
• Compulsion

Let's look carefully at these components in order to better develop our concept of work. In the process we must decide whether each of these elements is *necessary* to label an activity as work, as well as determine whether each is *sufficient*.

In order that you might better follow the discussion, and so you can be alert to the implications, let me tell you where I am going with this. I think you will discover, as I have, that the concept of work is so broad as to disqualify it as the ultimate objective of our economic lives. Work is often desirable, is generally productive, and may contribute to one's self-esteem. In short, it is usually a good thing. But . . . it isn't absolutely necessary we all do it.

OK, so what is it?

Work Is Something for Which One Gets Compensated

If somebody will pay you to do it, then it must be valued. Therefore, you are doing a valuable thing. Therefore, so the reasoning goes, it is good that you work.

Compensation as a Sufficient Criterion

If we regard this element as sufficient, it allows us to conclude that a professional baseball player works. This is true, however, only when he is on a team, and then only during the season. Of course, you might argue that the season's pay is designed to compensate for the full year. This is slippery, however. How do we view the player who has been cut from a team but not yet picked up by another team? Is he no longer working, even though he is engaging in exactly the same activities he would have, had he not been cut?

A similar point can be made with respect to teachers. If they are on a nine-month contract, do we say they don't work during the summer? Is the teacher whose contract has not been renewed for next year not working during the summer, while those with expected continued employment are?[8]

What about a professor who is on sabbatical?[9] I can provide a case in point. I am writing this book while on a sabbatical. (Remember—at this point we are only considering the issue of compensation, not productivity or the other factors.) If compensation is the issue, I am working (although my compensation was reduced, as is typically the case during a sabbatical). But what if I were plagued with a severe case of writer's block and never quite got started with my book? Would we still say I worked during this year? If compensation is a sufficient criterion, then I did.

Do beggars work? If enough people come by and drop something in their cup for them to survive, we might conclude they are being compensated. If compensation is a sufficient criterion, they are working.

Compensation as a Necessary Criterion

At the other end of the compensation spectrum, we have people who labor long and hard but earn nothing. What of the commissioned salesperson who never makes a sale? If compensation is a necessary criterion for work, we must conclude that person did not work during the period at issue. For those readers who regard this example as extreme, let's make the issue a little more complicated. What of the blind person selling pencils or a deaf person selling sign language cards?[10] Are you more inclined to say they are working? Note, however, in both cases, the compensation they receive probably bears little resemblance to the service they are providing.

And what of the homemaker? The person who cleans her or his own house, prepares meals, and raises the children—is this work, since it is generally not compensated?[11] For my part, I would say it is. I think a case can be made that child rearing is the most important work done by anyone in society.

Can a volunteer "work?" Not if compensation is a necessary element of work. Still, wouldn't most of us feel a hospital volunteer is "doing good work" or picking up trash in the city park on neighborhood clean-up day is "hard work?" During the recent floods in the Midwest, substantial work was done by volunteers filling and placing sandbags —all without compensation.

It seems at this point reasonable to conclude that compensation is neither a sufficient nor a necessary element of work. The fact we get paid does not per se mean we are working, and when we work we do not always get paid.

Work Must Be Onerous

Many people have suggested to me that work is something we don't enjoy doing. It is, therefore, something unpleasant. It is a chore or a drudge.

Onerousness as a Sufficient Criterion

If we don't like what we do, is that sufficient to say we are working? Surely not. There are those who "hang around the house" all day, bored and unhappy. They don't like what they are doing, but few of us would say they are working.

Onerousness as a Necessary Criterion

Is it necessary we not like what we are doing in order to be considered working? I think not. For many, their jobs are their primary source of pleasure in life. They would rather be working than playing. According to sociologist Robert Shrank,

> People like jobs mainly because they need other people; they need to gossip with them, hang out with them, schmooze.[12]

Work, for many people, is not onerous. For some, it is one of the most pleasurable things they do. There is greater difference between types of work—onerous versus enjoyable—than there is between work and leisure.

Work Is Something People Must Be Compelled to Do

Perhaps the essence of work is simply the fact we have to do it. Therefore, those activities in which we must engage, but prefer not to, are what we call work.

Compulsion as a Sufficient Criterion

If compulsion is a sufficient criterion, then any time we do something we don't want to do, we are working. Youngsters are working when their parents make them pick up their clothes. Students are working when they are compelled to study. A person who misses the last bus home and has to walk is working. The homeowner who dislikes mowing the lawn is working when doing so.

Compulsion as a Necessary Criterion

Shall we consider a person to be working only if he or she is compelled to do so? What then of the millionaire who continues to work just because it is enjoyable? Or the retiree who seeks employment in order to have something to do?

An Activity Is Work Only If It Is Productive

The image that probably comes to most minds when they think of someone working is that they are doing something productive. They are accomplishing a task, providing a service, or creating a product.

Productivity as a Sufficient Criterion

If productivity is sufficient to label an activity as work, then those who mow their own lawns and tend their own gardens "work," even if they are not compensated.[13] So certainly do homemakers and child rearers. This latter category is particularly important when we consider criticisms of our current welfare programs. In the current round of welfare reform, the solution to the woes of our Aid to Families With Dependent Children program is to "put them to work." By the productivity criterion, however, they *are* working. What could be a more important contribution than raising the next generation?[14]

Productivity as a Necessary Criterion

Are there some people who meet the compensation requirement, but would not be regarded as workers because they are not "productive"? We might have a variety of views of who these people might be, but I suspect we would agree there are some such people. How about the professional golfers? They (most of them) make money for what they do, but are they "productive"? A basis for answering yes would be that they provide entertainment. If so, we could consider them in a category with singers and actresses and painters. How about a salaried salesperson who sells nothing during a pay period? Working? Or an author who is given an advance on a book, but never quite gets the book written? A salaried fisherman who comes home empty-handed? Some may wish to put certain government bureaucrats in the category of those who are compensated but unproductive.

Although people are not always productive when they claim to be working, this is probably the most necessary element to a concept of work. We need to recognize, however, it may also be a sufficient element. That is, we need to recognize an activity as work, even if the person is not being compensated, the work is not onerous, and the person is not compelled to do it. Thus child rearing, volunteering, and home maintenance are all entitled to the label "work." Even a person receiving a guaranteed income who engages in one of these activities *is* working.

Summary

We all have some intuitive notion of what we mean by work. However, when we analyze the elements commonly regarded as components of this notion, we realize none of them is either necessary or sufficient to describe this concept. We may be left to conclude that work, like pornography, is something we can't define but we know it when we see it.

We must recognize, however, the wide range of activities which might be termed work. At one extreme we have someone like me sitting in my easy chair with my notebook computer on my lap in my warm house exercising my mind while writing this book. Or the professional golfer on a sunny day in Palm Springs playing in the Bob Hope Desert Classic. At the other extreme is a person working in a cold room in a dairy packing pounds of butter off an assembly line into cardboard boxes all day, or the street construction worker on a hot summer day running a jackhammer breaking up old concrete (these were both me at other points in my life).

My concern is with the difficulty that arises when we try to base a social norm on the nebulous concept of work. The idea that everybody who can should work is fraught with difficulties in application. If this is regarded as a social edict, the consequences for different people are too diverse. What one person has to do to comply with our edict bears little resemblance to what someone else does. Some are able to find "work" they enjoy, that is mentally challenging, comfortable, and rewarding. It may well be something they would choose to do even if they didn't have to "work." For others, the only option available is an activity that breaks down their body prematurely, that is neither satisfying nor enjoyable, and that they would never choose to do in the absence of a compulsion to "work."

As John Kenneth Galbraith puts it:

> We use the same term for hard, unpleasant, bitter, demanding effort and for what men and women are willing to sacrifice their own and other people's money, not to mention their leisure, health, family and sex life, in order to do. In using the word "work" to describe such wholly contrasting, even conflicting, designs for life, we are indulging in a uniquely transparent form of deception.[15]

A note of caution. It is easy to argue that "we" had to engage in onerous work at one time in our lives, so why shouldn't others. There is a quantum leap between doing these jobs as a stepping stone to something better and doing them with the prospect of never getting anything better. The nature of the work is quite different in the two cases.

DO PEOPLE NEED TO WORK?

For many if not most Americans, work is the *sine qua non* of their existence. As one author put it:

> If work is the pivot around which life in America revolves, it must follow that not to work is, in a way, not to *be*—or to be irrelevant. It is another example of what Leonie Walker, director of the Women Managing Wealth program in New York City, calls "the cruel karmic joke" of inherited fortune. The wealthy are in the position of having everything except what matters—a role, a job, a healthy, active way of life.[16]

As noted by this author, the concern for working is not just an income concern. Many feel a need to work for the sake of doing, not just of getting. According to the views expressed by one character in a Kurt Vonnegut novel:

> Men, by their nature, seemingly, cannot be happy unless engaged in enterprises that make them useful.[17]

According to a Media General-Associated Press poll taken in 1986:

> When asked what they liked best about their jobs, more people said "the work itself" or "the people I work with" than said they liked the money best.[18]

In today's society in the United States there is a widespread need for work because of the social norms with which most of us have been raised.[19] Let's be clear here. When I now speak of work, I am separating the concept from that of income. There is no doubt in our money economy, people need an income. But do they also have a psychological need to work?

> For many (if not most) of the people *in this culture*, work satisfies psychological as well as physical needs. Work is the principal avenue by which men achieve recognition, establish their independence and status, and realize their potential as creative individuals [emphasis added].[20]

According to Charles Murray, a significant benefit of work is that it confers social status:

> Why, at bottom, should working confer social status? Originally, there were two reasons. One was that nonworking people were a threat to the wealth and well-being of the rest of the community. The second was that nonworking people were visibly outcasts; they lived worse than anyone else. Once these

highly functional sources of status are removed, the vaunted "work ethic" becomes highly vulnerable. The notion that there is an intrinsic good in working even if one does not have to may have impressive philosophical credentials, but, on its face, it is not very plausible—at least not to a young person whose values are still being formed.[21]

Commenting on the fact people were settling for shorter hours and lower pay just so they can have a job, Professor Bruce M. Stave of the University of Connecticut stated:

> I can understand why people take the (lower paying) jobs. It's a work ethic we trace back to the Puritans. The average person would simply rather work than not work.[22]

But do people have an *intrinsic* need to work? I think not. There are numerous examples of civilizations where the activities of the vast majority of the people bore little resemblance to what we think of as work today. We are at or nearing the point in our society where work no longer must be crucial to our image of ourselves.[23]

MUST SOCIETY REQUIRE THAT PEOPLE WORK?

"Somebody has to do the work."
"We all have to do our share."

Most of us were raised on sayings like these. But have you ever taken the time to think about *why*? Well, I have and I've concluded that these sayings are very close to being anachronisms. They may have been true at one time in history, but today (or perhaps tomorrow) they no longer are.

A Brief History of the Work Imperative

Just why was it people had to work? *To survive.* It was necessary to hunt, gather, till the soil, pound the wheat, weave the cloth, strip the hide, carry the water, gather the wood, build the fire, and construct the shelter in order to provide the necessities. Where conditions were harshest, the amount of time spent engaging in these activities was greater. In some climes, a benign environment required very little effort to survive. A strong work ethic was naturally less likely to develop there.

As economies became more organized and work more specialized, each individual no longer had to engage in activities directly related to survival. However, everyone was expected to do something which facilitated the work of those who were tilling, building, and so on. In a money economy, the incentive was the need for cash in order to purchase the necessities from those who raised or sewed or built them. Within families, each member was urged to contribute, either by directly producing that which was needed or by earning money to be used to purchase necessities. This urging expanded to communities and even to nations. Americans have been asked to work hard to contribute to the well-being of their country. The urging has been greatest in wartime, but even in peacetime the need to compete with other countries has given rise to it.

This social need was institutionalized in religious beliefs with the emergence of the Calvinist doctrine. Work became something which was ordained by God. Man was expected to toil during life, with the expectation of a reward in heaven after death. The harder one worked, the greater the chance of this reward.

It is interesting to contrast this belief with the attitude toward work held by the ancient Greeks. Among the intelligentsia of that age, work was regarded as something beneath the dignity of humans. A truly enlightened being was expected to spend time in contemplation, not in labor. Fortunately for them they had slaves, and the slaves were regarded as less than human. Therefore, the slaves could do the work.

Reaping the Rewards of the Technological Revolution

In today's advanced societies there is the opportunity to return to the thinking of the ancient Greeks. Fortunately for us, we do not need to rely on slaves to accomplish this.[24] Technology can become our slave.

The primary benefit we have reaped from technology to date has been "more." More goods and more services. It is time for us to realize a more important benefit—"less." Less work. Of course, we have seen some of this in the form of a shortened work week.[25] The more important benefit for which I am arguing is less emphasis on the need to work at all. The historical imperative that everyone must work is no longer a social necessity. The demonstration of that point comes from agriculture.

Agriculture and the Need to Work

Everyone is well aware of the agricultural revolution. The advances in growing technology, from mechanization to insecticides, have been tremendous. The amount of food that can be produced by a small number of farmers is astounding.[26] What is perhaps even more mind-boggling is the prospect for further advances. Such techniques as hydroponic gardening, fish farming, and genetic engineering of plants and animals provide additional promise on a scale with the advances already realized. Between the past and the prologue, the need for workers to provide food has diminished greatly. I envision a time when it has become nearly zero.

Have you seen the "green monsters" currently available to till the soil? These machines are awesome—not only in their productivity but also in the comfort they provide to their operators. Now you may be thinking, "Sure, but somebody still has to drive them." But do they? How difficult will it be to add cybernation to agricultural automation?

A Note on Cybernation

Cybernation is not a household word, but it exists in most households. A cybernated system is one in which there is a feedback-control loop operating. Not only is the function which is being performed mechanized but so is the process of initiating and controlling that function. The system itself decides when to start operating and for how long. The prime household example of this? The furnace and its attendant thermostat. Heating of houses became *mechanized* when the homeowner no longer had to build and light the fire.[27] It became *cybernated* when the homeowner no longer had to turn on the furnace. The thermostat, sensing the temperature in the house, electronically sends a message to the furnace to begin heating. When the desired temperature is reached, the message goes out to shut down. About all that remains is for us to set the thermostat and to occasionally change the filter.[28]

The automatic coffee pot is another example. Not only does it make the coffee now, it even knows *when* to make the coffee. It senses the time of day (from an internal clock) and automatically starts brewing at the preset time.

Other examples of cybernation abound in factories. There are machines that sense when a part needs to be replaced, and may even make the replacement automatically. There are systems which sense the quality of the product being produced and make automatic adjustments when the quality falls below a predetermined level.

Now let's speculate on the potential applications of some of these techniques to agriculture. The sci-fi buffs among you can probably outdo me in this, but let me start you with some thoughts. We have already mentioned the mechanized plowing and planting devices (aka tractors) available to farmers. We then took note of the need for a human to drive them, and I asked whether this was really necessary. My conclusion is that in the not-too-distant future, it will not be.

How far-fetched is the following? Electronic sensors are placed at various locations in a huge farm field. A computer is programmed to analyze the soil temperature readings at a particular depth and incorporate the calendar date into its calculations. When the combination of this temperature and the date reaches a critical point, an electronic message is sent to the barn. The barn door automatically opens, the tractor is automatically started, and it heads out to plow. Oops, how does it know where to go? Well, five years ago the human farmer had driven the tractor around the field, following the normal plowing pattern. The onboard computer sensed and recorded the turns and lifting and dropping of the plow. The resultant program sends the tractor out on the same route. This same routine will apply at planting and fertilizing and harvesting times. Sure, there are a few "But what if's." Maybe the human farmer will have to get paged at the golf course occasionally because of a breakdown, but these occasions should become less frequent.

We now return to the issue of incorporating the benefits of this revolution into society. To dramatize my point, let's assume the technological change took place overnight. Imagine a very large farm on which there were numerous family members and hired hands. All worked long and hard plowing the fields and planting and reaping. Assume the work was all being done with hand tools. Overnight, the magical tractor appears. It is no longer necessary for anyone to work the fields. Come harvest time, the tractor fills the bins with the wheat or corn or rice. Who gets the food? Just the person who first laid eyes on the tractor? The strongest people? Why not everyone who lived there on the farm?

An alternative scenario with the same implications involves two neighboring farms. Both are run by individuals who must work full time in order to grow enough just to feed themselves and their families (assume they are simply consuming the fruits of their labor, not selling them in the marketplace). Owing to advances in technology it becomes possible for one farmer to manage both farms. Two basic alternatives arise. One farmer could farm both farms and the other farmer becomes idle, or both farmers share in the work, working only one-half time each. Assume farmer A really enjoys the work and farmer B hates it. They agree A will do the work and share the produce with B. B then plays golf all day and both are happy. Is this not a picture in microcosm of the entire economy as it could be?

And so in a society where so much food is being produced with so little effort, why should it not be shared with all those whose labor is no longer needed to produce that food?

We now have come to the end of the progression. From a life in which each person had to produce their own food or die, to one in which fewer people produced the food and sold it to others who had to work to earn the money to buy the food or die, to a life in which no one has to work to produce the food. Should people still have to work in order to get some of the food? True, under the market system they do. They still need money to pay the owner of the tractor for the use of that tractor.[29] Isn't this just an issue of distribution, however? As a society, is it still necessary we require people to work in order to survive? I think not.

Extending the Food Argument to Other Sectors

Mechanization and cybernation not only affect the food-producing sector of our economy; similar advances have been made in home building. Consider the significant efficiencies generated by factory-built components or even the relatively recent progress in automated tools. As one who spent many a hot summer day nailing sheeting for roofs, I can appreciate the time saved with automated staplers and hammers. As one who spends many a cold winter day contemplating the future, I can also imagine a time when even the human holder of the staple gun is replaced with a small machine that senses the location of the joists, follows them, and shoots a staple at predetermined intervals.

The progress in producing clothes is similarly significant and subject to further advances. Who knows—maybe we'll even one day be capable of mass-producing something other than "one size fits nobody" socks and hats.

Impacts of Further Technological Advances

The speed with which the advances I have mentioned will take place depends to a great extent on our attitude toward their impact on jobs. Labor is fighting a holding action on many fronts, trying to halt the spread of job-elimination machinery. It is becoming increasingly apparent, however, that technology is affecting not only those jobs traditionally regarded as the venue of "labor," but more and more also white-collar jobs. Banking and insurance provide prototypical examples of this.

Consider the impact of automated tellers on the need for human tellers. Remember, this job has traditionally been the means by which many young people enter the banking industry. In the insurance industry, the need for people to engage in record-keeping is eroding dramatically. Insurance agents are going on-line with their companies allowing direct contact with the underwriters. Even the underwriting function is being affected by technology. Just over the horizon is the widespread use of expert systems to make the decision whether to insure someone. As in so many areas of our economic lives, the humans doing these jobs argue that this decision process is an art which can never be computerized. This is just an example of wishful and humancentric thinking.

The pace with which humans are replaced by machines is slowed not so much by the technology as by the psychology. Our society is loath to replace too many positions because of the impact on the morale of the remaining humans. Kurt Vonnegut, in his novel *Player Piano*, developed (in 1952) his view of a society damaged by too much technology. One of his characters notes, for example, the impact on workers:

> It was so ridiculous to have people stuck in one place all day, just using their senses, then a reflex, using their senses, then a reflex, and not really thinking at all.[30]

And another points out:

> For generations they've been built up to worship competition and the market, productivity and economic usefulness, and the envy of their fellow men—and boom! it's all yanked out from under them. They can't participate, can't be useful anymore. Their whole culture's been shot to hell.[31]

There is also a concern about the impact on customers—not so much regarding service as regarding image. This will change.

Will Unemployment Lead to Lawlessness?

As a society we must be concerned about the impact of a guaranteed income on the behavior of members of our society. One concern is that such a program would lead to idleness, which will lead to lawlessness. I am not convinced this would happen. The connection between idleness and lawlessness is tenuous at best. The vast majority of "idle" people engage in either charitable or recreational activities. One of the people who expressed this concern to me is in fact a retired person. He fills his idle time with family activities and home maintenance and recreation. Like the vast majority of "idle" retired people, he is a law-abiding citizen.

I have another friend who owns some low-rent apartments. He cites the numerous occasions on which his tenants, many of whom are on welfare, have "trashed" his apartments. To him, this is evidence that receipt of a guaranteed income would lead to such behavior on the part of many more people. Again, the evidence is suspect. To conclude that the receipt of welfare was the *cause* of these people's behavior is to ignore the manifold factors which led them into poverty in the first place, as well as the negative consequences of being in poverty. This antisocial behavior is rooted in an absence of social values and in feelings of despair. There is no evidence to suggest that the behavior would not be even worse in the absence of welfare benefits.

The real factors which cause lawlessness are poverty, hopelessness, and feelings of alienation from society. The guaranteed income would be a positive force in this regard.

Effects of a Guaranteed Income

A guaranteed adequate income would be a step in the direction of removing the resistance to greater levels of unemployment. At least the income aspect of the lost jobs would be partly mitigated. Granted, there is still the psychological aspect of work; it will be difficult to change people's thinking about the meaning of one's existence in the absence of work. But it can and must be done. People must come to realize that holding a job is not the *sine qua non* of one's existence. According to Marshall McLuhan:

> What we call "jobs" represents a relatively recent pattern of work. When a man is using all his faculties we think he is at leisure, or at play.[32]

With a guaranteed income, we could cease fighting the rising tide of unemployment and greet the prospect of higher levels of unemployment not with fear and loathing but with pleasure.

> The guaranteed income that results from automation could therefore be understood to include that quite unquantifiable factor of joy and satisfaction that results from a free and full disclosure of one's powers in any task organized to permit such activity.[33]

IS WORK GOING TO BE AVAILABLE?

There is a widespread belief that technology will have no lasting impact on the availability of jobs. Those with this faith believe as many jobs will be created as will be lost, and the new jobs will be of higher quality than the old. I and others don't believe this is true. Consider the words of Ben Seligman:

> These are the first two myths of automation—that it upgrades workers and produces as many or more jobs as it destroys—and since they tend to assuage our concern, they are vicious.[34]

According to Theobald:

> In effect, therefore, economists have no valid theoretical structure to support their contention that unemployment can be avoided by increases in demand.[35]

Funiciello notes:

> In the early eighties, estimates in *Fortune* magazine, for instance, predicted the further decimation of production jobs by one third to one half by the end of that decade. By 1990, concurred economist Robert Theobald, "the installation of 10 to 20 thousand robots . . . will create up to 5000 new jobs for robot technicians, but the robots will replace 50,000 auto workers." Close, but no cigar. Ford Motor Company *alone* announced it would lay off 75,000 workers in 1992. . . . Also in 1992, IBM, which had once touted its job security, announced the layoff of 25,000 workers.[36]

Also:

> Although governments have been slow to recognize it, the industrial world's job crunch is due to more than just another blip in the business cycle. In Europe, Japan and Canada, as in the United States, many of the jobs being shed today will never return.[37]

> With tough global competition and rapid technological change now economic constants, high unemployment and insecurity will haunt the world's most prosperous countries for years to come.[38]

THE SERENDIPITOUS IMPACT OF TECHNOLOGICAL DEVELOPMENT

There are three major impacts of the technological revolution. First, people live better because of increased productivity. There is little argument on this point. The negative effects of pollution and crowding are more than offset in most people's minds by the availability of plenty of food, comfortable housing, inexpensive clothing, and abundant accessible recreation.

On the remaining two effects there is more debate. Effect number two is the elimination of jobs. As was suggested in the agriculture example, many fewer people are needed to do the work to create the necessary goods. The debate on this point comes from those who have a faith new jobs will be created to replace the old jobs. I don't share this faith.

The third impact of technology is the fact we no longer need as many people to do the work.

[A new statistic] measured not the people who were out of work but the jobs that those out-of-work people would never be able to find because they had disappeared completely from the economic landscape. By the fall of 1992, only 18% of the lost jobs had returned, although at such a late stage in every other recession for a half century, all the previous lost jobs had come back again.[39]

This is the mirror image of the second point. There are fewer jobs available because fewer people are needed to do the work.

The manufacturing sector of our economy produces, with no more workers, five times as many goods as it did at the end of World War II.[40]

According to one author:

What is disappearing is not just a certain number of jobs. . . . What is disappearing is the very thing itself: the job. . . . The modern world is on the verge of another huge leap in creativity and productivity, but the job is not going to be part of tomorrow's economic reality. . . . The conditions that created jobs 200 years ago—mass production and the large organization—are disappearing. Technology enables us to automate the production line, where all those job holders used to do their repetitive tasks.[41]

We can *create* plenty of what we need without requiring that as high a percentage of our population toil in the workplace. The challenge facing us is to decide how to *allocate*. One option would be to allocate jobs. We could limit the amount of time any one person could work, thus spreading the jobs around.[42] If we continue to ascribe to the view that a job is essential to a person's feeling of worth, this may be a necessity. However, the administration of such a program would be extremely cumbersome and unnecessarily interfere in the working of the market. As one author says:

> They [mainstream economists and politicians] insist employing most work-age citizens is not only desirable but attainable. As the popular slogan has it: "We can't afford unemployment." But the fact is, if the radical view is right, we *can* afford unemployment. Full employment, based in effect on permanent subsidies to those doing needless jobs, is what we cannot afford. Here and there in European think tanks and universities, scholars are toying with scenarios in which previously unthinkable levels of unemployment would become permanent. . . . We need to be thinking through the implications of an utterly new kind of society, where only research scientists, artists, entertainers, and athletes would be sure of finding useful "work."[43]

The other alternative, and the prescription of this book, is to find a way of providing an income to those for whom no jobs are available.[44]

A NOTE ON CREATING JOBS

Although I am arguing that society need no longer require all its citizens to work, I recognize that a high percentage of people want to work.[45] The traditional response to this need for jobs is to promote economic development. This was attempted by the Republican administrations in the 1980s through the "trickle-down" theory. Programs designed to encourage investment were expected to eventually result in more jobs. It is not clear this worked. Much of today's investment results in greater automation and hence fewer jobs.

Here is an alternative view. If what we really want is more opportunities for humans to engage in productive activities, it may be necessary to force job availability. This could be accomplished by *limiting* the use of technology in certain areas.[46] Here are some thoughts in that regard:

• More jobs could be created for loggers by limiting the use of heavy machinery in forests. There are a number of reasonable arguments for doing so. The damage to the environment is substantial; the noise is oppressive; and the rapidity with which the forests are cleared is excessive.

• More farming jobs could be created by limiting the use of herbicides. Hoeing of fields is hard work, but it is work and it is productive. The laws could be justified by the negative effects of herbicides on the environment.

• More jobs for young people could be created by limiting the use of golf carts on golf courses. Caddying has traditionally been a noble profession for young people. It is healthy and active. Prohibiting golf carts for all but those with a doctor's orders could be justified on the grounds that the carts are noisy and detract from others' enjoyment of the game. They also require paths which detract from the aesthetics of the courses.

• More jobs for artisans could be created by changing our purchasing preferences from mass-produced items to handsewn clothing or handmade pottery.

CONCLUSION

In brief, here are the major arguments of this chapter:

• Human beings do not have an intrinsic need to work.
• Individuals were historically driven to work by the need to survive.
• In western culture, a need to work has been strongly ingrained.
• This cultural tradition is a result of a societal need for people to work.
• Western society has developed the work ethic as a means of promoting a higher standard of living.
• Because of advances in technology, there is an insufficient number of jobs available to meet the demands of those who wish to work.
• Because of these same advances in technology, it is no longer necessary society insist all people work.

Our current welfare programs are based on the premise that society should determine who can be excused from working. The proposal of this book, the guaranteed adequate income, is based on the premise that individuals can be allowed to determine whether to work. I argue that the wealth and productivity in the United States is sufficient to support all its citizens at an adequate level, even if some choose not to work. The work that still needs doing in the United States will be attended to, even in the presence of a guaranteed income, because:

• The level of the income will be low enough that most people will still desire to work to improve their standard of living.
• The cultural bias in the United States is sufficiently strong in favor of work so most people will still choose to work to the extent work is available.
• Much of what we call work is pleasurable. Those who have the option of engaging in this type of work would still choose to do so even if the guaranteed income were sufficient to meet all of their material needs.

Acquisition is no longer the primary economic concern of society. Distribution is.

Notes

1. Work Song, *The Methodist Hymnal* (Nashville, Tennessee: Abingdon Press, 1939), p. 293, Verse 2.

2. "Work has turned into a modern religion for us and it costs us dearly. You can't conceive of a world without work, but work has expanded into our lives, damaging the family, our communities, which we no longer have time for." Deborah Wiley, "Humanizing the 'Modern Religion,'" *Des Moines Register*, April 3, 1995, p. 1A.

3. On the other hand, Bryant Gumbel, on the NBC *Today Show*, quoted a "wise man" who said: "If work is so good, why do people pay you to do it?"

4. I had to look this up to make sure it was the word I wanted. It translates as a "black beast" or a "bugbear"; my dictionary says a bugbear is "something that causes needless fear."

5. In the 1996 congressional debate over welfare reform, it was common for Republicans to emphasize that the work requirements included in the bill were designed to be of benefit to the poor, in that the requirements would make it more likely that poor people would work, and they would thus feel better about themselves.

6. Thomas Sowell makes the point that even the rich "work," so that we shouldn't try to distinguish between "the rich" and "the working people." "The Rich *Are* Working People," *Des Moines Register*, April 18, 1995, p. 9A.

7. One formulation of the concept of work was provided by Lutz and Lux in *The Challenge of Humanistic Economy*. They first cite two definitions of work used in James O'Toole (ed.), *Work in America* (Boston: MIT Press, 1973): (1) employment for pay; (2) an activity that produces something of value. Lutz and Lux say these represent two necessities: (1) to stay alive; (2) to actualize our human potential. They would like to see us eliminate as much as possible the first necessity, thus enhancing our freedom. But, they say, we should not eliminate the second. They go on to point out "first and foremost, as a necessary criterion of social welfare, the basic physiological needs will have to be satisfied for every citizen." Ibid., p. 170. This is in keeping with the spirit of a guaranteed adequate income.

8. Those applying our unemployment compensation laws have had to wrestle with this question over the years. Generally, teachers cannot collect unemployment benefits during the summer if they have a contract for the following year.

9. Most universities periodically (about once every seven years) allow professors to be excused from teaching and other duties if they propose to do something productive with their time.

10. Another note on political correctness. I am aware that there is a school of thought which argues we should not refer to someone as a "blind person." The argument is that to do so places a greater priority on the blindness than on the person. By this argument, a preferred alternative is "a person who is vision impaired." In this case, I choose to use the more conventional language. However in so doing, I do not intend to side with those who contend the whole issue is ridiculous. There is a point worth making in this regard, and we should all be sensitive to it. In this case, however, I do not choose to make the change. (I know—perhaps if I were vision impaired I would think differently about it. I'm still open to further arguments.)

11. It could be argued that the compensation is in the form of lodging and food provided by the breadwinner.

12. As cited in Lance Morrow, "Essay: What is the Point of Working?," *Time*, May 11, 1981, p. 93.

13. One might argue they are "compensated" by the pleasure they receive or the produce from their garden. However, the meaning I am giving to compensation here is a remuneration paid by someone else.

14. Granted, there are some welfare recipients who do not seem to be performing this task, or who don't perform it well. This is a separable issue, however.

15. John Kenneth Galbraith, "When Work Isn't Work," *Parade Magazine*, February 10, 1985, p. 10. Galbraith goes on to note that this "disguises a major inequity in our social arrangements. Those who least enjoy their work, who must be paid to show up, who do what we should call real work, get the least pay, under all normal circumstances, for what they do. Those who most enjoy their work, who greatly prefer work to idleness, who do what is only called work, normally get more money."

16. Peter Edidin, "Drowning in Wealth," *Psychology Today*, April 1989, pp. 34-35.

17. Kurt Vonnegut, *Player Piano*, p. 261.

18. "Americans Like Jobs; Pay Isn't the Main Reason: Poll," *Cedar Rapids (Iowa) Gazette*, December 1, 1986, p. 1A. As with most polls this is subject to a number of interpretations. One I favor is that more people thought the work was satisfactory than thought the pay was satisfactory.

19. According to Professor Frithjof Bergmann, a University of Michigan philosophy professor, "We've created a culture in which everything in life surrounds our work. Our job is the source of our dignity, self-respect, even our access to the world." Bergmann proposes a system in which people would spend six months on the job and six months off doing "real work" (doing "socially useful" tasks). "6 Months at Work, 6 Off, Proposed by Philosopher," *Cedar Rapids (Iowa) Gazette,* January 15, 1986, p. 2A.

20. Robert H. Davis, "The Advance of Cybernation: 1965-1985," in Robert Theobald (ed.), *The Guaranteed Income, p.* 65.

21. Charles Murray, *Losing Ground,* p. 185. In fairness, I should note that Murray makes this point as part of a discussion of the negative effects of our means-tested welfare programs. He feels it is these programs which are to a great extent responsible for undermining the work ethic.

22. *Cedar Rapids (Iowa) Gazette*, February 27, 1983, p. 14A.

23. "For the first time in the history of the world, masses of people in industrially advanced countries no longer have to focus their minds upon work as the central concern of their existence." Morrow, "Essay," p. 93.

24. In one sense, we are all slaves—slaves to the marketplace. In so saying, I have no intention of demeaning the horror of slavery in which one person has complete dominion over another's life. But there are similarities. With the exception of those who qualify for aid or have inherited wealth, each of us is forced to accept the work the market makes available to us in order to survive. Given a pure market economy with no welfare safety net, those who refused to work would be condemned to die. "Root hog, or die" is the unmistakable message of the market.

25. Actually, the long-term trend toward shorter work weeks has seen a slight reversal in recent years. "Harvard economist Juliet B. Schor said the average American worked 1,924 hours in 1989 compared with 1,786 hours in 1969." However, there is considerable belief that shorter work weeks are likely in the future." "There's no question that the long-term salvation of work lies in reducing work hours," said Thomas R. Donahue, secretary-treasurer of the 95-union American Federation of Labor-Congress of Industrial Organizations. "Shorter Workweek on Horizon," *Des Moines Sunday Register,* October 31, 1993, p. 1L.

26. According to the secretary of agriculture for the state of Iowa, each farmer in Iowa produces enough food for 279 people. WHO Radio, October 15, 1993.

27. In the furthest reaches of my memory is the coal delivery and the process of "stoking the fire" to keep it going. Soon, few Americans will even remember this.

28. Have you done this lately? Like me, you probably forget. Let this be your reminder.

29. Some may raise the issue that the tractor owner always has a prior claim on the product of the tractor. I disagree, and have so argued in Chapter 2.

30. Vonnegut, *Player Piano,* p. 13.

31. Ibid., p. 78.

32. Marshall McLuhan, "Guaranteed Income in the Electric Age," in Robert Theobald (ed.), *The Guaranteed Income,* p. 199. To put some historical perspective on this issue, McCluhan also notes: "In Shakespeare's day it was a charge against the players [actors] that they were little other than beggars and vagabonds because their livelihood derived from direct dependence on the public. . . . They had no *place* and no stake in society. They had no roles but merely transitory jobs." Ibid., p. 194.

33. Clarence E. Ayres, "Guaranteed Income: An Institutionalist View," in Robert Theobald (ed.), *The Guaranteed Income,* p. 205.

34. Ben B. Seligman, "Automation and the Work Force," in Theobald, *The Guaranteed Income,* p. 90.

35. Robert Theobald, "The Background to the Guaranteed-Income Concept," in Theobald, *The Guaranteed Income,* p. 101.

36. Theresa Funiciello, *Tyranny of Kindness*, p. 290.

37. "Can Anyone Spare a Job?," *Newsweek,* June 14, 1993, p. 47.

38. Ibid., p. 48.

39. William Bridges, *Job Shift,* p. 6.

40. Ibid., p. 5.

41. William Bridges, "The End of the Job," *Fortune,* September 19, 1994, pp. 62, 64. Bridges goes on to note, however, this is not all bad. "The job is a social artifact, though it is so deeply embedded in our consciousness that most of us have forgotten its artificiality or the fact that most societies since the beginning of time have done just fine without jobs," p. 64.

42. Another option is to keep people employed in useless jobs, such as the *madogiwazoku* ("window tribe") in Japan. These are white-collar workers who collect paychecks while sitting and looking out the window. "Can Anyone Spare a Job?," p. 46.

43. Scott Sullivan, "Life on the Leisure Track," *Newsweek,* June 14, 1993, p. 48.

44. "One of the most important things that policymakers need to do is to start transferring the security machinery from jobs to some more permanent basis." Bridges, *Job Shift*, pp. 186-187.

45. I am reminded of the logger's wife from Oregon who on national TV sent this message to President Clinton: "Don't send us money; send us jobs."

46. The cartoonist Tom Tomorrow suggested the use of technology to create more jobs. After suggesting that we might need to retrain displaced workers to be economists, but concluding that there may not be enough jobs to go around, he pictures people with virtual reality headgear on. One is saying "Hey—this is great! I'm sitting at a desk in an office," another remarks "I'm chatting with my coworkers by the water cooler," and the third comments "I'm opening my virtual reality paycheck." "This Modern World," *Des Moines Register*, September 26, 1993, p. 3C.

5

We Are What We Were

Are you worthy? Is everyone worthy? Why do I ask?

Present public assistance programs in the United States primarily take a "categorical" approach to deciding eligibility. To qualify, one must be deemed worthy or deserving of the benefits. For example, a poor single mother with an infant child generally qualifies, but a single person who is just "down on his (or her) luck" is not eligible.[1] I have previously presented an argument that a just system does not allow us to make such distinctions. Later in the book I argue for a guaranteed income which does not make such distinctions. To draw a conclusion on whether some people are more worthy or deserving than others, the question to consider is whether some people are better than others.

Many of us want to believe that poor people deserve to be in their condition. This allows us to believe that those of us who are not poor deserve to be doing well. Partly for this reason, we are circumspect in our public assistance programs, taking pains to extend benefits to only those whose status appears to be no fault of their own. Is a system such as this "just"? In Chapter 1 of this book, I answered no to that question. My answer was founded, in part, on a determinist viewpoint. In this chapter, I explain that view.

Until one takes a stand on whether there are good or bad people, one has a difficult time formulating a concept of justice. This is because one of the points at issue is whether any people deserve (deserve more than others, or deserve punishment, or deserve adulation). If one adopts the view (as I do) that we cannot separate people into "good" and "bad," then one dramatically limits the extent to which one can base justice on deserving. It is important to note at the outset this does not mean we cannot label *actions* as good or bad.

This is a difficult distinction to make, for two reasons. First, many have the view that we cannot separate people from their actions. True, but we do not need to *label* them by their actions. Don't we all know "good" people who have done "bad" things? We may well view our own children (or our own parents) that way at times. Second, this is a difficult distinction because most of us have a deep-seated need to label people. Only by having a category of bad people does it make any sense to have a category of good people. Since we ourselves want to be in that second category, we need some others to be in the first category.

For many, their religion enhances this view. The concept of sinner is synonymous with bad person.

Some of you may already have discarded the notion of good and bad people. The challenge of convincing others to do so is formidable. I can't prove to you that you're wrong. I can only share with you the ideas which have led me to do so. Those of you who are leaning in this direction may find enough reinforcement to accept it fully. I hope there are a lot of you. I strongly believe our interactions with our fellows will be bettered if we adopt this view.[2]

THE ESSENCE OF THE ARGUMENT

Three views are essential to the conclusions of this chapter. They are stated briefly below and expanded upon as the chapter develops.

1. There are no good/bad people.

This is a conclusion I have drawn and an assertion I make. The truth of it can't be proven.[3] The best I can do is offer some of the observations that led me to this conclusion and hope you will see their merits.

2. People engage in good/bad actions.

Herein lies the critical distinction. I accept this proposition and expect that most readers will also. It is not necessary at this point to determine just what constitutes a good or bad action. Certainly there is a diversity of opinion about many actions. What is one person's murder (bad) is another's mercy killing (good). Taking from the rich and giving to the poor (good) is regarded by others as thievery (bad). Is one's behavior laid back (good) or lazy (bad)? Is the life of the party (good) or simply a drunk (bad)? Is one on welfare taking advantage of an opportunity (good) or leeching off the system (bad)? Is one who continues to work hard after becoming wealthy ambitious (good) or greedy (bad)?

For purposes of this book it does not matter how you answer these questions. Suffice it to conclude we all feel *some* actions are bad and *some* are good.

3. People are not inherently good or bad

Fortunately it is not necessary for us to agree on whether people are inherently good or bad. Personally I tend to lean toward good, but it isn't likely I can convince those who disagree.[4] Depending on one's religious beliefs, a person may feel that mankind has "fallen from grace" or that we are all God's creatures. Either is acceptable with respect to the argument in this chapter. What I will argue against, however, is the notion that *some* of us are good and *some* of us are bad.

THE PATH TO THIS CONCLUSION

Many readers will have already trod the mental path that led them to this same conclusion. For those who have not, I offer the observations that pointed me in this direction, starting with the issue of child abuse. Although this is not directly related to our main issue—behavior which relates to poverty—I discuss it first because it provides a classic example of the point I wish to make.

I grew up with the view that child abusers were bad people. Anyone who would intentionally beat a helpless youngster, particularly his or her own child, must be bad—so bad we feel justified in condemning that person. Over the years, however, I have encountered more and more information about those who engage in these actions. What have we learned? Right! Almost all child abusers were themselves abused, often by their parents. This abuse most likely had an affect on the overall personality of the abused child. It also was the child's primary lesson in how adults deal with children.

Once I learned about the trauma encountered by a youngster who is abused, I became less critical of the adult into which this child grew. I am not saying I tended to be less critical of the *actions* of that adult. If anything, I became even more critical of those actions because I realized what a devastating effect they had on future generations. Nor did I come to believe we should *excuse* the actions.[5]

As a society, we must not tolerate this behavior, particularly because it tends to perpetuate itself. It is probably necessary to punish persons who engage in these actions. However, we should be understanding and compassionate towards those who themselves have suffered, even if that suffering has led to undesirable behavior. To look at the person and conclude "This is a bad person"—that we ought not do.[6]

Did the first abuse *cause* the second? It is unlikely one could prove the point either way. Some readers may wish to emphasize that not all abused children become abusers. It is true that all we have at this point is a correlation plus some *a priori* reasoning. The issue of cause aside, one observation seems undeniable: being abused predisposes one to abusing.

There is other evidence of the damning effects of child abuse. It may predispose one to criminal behavior in general. During a tour of Alcatraz prison, our guide quoted a former captain of the guards. After reviewing the files of all the men he had guarded (during the entire time Alcatraz was open), he concluded that "90 to 95 percent of the men had experienced severe mental or physical abuse before the age of 10. We'll never solve the problems of crime and violence until we solve this problem of abuse."

Abuse may also be a factor in "determining" poverty:

> What causes poverty in Des Moines? The obvious suspects are substance abuse, lack of education or an absence of role models for children, but a group of social and health-care workers at a recent forum most often cited "sexual and physical abuse." "If you've ever been abused," said the Iowa Department of Public Health's Mary Evans, one of the participants, "your self-esteem is zilch," and few who lack self-exteem succeed.[7]

A multitude of other factors ultimately influences behavior, but this in no way diminishes the importance of this observation.[8]

My next observation comes closer to the theme of the book. In the late 1960s, a bold effort was initiated to react to the urban riots in Detroit. A proposal to correct the conditions that led to the riots was to put the hard-core unemployed from the center city to work. To this end, those attempting to help provided a bus to transport any willing workers to an auto assembly line where they were guaranteed employment. The results of this program led to my second, major observation on this issue. The program was a failure. Of those who accepted the offer of employment, only a few continued working for more than a couple days. The newly employed walked off the job in the middle of a shift; they failed to show up for work on subsequent days; and often they refused to take even the most reasonable orders from their supervisors. The behavior seemed particularly strange since most of these young men were not eligible for any income support from the government.[9] It appeared that these were people who simply preferred to loaf rather than work. This seemed to be evidence that "those people" could not be helped. Even more damning was the conclusion that they didn't *deserve* to be helped. In the context of the earlier discussion in this chapter, they were labeled as bad people.

Further consideration of this episode, however, led many, myself among them, to recognize factors contributing to this unseemly behavior. Here was a group of people who had not been imbued with the rudimentary skills, attitudes, or behaviors necessary to succeed in a work environment. Such behavior as following a time schedule was not familiar to them.[10] The idea of taking orders from someone other than their mother was anathema to them.[11] I asked myself, and I ask my readers—how can we dismiss someone as undeserving because that person was behaving in a manner consistent with his or her experience?[12] Certainly one can criticize the actions, although that criticism is not as clear as it was in the case of the child abuser. Some might argue that many of us are driven by the clock, or that we too readily do what someone else tells us to. Most feel, however, that it is necessary for people to engage in certain behavior for the smooth running of an industrial society. The issue of whether the *action* was bad is not important here; what is important is that we not dismiss the *actors* as bad people. I have no quarrel with negative responses to bad actions. If everything one does is bad, all of our reactions will be negative. Even in this case, however, it is certainly not necessary—and I argue it is neither desirable nor reasonable—to label the *person* as bad. There may well be some salutary characteristics of the person which we simply have yet to observe. In addition, people can and do change. If someone changes for the better, it is awkward to say "Oh, now you're a good person."[13] Is it not preferable to realize they are the same person, but now engaging in good actions?

DETERMINISM

My own view on the good/bad people issue was developed long before I realized it was consistent with a broader philosophical view. That view is called determinism.[14] This is the name for a group of scientific and philosophical doctrines, all based on the conclusion that nothing takes place without a cause.[15] This doctrine has been hotly debated for centuries.[16]

It is important to note, early in this discussion, that it is not significant whether someone can identify the causes. All the determinist argument requires is a recognition that there *are* causes.[17] My version of determinism is not one which limits causes to those which are materialistic and exterior (environmental).[18] I am not espousing "Skinnerian" determinism in which "behavior modification" is the sole determinant. For my purposes, determinism allows the influence of genetics, as well as environmental influences. It also can incorporate the influence of a soul and a self.

This cause-effect view can be applied not only to the physical world but also to human behavior. Whether we can include human behavior as part of the physical world is not important here. I happen to think that we can. The more I learn about neurons and synapses in the brain, the more convinced I become of this. If you do not agree, however, we have no major problem. My view of the determinism argument does not require an entirely physical view of human behavior. All it requires is that *something* causes our actions (and that it was itself caused).

The Two Alternatives to Determinism

In one sense, determinism is based on a tautology, in that there can be no other view. Can there be a completely uncaused event? There are only two possible views, alternatives to determinism, which allow this. I'll refer to these as "randomness" and "divine intervention."

The Randomness Thesis

There is support among some scientists for a view that randomness plays a large role in the universe. According to this view, occasionally events occur that not only have no identifiable cause but indeed are not caused.[19] Some physicists are presently focusing on the decay of the proton as one such event. The contention is that this decay is completely random, independent of any events that precede it. If this be the case, so the reasoning goes, then a multitude of other events that may be marginally related to this decay could themselves be regarded as random.

A variation on this theme holds that, while events are never random, there are some which are nonetheless incapable of ever being predicted. According to this view, the very process of observation unavoidably alters the events themselves.[20]

The Divine Intervention Thesis

The divine intervention view is not so clearly contrary to a deterministic view. Under this thesis, there can be events that are not predicated on influences of this world. "God only knows" why they happened. However, as will be discussed later, it is not critical we *know* what the causes were to conclude events were caused. If the divine intervention was itself the result of preceding factors in the world (humans misbehaved so God sent a plague, for example), then one can still accept that the outcome (plague) was determined (by the bad behavior that led to the divine intervention). The only way in which this concept would conflict with determinism is if the intervention were arbitrary and capricious. Very few theists today hold that view.

There is another view of God that is even more in sync with the deterministic view: God set the universe in motion, but chose not to intervene subsequently. Therefore, all events are caused by God, but only in the sense of the establishment of the original state.

The important point to note, at this stage, is that a belief in God and a belief in determinism are not incompatible. The determinist argument is made without reference to a supreme being, but the conclusions are no different if the concept of God is woven into the argument.

Weather— A Comparison of the Three Views

Even as this chapter was originally being written, the midwestern United States was experiencing extraordinary rainfall and flooding. Why was this happening? The randomness thesis would suggest that these things just happen sometimes; they are theoretically unpredictable. A subscriber to the divine intervention thesis might suggest that the supreme being decided that this "plague" should be sent—perhaps because farmers had gotten too complacent or farmers in other areas of the world deserved higher prices (of course, this is pure speculation on my part—we could never know why the decision was made). The ancients explained various weather events as the actions of specific deities who were in charge of, for example, lightning.

A determinist looks for the causes—and increasingly finds them. During the life spans of those of my generation, humans have made incredible strides in identifying these causal factors. We have added a long list of weather-causing factors to our vocabulary and understanding. "Fronts," "closely spaced isobars," "gulf moisture," "El Niño," and "the ozone layer" are but a few. The use of radar to identify upcoming weather has tremendously enhanced our ability to predict the weather.

Although our ability to predict the weather is still somewhat limited, it has improved dramatically over my lifetime.[21] If one compares the forecasts of today with those of forty years ago, and then projects this progress forty years into the future, one can envision extremely accurate forecasts. Can we ever be error free in our weather forecasts? In theory, yes.[22] However, as someone once suggested, a hurricane occurs or does not occur because of one extra beating of the wings of a butterfly in the Caribbean. (The extra motion generated by this one beat, so the thinking goes, starts a series of events in motion that might ultimately lead to the hurricane.) We do know, however, that the warming of the Pacific Current can significantly affect midwestern weather. Once we know this, we are led to ponder just why the current warmed. This leads us backwards in time to events beyond our ability to recognize or perhaps even to ponder.

The critical point for the argument, however, is not how well we can predict, nor even how accurately we will ever be able to predict. The important point is the weather is *caused.* The more we learn about it, the more we are forced to recognize that it is. If one thus concludes the weather is determined, a person has a reason to believe the rest of the world may also be determined.

Human Behavior—Is It Determined?

Weather was perhaps an easy case with which to demonstrate the merits of the determinist argument. Let us now turn to what may be the most difficult case—human behavior.[23] In this section, I intend to make the case that, as the title of the chapter states, "We are what we were." The essence of this argument is: at any instant, our actions (and even our thoughts) are a product of what has happened to us in the past. That past includes what we inherited and what we have experienced.

Nature or Nurture—No Matter

There are many factors which affect human behavior. It is not critical we agree on which are the most important factors. It is important we agree that behavior is determined.

I am not espousing what some call "hard determinism." That view holds that inheritance is the sole determining factor.[24] Nor am I siding with those who claim that our behavior is strictly the result of our environment and upbringing. Neither of these views is consistent with the argument made here.

When some authors use the term determinism, they mean strictly biological determinism. For example, Lewontin et al. use the term *interactionism* to name the concept of determinism I am presenting.[25] They disparage biological determinism ("Biological determinist ideas are part of the attempt to preserve the inequalities of our society"[26]) and argue for a combination ("a full understanding of the human condition demands an integration of the biological and social in which neither is given primacy"[27]).

Can we deny that our genes have some effect on who we are? Can we reasonably conclude that our upbringing had no effect on who we are?[28] Assuming you answered no to both of these questions, the followup question has to be "What else influences our behavior?" Two possibilities come to mind. First might be the influence of God.[29]

What About God?

While at first glance the introduction of this factor may seem contradictory to determinism, it is not. It simply brings in one additional determinant of behavior. As discussed previously, the influence of God can be viewed in one of two ways. Perhaps She or He chooses to intervene and cause us to behave in a particular manner. This intervention could be before birth when we are endowed with God-given talents, or it could be periodically during our lives when it is felt we need changing.[30] The second view of God is that He or She originally put the universe in motion and allows it to develop in a preplanned manner. In either case, the belief is not contradictory to a determinist position. One must still conclude that a person's behavior is determined—albeit now determined by this third factor.[31]

At this point I suspect many readers have a couple of "But what about's?" that need consideration.

What About My "Self"?

The issue here is whether an "in-dwelling agent" develops out of the various causative factors. If so, according to one argument, this self makes decisions which affect the causal chain. My own view of determinism allows for and respects this self, but contends this self is a product of causal factors, and hence its decisions are also caused.

What About My Soul?

What is the impact on the determinist argument of the existence and influence of a soul? Perhaps you are among those who believe each of us has a soul which may influence our behavior, independently of what we inherited or what we have experienced. For you, this soul is the essence of one's being, the arbiter of right and wrong for each of us.[32] Religion is the foundation for a belief in the soul. Hence the existence of this soul is difficult to prove or disprove. Therfeor the function or operation of the soul is impossible to determine. It is fortunate, therefore, that its existence (or nonexistence) is not critical to the development of my position. I argue that if one indeed has a soul, and this soul does influence our behavior, this is simply one additional factor that determines behavior. Surely the concept of the soul includes a belief that it is something God gives to us. Recognizing this influence was outside our control, we are led to the same implications as those we would reach if we do not consider the soul.[33]

A similar view is that of philosophical libertarians, who claim human actions are not just the result of physical processes but are also caused initially by intentions. These intentions are not physical; that is, they are not part of the neural processes of the brain. We know these as our inner thoughts. Libertarians feel they have a sounder basis for their position than do determinists, partly because we all *know* that we have those inner thoughts. We do not yet *know* there are physical explanations for these thoughts.

The Evidence for Determinism

I cannot prove to you that determinism is the proper description of human behavior. I must acknowledge that it is, and probably will remain, a belief.[34] What I propose to do in the next section of this chapter is to share with you some of the recent findings regarding influences on human behavior. I focus on these findings for two reasons: (1) the one aspect of existence people are least likely to regard as determined is probably human behavior; and (2) the balance of the discussion in this book is concerned with human behavior.

Mental Illness

Just as we have seen dramatic strides in our ability to explain the weather, so have we witnessed such strides in explaining deviant human behavior. Behavior that society once regarded as "possessed" is now explained in terms of a chemical imbalance in the brain. Researchers have shown that even as subtle a behavioral characteristic as depression has a tie to a chemical imbalance.[35] The more we learn of these relationships, the more we must recognize the veracity of the determinist view.[36]

Another recent development in the realm of mental illness relates to those who "hear voices." A recent study has found there are waves emanating from the speech portion of the brain during the time these voices are heard. A possible implication is that in some sense these people are speaking to themselves.

Personality

Evidence is mounting that the characteristic most closely related to who we are—that is, our personality—has a distinctly genetic component. As one writer put it:

> Shyness, for instance, appears to have a genetic basis; assertiveness and hair-trigger anger probably do as well. Like it or not, predicts Dr. Lewis Judd, Chairman of the Psychiatry Department at the University of California at San Diego, "We are going to find that the attitudes we take, the choices we make, are far more influenced by heredity than we ever thought."[37]

Another expressed it as follows:

> Ancient and medieval ideas about our constitutional predisposition to certain character types . . . are rising again, in altered form, with data to back them up.[38]

> To the skeptical eye of the behavioral scientist, the results of these studies are stunning. About 50 percent of measured personality diversity—how we behave—can be attributed to genetics.[39]

Harvard molecular biologist Walter Gilbert, after noting the entire genetic record will someday fit on a single CD-ROM, says:

> We look upon ourselves as having an infinite potential. To recognize that we are determined, in a certain sense, by a finite collection of information that is knowable will change our view of ourselves. It is the closing of an intellectual frontier, with which we will have to come to terms.[40]

What are we discovering about the various impacts of our genes? Citing a study which suggested a possible "aggression" gene, one writer summarized:

> Crime thus joins homosexuality, smoking, divorce, shizophrenia, alchoholism shyness, political liberalism, intelligence, religiosity, cancer and blue eyes among the many aspects of human life for which it is claimed that biology is destiny.[41]

Twins

A study by the Minnesota Center for Twin and Adoption Research concluded that "the degree of genetic influence on behavioral characteristics [such as aggression and social closeness] tends to be around 50%."[42] This finding, like some of the others reported in this section, speaks to the issue of the relative importance of nature and nurture. As such, it does not directly impact the debate over determinism. However, it does provide one more bit of evidence that *something* identifiable causes our behavior.

IMPLICATIONS OF A DETERMINIST VIEW OF HUMAN BEHAVIOR

For many, the issue of concern with respect to determinism is not whether it is applicable to human behavior. The issue is, rather, the implications that will be drawn from accepting this view. The primary positive implication is this: each individual human is as worthy, as entitled to respect, as deserving of our concern as any other. This I find to be a positive result because it is so in tune with the religious views I learned early in life. I now have a basis for regarding others as equally worthy without the need to rely on the preachment they are "all God's children." I come to the same conclusion, but by what I regard as a more reasoned route.

Another important implication of determinism is to recognize that our interacting with others will have some influence on their behavior. If we have an image of how people ought to behave, we have the opportunity to help develop this image. We each are a part of what determines those with whom we come into contact.[43]

I recognize a negative implication also. Some may choose to use this realization as a cop-out for their behavior. As such, they may feel no pressure to change their antisocial tendencies, relying on the argument they are only doing what they are "determined" to do. As a society, we cannot allow this. However, it is neither necessary nor desirable to ignore the reality of determinism in order to avoid it. It is simply necessary for all of us to require each of us to act as though our behavior were not determined.[44]

If we accept the conclusion that behavior is determined, this can have an affect on our attitudes both toward others and toward ourselves.

Our Attitudes Toward Ourselves

Many people feel threatened by the notion of determinism. If they accept that "We are what we were," they fear that it diminishes their status as a special person. It seems to imply that they are simply automatons responding to programmed commands. In one sense, this is indeed the view argued here. The human brain is very much like a computer. It reacts to stimuli in a manner consistent with what it has learned.[45] To conclude otherwise is to run into an absurdity. Can it be that an individual decides, impulsively, to behave in a manner completely inconsistent with everything she or he has been taught or that is in her or his nature? Granted there are occasions when we observe people who appear to be doing this. However, these apparent contradictions exist because there are some things about the person we do not know. For example, a seemingly docile neighbor commits a violent crime. "How can this be? It is so 'unlike' that person." Generally, we discover later there was indeed something that triggered the outburst. Perhaps a recent experience brought to the fore a traumatic incident in childhood. Perhaps it was a chemical imbalance in the brain that altered behavior. Granted, we are not always able to *pinpoint* the exact cause. Some behavior continues to mystify us. This is not, however, because determinism is inappropriate; it is because we lack sufficient insight.

Those cases where we cannot identify a cause for seemingly inconsistent behavior leave us with two choices. On one hand, we may conclude that people do sometimes behave in a manner contrary to their nature (in which I include their nurture). If we conclude this, we might argue that it is the result of their souls or that God made them do it. Should we adopt this view, we are still taking a position consistent with determinism. The other possible reaction is to regard the behavior as strictly random. Those who believe in a universe that does not operate on a cause-and-effect basis (as discussed earlier) might adopt this view.

The more plausible choice for an unidentifiable cause of inconsistent behavior is that we simply are not able to identify the mysterious source. One of the reasons I find it more plausible is that we are increasingly identifying previously unknown causes of behavior. The realm of behaviors with undetectable causes has diminished dramatically in recent decades. While we may never identify all the causes, enough have been identified to date to convince me there *are* causes.

"But can't I change?" Yes, people can change. However, this change occurs as a result of some outside force. Were this not true, how would we explain the existence of counselors, ministers, missionaries, and teachers? Even those people who make a dramatic change, because they "found religion," do so because someone introduced them to the idea.[46] We are not "once formed, always the same." We can and do change; however, this change is itself determined. In addition, many changes are extremely difficult to make, even when help is provided. After watching a television program dealing with child abusers who were themselves abused, my mother-in-law commented, "They can change, can't they?" I don't argue with my mother-in-law, but I wondered, "Why is it that people who know how important it is to raise their children *right* can't see the significant effects of being raised *wrong*?"

"How can I be proud of myself if my behavior is determined?" I would contend that this view of human nature requires us to be circumspect in our feelings of pride. It is permissible to take pride in our accomplishments when these are the result of an effort on our part. However, one cannot be proud of oneself in the sense of being better than anyone else. There is no justification for having an arrogance or smugness about one's own place in society or in the universe.[47]

If we conclude, therefore, that our own behavior is caused, how does this impact our view of ourselves? For many, the trauma comes in the apparent conflict with the notion of free will.

Determinism and Free Will

The subject of free will has been the basis for philosophical discussions for centuries.[48] The argument may take one of two forms: (1) Whether God gave us a free will independent of his dictates; and (2) Whether we have a free will, independent of other factors which influence our decisions. The argument herein does not require that we take a stand on the first of these issues. The issue of whether God dictates our every move or allows us to make this determination for ourselves is moot in this discussion. In either case, we can still conclude that our behavior is determined, either by God or by our free will which was given by God.

The critical issue in the current discussion is whether our free will can operate independently of other factors that determine our behavior.[49] Unless they take this to be the case, many persons feel that their sense of "humanness" is diminished.[50] We all want to feel that, at any instant and on any issue, we can decide to behave in whatever way we wish. Were we to prefer a course of action quite contrary to anything we have done before, we could take that course.[51]

Determinism is not inconsistent with this view of ourselves. It only requires that we accept that *something* in our background is influencing the choice we make. It still allows for the conclusion that *I* made the choice. *I* am in control of these choices. That *I* am the product of my inheritance, upbringing, and perhaps the influence of God does not diminish this conclusion.

The only exception is where there is some outside physical force immediately compelling our movement. That is, if someone lifts us and carries us somewhere we don't want to be, this is not within our control. Note that this is not the same as someone "twisting our arm" to get us to comply. In this latter case, we still make the decision. We are programmed to conclude that if the pressure (either physical or mental) is great enough, we will comply. The important point is that we still make the decision. We make it with our free will.

A couple of difficult cases present themselves at this point. One is the issue of mental illness. If a person behaves in a psychotic manner because of a recently acquired psychosis, is she or he acting out of free will? My answer is yes. This is simply one of the factors influencing who a person is. True, the influence may be temporary and reversible, but until the time it is reversed, that person's behavior is still determined by the mental illness.

A similar case is brainwashing. It is common to view behavior that results from brainwashing as somehow different from other behavior. We don't feel the individual is responsible for that behavior. I argue this distinction ought not to be made. The brainwashing is simply one factor influencing the person's behavior. We must regard it no differently than more subtle and less identifiable factors which, over long periods, have influenced a person's behavior. Granted, there is the possibility of quicker reversal of the influence of brainwashing, but this is only a difference of degree, not of form.

Those who view brainwashing as a distinct type of influence on behavior ignore the fine line between brainwashing and other behavioral influences. On occasion, someone makes a great deal of effort to determine whether a person has been brainwashed. If we conclude the person has been, this leads us to believe that the person is somehow less responsible for his or her behavior. From a determinist point of view, however, this distinction is irrelevant.

A belief in determinism is not inconsistent with a belief in free will. *I* exercise my free will. The *I* to which *I* refer here is no esoteric philosophical concept. I, Mike Murray, choose to write these words. I am free to do so or not. I am free to ignore the fact that my editor would not like the fact that I use "the fact that" twice in this sentence. This *I* is the totality of the individual, not the ego or the id or an "indwelling agent." However, and here is the crux of the issue, The things *I* do or think are a product of influencing factors, and thus are determined. *I* am a product of my inheritance and my environment, but *I* make the choices.[52] Lewontin and his colleagues expressed this view similarly:

> What characterizes human development and actions is that they are the consequences of an immense array of interacting and intersecting causes. Our actions are not random or independent with respect to the totality of those causes as an intersecting system, for we are material beings in a causal world. But, to the extent they are free, our actions are independent of any one or even a small subset of those multiple paths of causation; that is the precise meaning of freedom in a causal world.[53]

Is a Determinist a Fatalist?

Yes and no. The answer to this question depends on what one means by "fatalism." The nineteenth-century British philosopher John Stuart Mill has identified two forms of this concept:

> Pure, or Asiatic fatalism . . . holds that our actions do not depend on our desires. Whatever our wishes may be, a superior power, or an abstract

destiny, will overrule them, and compel us to act, not as we desire, but in a manner predestined. . . . The other kind, Modified Fatalism I will call it, holds that our actions are determined by our will, our will by our desires, and our desires by the joint influence of the motives presented to us and of our individual character; but that our character having been made for us and not by us, we are not responsible for it, nor for the actions it leads to, and should in vain attempt to alter them. The true doctrine of the Causation of human actions maintains, in opposition to both, that not only our conduct but our character, is in part amenable to our will; that we can, by employing the proper means, improve our character; and that if our character is such that while it remains what it is, it necessitates us to do wrong, it will be just to apply motives which will necessitate us to strive for its improvement and so emancipate ourselves from the other necessity.[54]

I agree with Mill one can be a determinist without adopting the "pure"view of fatalism. I accept the Modified View as a necessary consequence of determinism, with a clarification. When Mill says we "in vain attempt to alter them," he is right with respect to the moment. What I do in this instant is a function of who I am, and I can't change that. However, any implication that we can *never* change our character, and thus our actions, is an overextension of the view. I subscribe to Mill's "true doctrine" with one caveat. He seems to imply we can change ourselves. As I point out above, we can change, but some outside stimulus is needed.

Am I a "Good Person?"

One of the unavoidable implications of determinism is that we cannot view ourselves as better or worse people than others.[55] For many, this detracts from their view of themselves. This is particularly true of successful people. Those who have been successful want to believe they are responsible for that success and deserve credit (if only from themselves) for it. To suggest they are successful because of who they are, but that "who" is a product of factors beyond their control, is to challenge their affirmative self-view[56]

Of course, a determinist view is soothing for those who have berated themselves for their lack of success. This is not to suggest we should cease trying to be better. Rather, it allows each of us to cease "beating ourselves up" over our lack of success. The goal is to play as well as we can with the hand we are dealt, but recognize we could only do so much with our hand.

Our Attitudes Toward Others

Determinism requires a compassionate view toward others. No matter how unacceptable the behavior of another, we recognize that behavior is the result of preceding influences over which the individual had no control. Therefore, while we may speak of bad behavior, we cannot speak of bad people. The other side of the coin is that we also cannot speak of good people. People may engage in behavior that we prefer, but that doesn't make those people better than others.[57] Again, we can decry the behavior without impugning the person.

Can we change other people? Certainly. While it is true that a person's behavior at any instant is a function of influences up to that time, it is not true that *future* behavior need be the same. Every action we take has a consequence and that consequence is part of what influences our future behavior. This is, of course, a great part of how we learn. Therefore, when each of us reacts to others (our children, for example), we are influencing their future decisions and actions.

This point also applies to society as a whole. Individuals observe actions taken by groups (e.g., governments) and adjust their behavior accordingly. The operation of the criminal justice system is a prime example. As a society, we intend for our penalties to influence the behavior not only of the penalized person but also others who may be contemplating certain behavior. For example, those who know someone who has recently received a traffic ticket in a certain area will most likely adjust their driving behavior in that area.[58] As another example, our welfare system can impact behavior. If, as a society, we provide benefits only to unmarried single parents, this will have an influence in the direction of encouraging child bearing by unwed parents.

To summarize, determinism does not imply that a person's behavior is fixed forever by a certain set of antecedents. That set is constantly being altered and people adjust their behavior accordingly. We can and do change our attitudes and actions. A determinist viewpoint suggests, however, that some new influence is required for that change to be made.

Determinism and Religion

Determinism itself is not a religion. It is true that throughout this discussion I have used the term "I believe." However, that is simply in acknowledgment of the fact that some of the contentions cannot be proved. I do not, however, simply take them on faith. These are beliefs that are developed through observation and reasoning. If the reader makes the same observation and uses the same reasoning, she or he should arrive at the same conclusions. If not, I cannot convert that reader.

Fortunately the conclusions of determinism are consistent with many of the teachings of our major religions. For example, the second commandment given by Jesus was: "Thou shalt love thy neighbor as thyself."[59] One who agrees with the determinist conclusions is led to do exactly this. Recognizing that my fellowmen and women are, like myself, the product of factors beyond their control, I am led to regard them (all of them!) as highly as myself.

CONCLUSIONS

In his inaugural address on January 20, 1993, President Clinton stated "But for fate, we, the fortunate and the unfortunate, might have been each other." He may have been commenting primarily upon the fortuitous consequences of our efforts, but the statement also reflects an understanding of the fate involved in our ability to make those efforts.

One of the consequences of adopting the determinist view is that it helps to eliminate the "them versus us" attitude which is far too prevalent in discussions of public assistance.

I hope that readers will, at this point, see the merits of the determinist argument. It just makes sense. It is one of those views which many don't want to believe because it does not coincide with the way in which we wish to view ourselves (and perhaps others). Nonetheless, there are always some things we want to believe and others we should believe.[60]

In Chapter 1 I developed a concept of justice which incorporated the determinist view. This notion of justice will form the basis for a proposal for a major change in our economic structure. A major basis for my proposal is a desire to see that every American has the opportunity to feel good about him or herself because she or he has an income provided, without discrimination, solely as a recognition of his or her worth as a human being.

Notes

1. This is true with respect to current federal programs; after the 1996 welfare reform legislation, states may change this. However, it is quite unlikely that the state rules will be less restrictive in this respect.

2. This includes not only our attitudes toward economic justice but also our attitudes toward criminal justice.

3. "Proof" is at any rate an elusive concept. Nothing can be proven unless the "provee" accepts the criteria for proof as laid out by the "prover."

4. It may be that this is a view people accept simply because it makes them feel better.

5. Talk show host Rush Limbaugh, on his September 23, 1993, program decried the tendency of liberals to excuse people's behavior. He noted that people who abuse their children were often abused by their parents, but argued that this should not give them license to do whatever they want to. I agree.

6. Many readers will recognize in this argument the classic Christian admonition to "hate the sin; love the sinner." I liked the point made by a caller

to a local talk show, who said, in a discussion of stigmatizing unwed mothers, "We should hate the sin, not the sinner. If not, what is the statute of limitations on stigmatizing?" The point is also made in a country-western song in which someone who had done some bad things is told by both earthly and heavenly fathers that a father doesn't only love his son now and then; he loves them without end.

The same subject was broached in another of the primary sources of insight into human nature, daytime talk shows. During an Oprah Winfrey show (I saw the rerun on December 11, 1993), the guest, Attorney Andrew Vachss, was asked with respect to child abusers: "Do you hate them or hate what they did?" He replied "For me? You hate them. 'Hate the sin but love the sinner' is for people who make a mistake. For people who deliberately hurt you, you hate them." A determinist view does not allow this distinction. (I didn't get the sense Oprah—herself a victim of child abuse—agreed with it, either.)

7. "Abusive Past Is Identified as Primary Cause of D. M. Poverty," *Des Moines Register*, March 30, 1994, p. 1A.

8. In fact, as will be seen in a later discussion, it reinforces the argument.

9. Since they were single, and thus did not fall into an eligible category.

10. Certainly some of this information was imparted in early school years. I believe, and this evidence would seem to confirm, that the experience in the home environment had a much greater impact.

11. The fact that most of these participants were black and most of the supervisors were white exacerbated this problem.

12. Jimmy Breslin equated this behavior to attitudes he had observed among some of his relatives in Northern Ireland. After trying unsuccessfully to get a young relative to take a job, he noted "I decided that he had a social disability which impeded him from working every bit as much as a broken leg prevents us from walking." He noted in conclusion, "What it comes down to is that you cannot muck about a race of people, black or white, for 300 years and then expect them to be able to perform normally." "Dirty, Too Lazy to Work, Living Only for Drink and Welfare," *Des Moines Register*, June 21, 1976, p. 8A.

13. I recognize there are some religions which espouse the view that the whole person changes when he or she has a "religious experience." If you believe that, we will have to agree to disagree on this point.

14. A very readable discussion of this concept can be found in *Free Will and Responsibility* by Jennifer Trusted. Trusted makes a distinction between physical determinism ("all events, including human actions, are completely explicable . . . in terms of . . . physical laws"); teleological determinism (in

which human actions require explanation in terms of ultimate causes); and libertarianism (which allows for an individual freedom of action which can be independent of physical causes), p. ix. I use determinism in the first sense. However, acceptance of the second view does no harm to my final argument. Note that the term *libertarian* is also used to describe a political philosophy, and is so used elsewhere in this book.

15. Sometimes expressed by the Latin phrase *ex nihilo nihil fit* (''from nothing nothing comes'').

16. The debate has been influenced, among others, by Hume, whose criticism of causality caused a loss of support for determinism; the Calvinist doctrine of predestination, which says acts of man can be as rigidly necessitated by supernatural causes as they might be by natural causes; and by Spinoza, who noted that our feeling of freedom results from our being conscious of our actions but ignorant of the causes that determine them.

17. Actually, the causality version is not the only view of determinism. Bernard Berofsky (see References) suggests that determinism can be viewed in terms of foreknowledge, explanation, or causality.

18. Indeed, Sidgwick makes a distinction between determinism and materialism. He says the latter limits causes to physical events. *The Methods of Ethics*, p. 62.

19. This view is sometimes referred to as the ''principle of indeterminacy,'' cf. Trusted, *Free Will and Responsibility,* chap. 8.

20. The subtleties of this view are beyond my ken. It is elaborated on in ''Is the Moon Really There When Nobody Looks? Reality and the Quantum Theory,'' N. David Mermin, *Physics Today*, April 1985, pp. 38-47.

21. Many people find joy in pointing out the shortcomings of weather forecasters. This may be because they secretly want the forecast to be inaccurate. To conclude that the future weather will be known with certainty is to change our way of viewing the world.

22. The weather provides an example of the difficulty in identifying all the causes. The current interest in chaos theory reflects a recognition that some phenomena appear to be random but may actually embody some pattern. As one observer put it, ''But weather, like a wildly bouncing football, still obeys the law of physics, however erratic its pattern. And there's an equation that explains the summer of 1993. But it could take the space of every blackboard ever bolted to a schoolhouse wall to solve an equation that accounted for every variable influencing the outcome.'' Bill Leonard, ''Iowa Soaks While Carolina Sizzles,'' *Des Moines Register,* August 3, 1993, p. 13A.

23. Those who prefer to base their philosophy on lyricists may wish to refer to the words by Oscar Hammerstein II in the song, "What's the Use of Wond'rin" from the musical *Carousel*. "Somethin' made him the way that he is, Whether he's false or true." This is a succinct version of the point being made in this chapter: something made us all the way we are.

24. This is not the only meaning given to the term "hard determinism." "William James (1842–1909) coined the terms 'hard' and 'soft' determinism to distinguish those determinists who thought that the ordinary moral attitudes could not be justified (hard determinists) from those who thought that they could be justified (soft determinists)." Trusted, *Free Will and Responsibility*, p. 39.

25. cf. Richard Lewontin, Steven Rose, and Leon Kamin, *Not In Our Genes: Biology, Ideology, and Human Nature.*

26. Ibid., p. 15.

27. Ibid., p. 75.

28. As examples of the influence of environment I offer the following: (1) Jim Sundberg's comment about the reasons for baseball pitcher Nolan Ryan's success: "It probably goes back to his childhood, his upbringing and his work ethic." As quoted in *Des Moines Register*, October 3, 1993, p. 11D; (2) Libby Raymond Yapp, reflecting on her work with children from disadvantaged backgrounds: "The most heartening thing to me, however, was that the precious preschoolers were every bit as smart, pretty, lovable and creative as my own kids. The 'raw material' was there for living decent, dignified lives. But statistics showed that it was their parents grinding poverty that eventually would fell most of them." *Des Moines Register,* March 6, 1988, p. C1; (3) Phoebe Wall Howard, writing in *Des Moines Register*, reports on interviews with mothers in a halfway house: "Growing up, they struggled to understand what landed them in foster homes while other children worried about clothes. They shook mothers who were passed out drunk on the couch. They waited for letters from fathers who never wrote. . . . One woman described having been sexually abused by her mother's boyfriends. . . . A woman described being dumped at a neighbor's as a child while her mother went off with truckers for days at a time." "The Legacy of Poverty," *Des Moines Register*, August 30, 1993, p. 1A; (4) Sylvester Monroe, commenting on conditions in the inner city: "Nowhere is the damage wrought by racial discrimination and isolation more evident and painful than in the schools." Speaking of a student at his alma mater, Monroe says: "Both of us also had the good fortune of landing in Leroy Lovelace's classroom." It was that "good fortune" which contributed to Monroe's success. "Breaking Out Then and Now," *Time*, October 5, 1992, p. 59.

29. I realize that readers of the book will undoubtedly include both believers (theists) and nonbelievers (atheists). References to God will, of course, only be relevant to the former.

30. We might note in passing an alternate explanation as often expressed by one of comedian Flip Wilson's characters: "The devil made me do it."

31. Alternatively, God's involvement can be thought of in one of the following three ways: (1) God has determined in advance how things are to be; (2) God simply allows things to happen; or (3) God foresees what will happen in the future. Note that none of these is inconsistent with the implications of determinism.

32. This concept is referred to by the philosopher Immanuel Kant as the "autonomous will." See discussion in Trusted, *Free Will and Responsibility*, p. 64.

33. Occasionally someone has argued that our souls are something for which we are responsible, as though we choose them. If that is your view, we may be at loggerheads on this issue.

34. Students of philosophy will recognize that my presentation amounts to a "self-sealing argument." As such, it is not subject to being disproven, thus it has no content as an argument. I can only hold it as a belief. In a more positive sense, I could refer to it as apodictic—that is, I am just pointing out something which is evident beyond contradiction.

35. Note that even if we regard a person as "possessed," we still are adopting a determinist position. The behavior is determined by the "possessor."

36. From a determinist perspective, a criminal justice system that attempts to excuse behavior because of mental illness is itself insane. Its results are arbitrarily based upon the extent to which certain behavior has thus far been proved to be related to certain illnesses. Aristotle thought people should be excused only if their behavior was forced, i.e., caused by an outside agent. He did not know what we now know about behavior being "forced" by an internal agent, e.g., a chemical imbalance. A determinist argues that there was some cause for any criminal behavior and that whether it is identifiable should make no difference.

37. J. Madeleine Nash, "The Frontier Within," *Time,* Special Issue, Fall, 1992, p. 82.

38. Melvin Konner, "Under the Influence," *Omni,* January 1990, p. 63.

39. Ibid., p. 90.

40. As cited in "The Genetic Revolution," *Time,* January 17, 1994, p. 53.

41. Dennis Overbye, "Born to Raise Hell?" *Time*, February 21, 1994, p. 76. In this essay, Overbye cautions about the implications of this research, but does not deny the possible genetic influence.

42. As reported in "Exploring the Traits of Twins," *Time*, January 12, 1987, p. 63. The article also notes, "Some scholars, such as Princeton psychologist Leon Kamin, fear that the Minnesota results will be used to blame the downtrodden for their own condition." The argument in this book is that just the opposite conclusion should be reached.

43. The evidence continues to accumulate, however, that this opportunity is infinitely greater when the "other" is very young. "As the twig is bent, so grows the tree." This could be the determinist credo.

44. According to Sidgwick, as members of society, we must act on the belief that the actions of others can be explained by "the principle of causation by character and circumstance." Sidgwick, *The Methods of Ethics*, p. 284.

45. When we are taught views which conflict with each other, is what we ultimately learn still determined? Certainly. We adopt the view most consistent with our previous learning.

46. Even if you insist on arguing that in some cases "Jesus came into their lives" without any influence from other people, I will still contend that this is consistent with my argument.

47. Some might refer to this as "unseemly pride."

48. In 1874, Sidgwick summarized the then-current state of the apparent conflict between determinism and free will: "On the Determinist side there is a cumulative argument of great force. The belief that events are determinately related to the state of things immediately preceding them is now held by all competent thinkers in respect of all kinds of occurrences except human volitions. It has steadily grown, both intensively and extensively, both in clearness and certainty of conviction and in universality of application, as the human mind has developed and human experience has been systematized and enlarged. Step by step in successive departments of fact conflicting modes of thought have receded and faded, until at length they have vanished everywhere, except for this mysterious citadel of will." Sidgwick, *The Methods of Ethics*, p. 284.

49. Berofsky describes the issue as follows: "Given any action there are three possibilities. The first is that it is random and I am not, therefore, free. Second, the action may be (completely) determined, and none of the determining factors is me. Again, I am not free in performing this action. Finally, I am the cause of my action even though the action has conditions distinct from me."

Bernard Berofsky, *Determinism*, p. 65. He goes on to state his view that "agent causality is sufficient for freedom," p. 67. This is consistent with my argument.

50. To decide that man has no free will would be to offend many. Some are even offended by raising the question. "[St. Thomas] Aquinas asserted that anyone who questioned the possibility of free will was undermining morality and, in addition, was a heretic." Trusted, *Free Will and Responsibility*, p. 22. Aquinas also argued the fact that man could be persuaded to act in a particular way was evidence of free choice. ("Man has free choice, otherwise counsels, exhortations, precepts, prohibitions, rewards, and punishments would all be pointless," as cited in Thomas Gilby, *St. Thomas Aquinas, Philosophical Texts*, p. 261. A determinist would argue, however, that this persuasion was simply another input which helped determine the behavior (and whether this input was or was not accepted is itself "determined"). In addition, the extent to which the individual was receptive to this input was determined by other factors—e.g., a parent who said "Never trust strangers" or "Doubt everything your professor tells you."

51. A well-educated friend suggested I am creating a "straw man" at this point. He said no one really holds this view. My experience suggests otherwise. One is often forced to take this position in order to avoid accepting the implications of determinism. Nonetheless, if you feel, as my friend does, that this is a "nonposition," then we have no argument at this point. Our next encounter will be on the field of "implications."

52. There is one point on which some believers in free will and I must agree to disagree. Those who believe free will is a uniquely human concept will want to argue that some aspect of the concept is not consistent with determinism. Otherwise, it requires us to apply the same arguments to other animals.

53. Lewontin, Rose, and Kamin, *Not In Our Genes*, p. 289.

54. John Stuart Mill, *An Examination of Sir William Hamilton's Philosophy*, as presented in Sidney Morgenbesser and James Walsh (eds.), *Free Will*, p. 66.

55. I am reminded of the Stuart Smalley character on the *Saturday Night Live* television program who so desperately needed to conclude, "Darn it, I'm a good person."

56. This need we have to feel better than others has been nowhere more poignantly displayed than by a character in the movie *Mississippi Burning*. As I recall, the sheriff recounts a story of how his father killed a mule belonging to a black neighbor. When asked why he did it, the father replied, "He had a mule. I didn't have one. If I'm not better than a [expletive deleted], who am I better than?"

57. There is an important implication here for child rearing. Parents can emphasize to their children that certain behavior is unacceptable. However, they should avoid implying that engaging in that behavior makes the child a ''bad person.'' Children need to be assured of the parents' love and support for them, even while certain acts are being rigorously criticized.

58. A controversial aspect of criminal justice is the death penalty. Does the imposition of this penalty influence behavior? There is literature suggesting this governmental action has no impact on the murder rate. However, even if this is true, one should not regard it as a refutation of my general argument. It only suggests that this particular action does not have the anticipated effect.

59. Matthew 23:39. The same admonition is found in the Old Testament in Leviticus 19:18.

60. At one time, people did not want to believe the earth revolved around the sun.

6

Why the Guaranteed Adequate Income

The foundation has been laid. It is time to give the specific arguments for a guaranteed adequate income. First, a quick review of the argument thus far. I presented the concept of determinism to suggest a view of human nature inconsistent with our current, categorical welfare programs. Each of us is a product of our past and neither entitled to praise nor deserving of blame for who we are. Thus, a welfare system which attempts to distinguish the deserving from the undeserving does not logically follow.

I noted that the citizens of the United States wish to have a just society. It is necessary to concern ourselves with economic status in order to provide a just system. This does not mean everyone has to have the same amount, but it does mean everyone must have some minimum income.

We saw how our current public assistance programs are in dire need of significant reorientation. Undesirable gaps are left, since some poor fail to qualify under one of the categories of entitlement. The administrative costs are too high, primarily because of the need to preclude the undeserving from benefits and the frequent use of in-kind benefits.

I made a case that our private market system is the best for creating wealth and economic development, however it earns a failing grade as a means of justly distributing the wealth. The people must play a role through government to rectify this injustice while retaining the favorable features of the system.

Because any income distribution system will, in part, be evaluated in terms of its impact on work, the notion of work was addressed separately. My twin conclusions are that society need no longer insist all of its members work in the traditional sense; and the need for work as felt by individuals is not inherent, but culturally inculcated. Therefore, if fewer people choose to work because of a guaranteed income, that will not be

153

disastrous. It may even be beneficial if, as is expected, the number of jobs available continues to decline.

It is not absolutely necessary that the reader agree with me on all these points in order to support a guaranteed adequate income. There are other paths by which one can reach this same conclusion. However, they do provide a sound base on which to build a program.

THE BASICS OF A GUARANTEED ADEQUATE INCOME

Yes, the guaranteed adequate income is what the name implies. It is a minimum income guaranteed by all of us to each of us:

- *Who* receives it? Every man, woman and child is entitled to do so.
- *Who* pays for it? You and I, the taxpayers.
- *What* is provided? Cash, through a periodic check or electronic funds transfer.
- *How* is it paid? Through the government—either the Internal Revenue Service or the Social Security Administration.
- *When* is it paid? With the use of electronic funds transfers, weekly payments would be reasonable.[1]
- *How much* is provided? An adequate amount, fluctuating with the state of the economy. OK, you want a number? How about $6,000 for an adult and $2,000 for a child annually? Too much *you* say? And *you* say too little? No matter—I'm not the dictator. We'll let our elected representatives determine the final amount. The concept is what is important now.
- *How* is it funded? I show how a change in the federal income tax to a 35 percent flat tax, when combined with the savings from eliminating all current welfare programs, could fund the proposed level of benefits. I also argue that a value added tax (VAT) would be a desirable option and would allow a reduction in the income tax rate. Details on funding this program are in a later chapter.

THE "SOUND BITE" ARGUMENT

The United States is a sufficiently wealthy country that we can afford to guarantee that everyone's income will be adequate to ensure her or his ability to survive, to have an opportunity to enjoy life, and to participate in the running of our free society. The eminent economist John Maynard Keynes recognized such a time would come when he wrote:

> When the accumulation of wealth is no longer of high social importance, there will be great changes in the code of morals. We shall be able to rid ourselves of many of the pseudo-moral principles which have hag-ridden us

for two hundred years, by which we have exalted some of the most distasteful of human qualities into the position of the highest values. We shall be able to afford to dare to assess the money-motive at its true value. All kinds of social customs and economic practices affecting the distribution of wealth and its rewards and penalties which we now maintain at all costs, however distasteful and unjust they may be in themselves . . . we shall be free at last to discard.[2]

The majority of people in the United States are sufficiently compassionate to desire this for all citizens. A guaranteed adequate income is the most effective and efficient means of achieving this goal.[3]

WHAT A GUARANTEED INCOME PROVIDES TO INDIVIDUALS

Freedom

The United States is a free country. We pride ourselves on this fact. Citizens are free to go where they will, say pretty much what they will, and engage in a wide variety of activities. We are free to participate in the political process and even are free to *not* participate in that process, a widely exercised freedom.

One freedom we lack presently, however, is the freedom from work. The compulsion to participate in the work force continues. For many of us, that compulsion seems inconsequential in view of the wide range of job choices open to us. Freedom to choose our employment overrides any concern that we lack the freedom to choose to not work. For others, however, this limitation on freedom is quite significant. Those whose job opportunities are limited feel the compulsion to work impinges dramatically on their freedom. How often have we heard it said of the jobless "Why don't they get a job at McDonald's?" The implication is that even though this choice of occupation is the only one open to them, they must take it. In other words, if you wish to survive, you must work at a fast-food restaurant. The issue is not whether this is desirable work. The point is that if this is one's only choice in order to survive, one's freedom is seriously curtailed.

Many people in the United States enjoy a significant degree of economic freedom. Some have inherited money, some are bright enough or talented enough to do almost anything they desire to earn a living, some have just been lucky, and others have been able to save enough to achieve financial independence. For a large group of our fellow citizens, however, none of these applies, and chances are none ever will. For them, a GAI would immeasurably enhance their freedom.[4]

Security

Security is one of the first advantages of the GAI. The *guarantee* of a continuing income provides a psychological benefit on a par with the economic benefit provided by the income itself.[5]

An often-cited characteristic of poor people is their failure to plan for the future. Some have regarded this as part of the culture of poverty, but it is rather a function of the *situation* of poverty. The bleak outlook for the future would cause any of us to live for the moment. This is why some poor people concentrate on buying clothes or cars rather than saving for a home. If the odds of ever obtaining a home are sufficiently small, the rational response is to go for something obtainable. We would all react this way.

Given a change in their situation, poor people, like the rest of us, would lose this artifact.[6] What better way to create this change than to guarantee a future income? Now saving becomes a potentially productive activity. Now every individual can envision the very real possibility of accumulating some wealth. The security of the income will have a dramatic, positive impact on behavior.[7]

Borrowing Power

An adjunct to the security the individual feels is the security with which the banking community will now view the individual. The status conferred by an income, coupled with the assurance of its continuation, creates a quantum leap in the perceived merit of a potential borrower. Access to credit is an enormous plus in one's ability to succeed economically. This is one reason the rich get richer: they not only have their own money, they also have the ability to use other people's money.

The various ways in which credit can be used to enhance one's economic position are all too often transparent to those who have it. Not only does it provide access to money but it also provides a means of saving and even making money. The ability to purchase a newer auto and thus reduce the maintenance costs on an older car is one example. The newer car with its better brakes and better tires is less accident prone, thus fewer repair costs are incurred.

Home ownership is one of the best ways of improving economic status. Almost no person in the United States can purchase a home today without access to credit. In addition, it provides an escape from one of the catch-22s of our economic system: the fact that a favorable point on a credit report is the ownership of a home. In other words, this gives one greater access to credit. But to achieve this status, you must have access to credit in the first place.

There are two issues which may arise in this regard, with which I have dealt elsewhere in the book. The first is whether poor people would use the credit wisely. I have argued that this is a nonissue. It presumes poor people are different from the rest of us. They are not—they are simply people with inadequate income and, more important, without a sense of economic security. They also appear different because they have been required to prove themselves different in order to qualify for government benefits. That is, they must prove they have been unable to succeed in the economic system. Removing the indignity of having to qualify as a pauper will have a positive impact on the self-concept of the poor. Change these factors and most of the difference is removed.

Changing the rules so that poor people have greater access to credit is an alternative to a guaranteed income. This could be done by requiring lenders to make riskier loans to welfare recipients, with perhaps government backing. (We already have some of this with our FHA insured loans.) I strongly disagree with this approach for two reasons. First, it is an unwarranted intrusion into the workings of the free market. Second, it creates a government program with undesirable administrative costs.

The GAI in this, as in so many ways, is the most efficient means of attacking the problem without undue interference in the market.

Opportunity

Much of the opportunity provided by a GAI is incorporated in these concerns of freedom, security, and borrowing power. There are, however, some additional aspects worthy of note—the opportunity to move and the opportunity to retrain.

In Chapter 3, I noted how the market can be made to work more effectively by giving individuals the means to move to where the jobs are. The flip side is the benefit to individuals. With the income and security provided by a GAI, those who find themselves in geographic locations relatively devoid of job opportunities can more easily move to where the work is.

In addition, those whose skills are not demanded by the market can use the security provided by the GAI to change their skills. A regular guaranteed income can provide the much needed opportunity to return to college or learn a new trade. It could also enable someone to develop skills on his or her own. Here is another example of how government programs suffer from bureaucratic inefficiency. Many of our education support programs provide funds only if the recipient partakes of government-approved educational programs. As a result, rules must be developed and enforced to establish which programs are approved. With a GAI, individuals would be free to determine for themselves what type of job preparation to undertake.

Dignity

A guaranteed income is based on an entirely different philosophy from our current public assistance system. The current system requires recipients to show they have failed in our economic system. One must not only confess one has failed but also must go to substantial effort to *prove* that is the case. The means test is a demeaning experience. Those who have gone through it bear witness to that fact. One describes it as follows:

> Think of the worst experience you have ever had with a clerk in some government service job—motor vehicles, hospital, whatever—and add the life threatening condition of impending starvation . . . and you have some idea what it's like in a welfare center.[8]

Once one has prostrated him or herself before the rest of us to claim entitlement to benefits, that person continues to be labeled as one of "them"—welfare recipients.

> We were ensnared in the ugliest system for responding to people in dire need that could be imagined. It was beyond belief, a bottomless pit of cruelty. Recipients were treated like untouchables in the newspapers, by all the politicians who opened their mouths about us, and by every institution we came into contact with.[9]

The guaranteed income would be provided without an application. As a matter of fact, under my plan a person applies only if he or she chooses to *not* receive it. Recipients would rarely be distinguishable from the vast majority of citizens. Since the benefit is regarded not as a special privilege but as a benefit available to all citizens, the "second-class citizen" stigma will become a long overdue artifact of less considerate generations.

A GUARANTEED INCOME IS NOT FOUNDED ON A RIGHT

Do United States citizens have a *right* to a guaranteed income? I do not base my case on such a claim. As I discuss elsewhere in the book, the notion of rights is so ill-defined and subject to debate as to render it ill-suited for a basis for this program.[10]

Instead, I start from the premise that those of us who have access to income and wealth, and thus some extent of control over its distribution, desire to see our fellow citizens cared for. The GAI turns out to be the best means of actualizing this preference.

There are, however, a number of people who have argued for a guaranteed income as a right. Theobald is among those who regard it as a right:

It is therefore essential that the areas of agreement and disagreement among those supporting direct payments to the poor should be sharply differentiated. The first area of agreement is that the initial step on the way to eliminate poverty is to supply money rather than moral uplift, cultural refinements, extended education, retraining programs or makework jobs. In addition, it is agreed that the prime criterion for the distribution of funds should be the poverty of the individual rather than whether Congress is willing to pass special legislation supporting him. . . . There is another area of agreement which is crucial. It is seen as vital that funds should be provided as an absolute right.[11]

Another cogent argument for economic rights was presented by Jon N. Torgerson in his article "Taking Economic Rights Seriously." The essence of his argument is that economic and social rights are necessary in order for everyone to exercise their civil and political rights.[12]

A third reasonable basis for regarding this share as an economic right was provided by Edward Bellamy, in his novel *Looking Backward: 2000-1887*. The character Julian West asked:

"How could they who produced nothing claim a share of the product as a right?" His host responded that they were co-inheritors of the "achievements of the race, the machinery of society" and so equally entitled to their share of its benefits.[13]

Finally, consider the comments of columnist Tom Wicker:

President Arjay Miller of the Ford Motor Company recently endorsed the idea of a negative income tax as an alternative to welfare. His major complaint about the welfare program was that it does not do the necessary job [helping all the needy]. Really compassionate and effective reforms to do something about poverty in America would recognize, first, that large numbers of the poor are always going to have to be helped. . . . Thus the aim of getting everyone off the welfare roles and into "participating in our affluent society" is unreal and a pipe dream. These principles would create something like a "right to income" for everyone, and that is the only way, in the long run, that poverty can be eliminated in America. . . . The inescapable truth is that the day of the self-reliant pioneer is at least a half-century in the past.[14]

It is tempting to adopt the "income as a right" basis for a GAI. However, because of the philosophical difficulties associated with proving a right, I will instead present a similar case using the notion of a "social dividend" as the basis for granting an adequate income to all citizens.

THE SOCIAL DIVIDEND ARGUMENT

A simple and widely accepted basis for supporting the GAI is the desire to share. Whether this desire is rooted in religious teachings or in a humanistic concern for our fellows does not matter. I believe most of us have it. The issue is how we should operationalize this desire. Three aspects are important: what we should share, with whom we should share it, and the mechanism used to accomplish it.

What Is to Be Shared?

The "social dividend" metaphor is used to equate this sharing with the sharing received by owners of a corporation. These owners are entitled to a portion of the profits of their company. This share is sometimes reflected in increased value of their stock and sometimes in a dividend paid in cash. In widely held corporations, the stockholders rarely do anything to affect the profitability of the company. Their only contribution is their initial investment.

Similarly, we should regard citizens of the United States as owners of the country. Their "equity" is obtained by virtue of having been born here or been granted citizenship. As such, all are entitled to a share of the national product.[15] Remember, this share is not something "they" claim; it is rather something we, as fellow citizens, choose to confer upon each other. Again, the corporate dividend analogy. No individual shareholder can say to the corporation, "Hey, you owe me!" Rather, the majority of shareholders, through management, decide to share the profits.

For some among us, this line of reasoning will be sufficient. We will wish to share with all our fellow citizens just because they are. For others, an additional view may be needed. I suggest the following. A significant input to the output of the country is the use of natural resources. As discussed elsewhere in the book, these resources include not only the ores from the mines but also the soil, the air and water, and the available plant and animal life. Each citizen is equally entitled to benefit from the use of these natural resources. This is the closest I will go to a notion of rights. If land, water, minerals, plants, and animals had not been claimed for use in our production economy, each citizen would have an undisputed right to benefit from their bounty.[16] That right should be transferred to the money sector in the form of a guaranteed adequate income.

Who Should Get a Share?

Everybody? Yes, everybody. It is time to end the "they versus us" mentality that infuses our current public assistance programs. We are all entitled to share. There are no good guys and bad guys. Only people. The reason I spent so much time on determinism in Chapter 5 was to emphasize this point. We each are what we were. Sure, some of us do some things the rest of us like better than what others do, but we are equally worthy human beings.[17] For those who get their guidance from their religion, this is a common theme. For others, the logical argument demonstrates the merits of this view.

How Much Should Be Shared?

Just enough. An adequate amount. I'll be more definite in Chapter 8 on my specific plan. For now, I simply note there is no "right" amount. It should be a function of three factors. First, it should be enough. Enough for a person to meet physical needs and be able to participate in the workings of our free society. It should be enough to enable the person to *have an opportunity* to enjoy life, free from the fear of starvation. Second, it should not be too much. As a society, we must retain the economic incentive to encourage productivity and innovation. Although some of this will accompany a person's desire to be productive for its own sake, that is not enough. The additional economic incentive is still needed. It is on this point I differ from the egalitarians. Although I acknowledge the merits of their arguments from the standpoint of justice, I give credence to the practical need to provide incentives over and above the guarantee.

Third, the income should be a function of the wealth of the country. It must be allowed to fluctuate with the economic times. Just as in those earlier times when incomes depended upon the natural climate, so, in the current economic state, well-being should fluctuate with the economic climate. One of the virtues of a GAI is that it is so amenable to this type of adjustment.

The type of adjustment is also extremely desirable, and can be seen by contrasting with our current system. Under our present welfare system, when times get tough, programs are changed to eliminate benefits entirely for some people. Under the GAI, everyone would continue to get benefits, albeit at a reduced rate. This is a much less idiosyncratic system and provides significantly greater economic security for our citizens.

How Should the Shares Be Distributed?

Through the government mechanism. Not "from" government; the government has no money. The money comes from the people, who pay taxes. The preferred means for distributing the shares is through the government mechanism.[18] Surely, private charity is nice, but it has some drawbacks. They are failure to assure universal participation, a stigma attached to the receiver, and existence of a "hit-and-miss" nature.

The primary benefit of using the government mechanism is the opportunity to compel participation on the part of sharers. Granted, this takes away some of the joy of giving, but there is more to be gained than lost. The primary benefit comes in knowing others are also doing their share. This removes the "Why should I when others are not?" syndrome.[19]

A major disadvantage to private charity is that it is just that—charity. While this makes the sharer feel good, it demeans the recipient. A governmental program based on the notion of universal sharing in the bounty of society removes this stigma.

Perhaps this would be a good place to deal with the often-heard comment "Nobody owes them a living." I agree. But we do owe them a chance to live. In a money economy, the absence of money is the absence of this chance. To deny a share of the wealth in today's society is tantamount to denying access to water or game or fruit in a primitive society.

The final benefit to using the government mechanism is its universality of coverage. Private charities suffer from a hit-and-miss approach. Benefits go to those who are deemed worthy by people who are in a position to give or raise money. This assessment of worthiness changes from time to time. Those whose particular appeal for help is not popular are left out. A government program based on the social dividend concept is universal, and so it should be.

We should note in passing that one reason for redistributing funds through government is that we have available the means for doing so. One author suggests the rise of taxation was facilitated by the advent of public administration which provided the means by which to collect the taxes.[20] In the same manner the rise in the availability of electronic funds transfer and the nearly universal use of checking accounts will facilitate the distribution of shares.

THE WORK REDUCTION ARGUMENT

Will a guaranteed income reduce the incentive for people to work? I expect it will and I certainly hope it does. For many people, however, this possibility is the primary basis for their opposition to a guaranteed adequate income. I, on the other hand, regard it as one of the plan's virtues. As I argued in Chapter 4 on work, we have reached a point in the United States where it is no longer necessary for everyone to work and where the number of jobs available is less than the current demand for work. Our reaction should be to find a means for some members of society to gracefully excuse themselves from the work force. We must allow them to do so with dignity, by recognizing that work is not the sole or even primary purpose of a person's existence. The guaranteed income is the means by which we can accomplish these goals.

Nonetheless, for those concerned about the possible impact of a GAI on work,[21] there is a large body of evidence available. Most of this was accumulated during one of the most ambitious social research projects in history.[22] Conducted mainly during the 1970s, and funded by grants from the federal government, this project provided a guaranteed income to thousands of low-income people in different parts of the country. The effects on behavior were recorded and analyzed. The result? It depends upon the person to whom you talk. The most common assessment appears to have been that the reduction of work incentive was greater than the proponents of a guaranteed income anticipated. The conventional wisdom is that these results dealt a severe setback to discussions of the guaranteed income concept.[23]

I, however, am among those who found the results satisfactory. Certainly, there was some work reduction, but the reasons for that varied. Many second-income earners chose to reduce their participation in the job force, in many cases in order to stay home and care for family. Some recipients used the opportunity to conduct a longer search for a more satisfactory job. Still others financed continuing education with the funds. Finally, there were those who simply chose more leisure. That's OK by me. For those who wish more detail on the outcomes of the studies, I have provided it in an appendix to this chapter.

It is important to remember that many people work because they want to and not because they have to. Whether economic incentives are necessary to get people to work depend on (1) the individual's attitude toward work and (2) the nature of the work available. Demonstrative of the ''I'd work even if I didn't have to'' attitude is the reaction of the Michigan couple who, in 1993, won the largest lottery payoff ever at that time—$111 million. They said they would keep their jobs. He is an English teacher and she is a nurse. Both most likely find their work stimulating and rewarding.[24] For those who do not find their work so satisfying, a guaranteed income will provide them with the opportunity to choose a low-income but adequate lifestyle rather than the slavery of a job which they detest.

A GUARANTEED INCOME IS CONSERVATIVE

Over the many years during which I have discussed this concept with others, the quickest rejection has come from those who consider themselves political conservatives. This is unfortunate since the GAI is actually consistent with many strongly held conservative positions. I feel, therefore, a special need to discuss the many ways in which a GAI is consistent with the views of those who consider themselves conservatives. First, it reduces the level of government bureaucracy with its attendant administrative costs. Second, it minimizes government interference in people's lives. Third, it has a minimal impact on the workings of our market system. Fourth, it emphasizes private property.

Reducing the Level of Government Bureaucracy

In Chapter 2, the problems with our current public assistance programs were presented. Among these is the tremendous expense incurred in administering the programs. This expense is necessitated, to a great extent, because the programs are categorical in nature. That is, people must fall into an eligible category (e.g., disabled) in order to receive benefits. This requires rules to establish criteria and government employees to apply the criteria. Perpetual observations must be made to determine whether recipients continue to be eligible and are meeting program guidelines.

The use of in-kind benefits also entails considerable administrative expense. For example, in the Food Stamp Program, rules are written establishing what can be bought with the food stamps and then these rules must be applied. In addition, there is the cost associated with printing and distributing the food stamps themselves.

The GAI, on the other hand, would be a universal program.[25] The only eligibility criterion would be citizenship. It could be administered either by the Internal Revenue Service or the Social Security Administration. The administrative costs associated with Social Security—in the range of 1 1/2 percent when Medicare is not counted— are those which can be expected in a GAI program. Since the GAI will lend itself to the use of electronic funds transfer, these administrative costs could be further reduced.[26] Also, since this would be strictly a cash program, there would be no bureaucracy (such as that necessary, for example, in the housing programs) associated with these benefits.

Minimizing Governmental Interference in People's Lives

Not only are the current programs costly in terms of the government bureaucracy required but they are also costly in terms of the impact on individual lives. They require trips to the welfare office, filling out complicated forms, compliance with income and wealth guidelines, and finally, spending money or stamps in preapproved ways.

With the recent welfare reform, we add to this the requirement to participate in specified training programs and to apply for and take specified jobs. I discuss these workfare programs in Chapter 2. I recognize they have wide popular appeal. Nonetheless, whatever one feels about these reform attempts, one must recognize the extent to which they allow government rules and employees to dictate behavior to individuals. This must be anathema to libertarians and undesirable to conservatives.

With a GAI, the interaction with government would be no greater than it is now for income tax purposes. The same forms which are used to determine how much we must pay in taxes can be used to determine how much we can receive in benefits.

associated with eliminating poverty, a guaranteed adequate
the most efficient means of accomplishing this. Virtually all
y collected in taxes will be used to provide the poverty-reducing
Using the overhead costs of the Social Security program as our
e can expect less than 2 percent of the funds to be used for
trative costs.

her inefficiency in our current programs is the duplication of
. Once one becomes eligible for benefits under one program, that
has access to numerous other programs as well. This is why we
ses of people receiving government benefits which put them in a
favorable economic position than others who are working for a
. By substituting a single income-maintenance program, the GAI
d eliminate this inefficiency also.

ome argue that a different inefficiency would accompany the
ranteed income, as I propose it. They point to the necessity to pay
e benefits even to those above the poverty level. While this will
ed happen under my plan, it is a necessary consequence of the goal
retaining a work incentive. Personally, I am willing to accept some
ple receiving benefits, even though they are above the poverty level,
exchange for (1) ensuring that all people who need income receive it
e effectiveness argument), and (2) keeping the effective tax rate low
ough to provide a work incentive. In addition, these "inefficient"
enefits to lower-middle-income earners do have the benefit of further
reducing the disparity in income distribution. This is not an undesirable
consequence.

CONCLUSION

In this chapter I have presented my reasons for supporting a guaranteed
adequate income. Many before me have argued for similar plans, but I
arrive at a plan which is at once simpler and more comprehensive. In the
next chapter, you'll see the most prominent, previous proposals for
various forms of guaranteed incomes; my plan is presented in Chapter 8.

A major psychological benefit would be the elimination of the stigma
associated with "going on welfare." Everyone in the country is eligible
for the benefits, so no group of people can be singled out as welfare
recipients. Since some benefits will be received even by those who are
working full time (because of the need to provide a work incentive),
there will be no clear line between recipients and nonrecipients.

Minimizing the Impact on the Market System

To be a conservative in the United States today is to have faith in the
market system. The market system is the best we know of for
accumulating wealth and creating prosperity. It is also better than
anything we know of for distributing wealth. However, it is not without
its faults. One of these faults is the inability to provide economically for
those who have little or nothing to offer the market. It is generally agreed
that government must play a role in rectifying this inadequacy. The GAI
is the least intrusive method of accomplishing this goal.

Reduced Demand for Socialist Enterprises

At first glance, some may regard the GAI as a socialist program. It is not.
A socialist system promotes enterprises in which the government owns
the means of production and hires the employees. By instituting a strictly
cash transfer program, we *eliminate* many socialist activities. For
example, much of our current welfare dollar is spent for advice and
counseling for welfare recipients. This is socialized family counseling.
Our public housing programs are socialism in action. As I have noted
elsewhere in this book, I am not among those who equate socialism with
the devil. But for those who do, this program should be their cup of tea.

By making cash available to a wider segment of our population, we
create a demand for more goods. It is my belief these goods can, should,
and will be provided by the market. Through the competitive mechanism,
a higher quality and lower price will be achieved than is likely when the
enterprise is run by government. The main reason we have government
enterprises is because some people cannot afford to partake of market-
provided goods. The more we remedy this problem, the greater can be
our reliance on the market.

Public schools provide a good example of this last point. If everyone
in the country could afford to pay the tuition of adequate private schools,
there would be little need for the government to get involved in
education. For those who believe government does a lousy job in this, as
in other areas, the GAI would be a welcome change. It is possible that by
introducing competition into this sphere, we could improve the quality
and reduce the cost of education. The same point can be made with
respect to health care. The current drive for national health insurance
would be considerably muted if everyone could afford to pay for private

health care (probably through the purchase of private health insurance). For those who want to maximize the use of the private sector, this should be a desirable alternative.

Elimination of the Need for Minimum Wage Laws

A guaranteed adequate income can also have a positive effect on wages, eliminating the need for the intrusion of minimum wage laws. These laws are currently regarded as necessary in order to ensure that employed people earn a decent living. However, they have an undesirable effect on the market for wages. For example, because they are applied uniformly to all occupations, they override the market evaluation of the proper wage for different jobs. With a GAI, sellers of their labor will be in a better position to choose those jobs which promise the best combination of working conditions and salary.

Maintaining the Concept of Private Property

Personally, I'm not a zealous exponent of the idea of private property. Oh, I know there are a lot of merits to it. People tend to take better care of things they own, for example. But on balance, I think it is primarily a notion developed and supported by those who have the property, to help ensure they can keep it and pass it on to their preferred recipients. Nonetheless, for those readers who avidly defend this notion, the GAI is ideal. It allows more people an opportunity to acquire property. Granted, it continues the practice of taking some property from people in the form of taxes, but this would appear to be a given. Given we're going to tax some to help others, the GAI does so with the minimum intrusion into the notion of private property.

EFFECTIVE AND EFFICIENT

It is important in any program to consider these two objectives. An effective program is one which accomplishes its goal. Success on this criterion is measured by the ratio of accomplishment to objective. An efficient program is one which minimizes the costs associated with accomplishing the goal. Success on this criterion is measured by the ratio of outputs to inputs.

Effectiveness

One of the major problems with our current programs is the existence of gaps. There are many poor people who, because of the categorical nature of the programs, receive no government benefits. This includes many

working poor. By eliminating these would be much more effective.

If our main objective is (and I be absolute poverty in the United States, a the most effective means of accomplishin the level of the income at the predetermin accomplishment is 100 percent of the objec program there will still be *relative* povert lowest 10 percent or 5 percent. Unless we cr goal I argue is neither possible nor desira always exist.

I recognize that in the process, we may we Murray refers to as "latent poverty." This is th of people who would have been poor but for go regards increases in this figure as evidence of the policies in the 1960s and 1970s. His concern is refl

> The reason for calling this the most damning of the sta
> independence—standing on one's own abilities and acc
> paramount importance in determining the quality of a far.

In this quote lies the essence of why two Murrays fro quite different views about the future of government inco programs. Mike Murray has no quarrel with Charles M says, "Hardly anyone, from whatever part of the political disagree" with the above statement. The difference is he build a program on the continued, widespread acceptance (indeed is anxious to reinforce this mind-set).

I, on the other hand, strongly believe this view is, itself, problem. To continue to base one's worth on one's ability to s the economic sphere is to continue to damn those who will neve in this way. It is also to overlook the manifold human virtues whi appropriately should define our worth—one's compassion, lo concern for others for examples. To these we could add the abi contemplate and to create. All of these virtues are poorly rewarded economic system. They are, however, among the factors that truly do our humanity.

The GAI will not only effectively eliminate poverty, it will also evidence that we have been effective in relegating the "economi success-measures-human-worth" syndrome to the scrap heap of once necessary-but-no-longer-desirable ideas.

Efficiency

An efficient program is one which accomplishes the goal with the minimum waste of resources. If one of our objectives is to reduce the

APPENDIX

RESULTS OF NEGATIVE INCOME TAX EXPERIMENTS

These massive social experiments were funded by grants from the federal government. They were conducted initially in New Jersey, in rural areas (Iowa, North Carolina), and in Gary, Indiana. The final and largest studies were the Seattle and Denver Income Maintenance Experiments (SIME/DIME).

Support rates in the New Jersey study were 75, 100, and 125 percent of the poverty level, and tax rates were 30, 50, and 70 percent. The SIME/DIME experiment had support levels from 95 to 140 percent of the poverty level, and tax rates from 50 to 80 percent (the latter rate included a declining rate as income rose).

SIME/DIME imputed a 5.75 percent return on some components of net worth (stocks, savings accounts, equity in owner-occupied housing and other real property) as countable income. Benefits were available only to households (more than one person), not to single individuals (except where divorce occurred during the experiment, in which case benefits continued to single individuals, but benefits were limited to $1,000 per year).

It was assumed that only families of these types were likely to be included in any permanent income maintenance program for political reasons.[28]

Disabled were omitted, because their labor supply responses were expected to be different and would confound the results. The age limitation was between eighteen and fifty-eight.

LABOR SUPPLY EFFECTS

Initial reports of the results of this study were quite sanguine.

What we found was that people forecasting a negative income tax would be a disaster apparently are wrong. . . . We're not saying the payments cause people to run out and get jobs. It's just that if the country wants to come up with legislation to increase people's income—to bring them up to a subsistence level —they're not necessarily going to become any less diligent than the rest of society. . . [A] reduction of only 12 percent suggests that the introduction of a national negative income tax program will not give rise to a tidal wave of voluntary idleness.[29]

While this initial optimism was overshadowed by subsequent more negative results, the interpretations could still be relevant. Even the later results hardly presage a "tidal wave of voluntary idleness."

An extrapolation of results to a nationwide NIT program suggested percentage decreases in annual hours of work of 6 to 11 percent for husbands, 23 to 32 percent for wives, and 0 to 15 percent for single female heads of families.

> The least generous program tested (one with support level equal to 50 percent of poverty level and a 70 percent tax rate) would cost $4 billion less than the current welfare system, provided there is no supplementation of lost welfare benefits by states.[30]

A relatively generous program (support equal to the poverty level and a 50 percent tax rate) would cost $30 billion more than the current system.

> In the set of programs tested, labor supply responses accounted for one quarter to one half of the total cost of the program.[31]

The benefits were provided for different durations. The estimated reduction in desired hours of work was found to be larger for persons enrolled in the longer duration (five-year) program.

Long-Term Implications

A major issue in interpreting these studies is whether the observed work reduction would be greater or lesser with a permanent program. I argue intuitively that one is more likely to regard a temporary NIT as an opportunity for vacation or retooling, whereas this effect would soon wear off in a permanent program. The prospect of temporary leisure is much more pleasurable to most people than is the prospect of a lifetime without productive activity.

Charles Murray has concluded, however, that most researchers feel the NIT experiments understate the work disincentive effect. The primary reasons he cites for this are two. First is the fact that the comparison was made with a group of people receiving traditional welfare benefits, and presumably already experiencing some work disincentives. Second is that because of the short-term nature of the program, people are less likely to "burn bridges behind them" if they know the guaranteed income will end shortly. He said there was only one paper he had encountered which dissented from this general view.[32]

In that paper, Charles Metcalf shows theoretically that the income effect of a temporary NIT is understated relative to a permanent program,

A major psychological benefit would be the elimination of the stigma associated with "going on welfare." Everyone in the country is eligible for the benefits, so no group of people can be singled out as welfare recipients. Since some benefits will be received even by those who are working full time (because of the need to provide a work incentive), there will be no clear line between recipients and nonrecipients.

Minimizing the Impact on the Market System

To be a conservative in the United States today is to have faith in the market system. The market system is the best we know of for accumulating wealth and creating prosperity. It is also better than anything we know of for distributing wealth. However, it is not without its faults. One of these faults is the inability to provide economically for those who have little or nothing to offer the market. It is generally agreed that government must play a role in rectifying this inadequacy. The GAI is the least intrusive method of accomplishing this goal.

Reduced Demand for Socialist Enterprises

At first glance, some may regard the GAI as a socialist program. It is not. A socialist system promotes enterprises in which the government owns the means of production and hires the employees. By instituting a strictly cash transfer program, we *eliminate* many socialist activities. For example, much of our current welfare dollar is spent for advice and counseling for welfare recipients. This is socialized family counseling. Our public housing programs are socialism in action. As I have noted elsewhere in this book, I am not among those who equate socialism with the devil. But for those who do, this program should be their cup of tea.

By making cash available to a wider segment of our population, we create a demand for more goods. It is my belief these goods can, should, and will be provided by the market. Through the competitive mechanism, a higher quality and lower price will be achieved than is likely when the enterprise is run by government. The main reason we have government enterprises is because some people cannot afford to partake of market-provided goods. The more we remedy this problem, the greater can be our reliance on the market.

Public schools provide a good example of this last point. If everyone in the country could afford to pay the tuition of adequate private schools, there would be little need for the government to get involved in education. For those who believe government does a lousy job in this, as in other areas, the GAI would be a welcome change. It is possible that by introducing competition into this sphere, we could improve the quality and reduce the cost of education. The same point can be made with respect to health care. The current drive for national health insurance would be considerably muted if everyone could afford to pay for private health care (probably through the purchase of private health insurance). For those who want to maximize the use of the private sector, this should be a desirable alternative.

Elimination of the Need for Minimum Wage Laws

A guaranteed adequate income can also have a positive effect on wages, eliminating the need for the intrusion of minimum wage laws. These laws are currently regarded as necessary in order to ensure that employed people earn a decent living. However, they have an undesirable effect on the market for wages. For example, because they are applied uniformly to all occupations, they override the market evaluation of the proper wage for different jobs. With a GAI, sellers of their labor will be in a better position to choose those jobs which promise the best combination of working conditions and salary.

Maintaining the Concept of Private Property

Personally, I'm not a zealous exponent of the idea of private property. Oh, I know there are a lot of merits to it. People tend to take better care of things they own, for example. But on balance, I think it is primarily a notion developed and supported by those who have the property, to help ensure they can keep it and pass it on to their preferred recipients. Nonetheless, for those readers who avidly defend this notion, the GAI is ideal. It allows more people an opportunity to acquire property. Granted, it continues the practice of taking some property from people in the form of taxes, but this would appear to be a given. Given we're going to tax some to help others, the GAI does so with the minimum intrusion into the notion of private property.

EFFECTIVE AND EFFICIENT

It is important in any program to consider these two objectives. An effective program is one which accomplishes its goal. Success on this criterion is measured by the ratio of accomplishment to objective. An efficient program is one which minimizes the costs associated with accomplishing the goal. Success on this criterion is measured by the ratio of outputs to inputs.

Effectiveness

One of the major problems with our current programs is the existence of gaps. There are many poor people who, because of the categorical nature of the programs, receive no government benefits. This includes many working poor. By eliminating these arbitrary categories, the program would be much more effective.

If our main objective is (and I believe it should be) to eliminate absolute poverty in the United States, a guaranteed adequate income is the most effective means of accomplishing this. It is only necessary to set the level of the income at the predetermined poverty level and *voila!* the accomplishment is 100 percent of the objective. Of course, even with this program there will still be *relative* poverty, since there will still be a lowest 10 percent or 5 percent. Unless we create an egalitarian society, a goal I argue is neither possible nor desirable, this phenomenon will always exist.

I recognize that in the process, we may well increase what Charles Murray refers to as "latent poverty." This is the measure of the number of people who would have been poor but for government assistance. He regards increases in this figure as evidence of the failure of our welfare policies in the 1960s and 1970s. His concern is reflected in the following:

> The reason for calling this the most damning of the statistics is that economic independence—standing on one's own abilities and accomplishments—is of paramount importance in determining the quality of a family's life.[27]

In this quote lies the essence of why two Murrays from Iowa arrive at quite different views about the future of government income maintenance programs. Mike Murray has no quarrel with Charles Murray when he says, "Hardly anyone, from whatever part of the political spectrum, will disagree" with the above statement. The difference is he is willing to build a program on the continued, widespread acceptance of this view (indeed is anxious to reinforce this mind-set).

I, on the other hand, strongly believe this view is, itself, part of the problem. To continue to base one's worth on one's ability to succeed in the economic sphere is to continue to damn those who will never succeed in this way. It is also to overlook the manifold human virtues which more appropriately should define our worth—one's compassion, love and concern for others for examples. To these we could add the ability to contemplate and to create. All of these virtues are poorly rewarded in our economic system. They are, however, among the factors that truly define our humanity.

The GAI will not only effectively eliminate poverty, it will also be evidence that we have been effective in relegating the "economic-success-measures-human-worth" syndrome to the scrap heap of once-necessary-but-no-longer-desirable ideas.

Efficiency

An efficient program is one which accomplishes the goal with the minimum waste of resources. If one of our objectives is to reduce the overhead associated with eliminating poverty, a guaranteed adequate income is the most efficient means of accomplishing this. Virtually all the money collected in taxes will be used to provide the poverty-reducing income. Using the overhead costs of the Social Security program as our guide, we can expect less than 2 percent of the funds to be used for administrative costs.

Another inefficiency in our current programs is the duplication of benefits. Once one becomes eligible for benefits under one program, that person has access to numerous other programs as well. This is why we see cases of people receiving government benefits which put them in a more favorable economic position than others who are working for a living. By substituting a single income-maintenance program, the GAI would eliminate this inefficiency also.

Some argue that a different inefficiency would accompany the guaranteed income, as I propose it. They point to the necessity to pay some benefits even to those above the poverty level. While this will indeed happen under my plan, it is a necessary consequence of the goal of retaining a work incentive. Personally, I am willing to accept some people receiving benefits, even though they are above the poverty level, in exchange for (1) ensuring that all people who need income receive it (the effectiveness argument), and (2) keeping the effective tax rate low enough to provide a work incentive. In addition, these "inefficient" benefits to lower-middle-income earners do have the benefit of further reducing the disparity in income distribution. This is not an undesirable consequence.

CONCLUSION

In this chapter I have presented my reasons for supporting a guaranteed adequate income. Many before me have argued for similar plans, but I arrive at a plan which is at once simpler and more comprehensive. In the next chapter, you'll see the most prominent, previous proposals for various forms of guaranteed incomes; my plan is presented in Chapter 8.

and that the gross and compensated price effects are overstated.[33] I interpret this to mean that the impact of expectations of future income in a permanent program would have a greater effect on causing one to seek employment than would this effect in a temporary program.

According to another group of researchers:

> We argue that these findings do not necessarily imply that the reduction in desired hours of work associated with most feasible types of permanent nationwide NIT programs would be larger than the reductions simulated on the basis of the SIME/DIME results. This is because of the relatively generous support levels of SIME/DIME (compared to most welfare-reform proposals), and the fact that support levels are underestimated in a temporary experiment while tax effects are overestimated.[34]

I am willing to concede that the evidence on balance shows a fairly sizable reduction in hours worked. As I indicated in the text, however, I feel this may well be a virtue rather than a liability of the GAI.[35]

PROBABILITY OF EMPLOYMENT

Researchers were interested not only in how many hours the subjects worked but also in how likely it was they would be employed at all. As Shown in Appendix Table 6.1 the probability of employment (in the "steady state"—that is, on an ongoing basis) changes as follows:

Table 6.1

Probability of Employment

	Without NIT	With NIT
Husbands	.805	.757
Wives	.423	.342
Single female heads	.569	.457

Source: Philip K. Robins, Nancy Brandon Tuma, and R. E. Yeager, "The Seattle and Denver Income Maintenance Experiments: Effects of SIME/DIME on Changes in Employment Status," *Journal of Human Resources*, Fall 1980, pp. 560-561.

According to the authors of one study:

> These predictions suggest that the decreased probability of employment under an NIT program is mainly (for wives, almost solely) due to longer spells of nonemployment. This means that the introduction of an NIT program has not greatly increased the overall rate at which people (especially wives) leave employment.[36]

Another author comments:

> Reduction in total hours of work most often reflect a reduction in the likelihood of being employed at all. The total reduction in work hours stems from a rather large response by a small number of men. Therefore, the negative income tax does not appear to have a pervasive effect on the work ethic of the low-income male population.[37]

Robins et al. also take note of the possibility that the longer spells out of work are beneficial:

> In the present study we observe longer spells out of work among persons eligible for counseling and education/training subsidies, which suggests that the longer spells out of employment are used at least partly for investment in human capital [i.e. to improve one's employability].[38]

EFFECTS ON MARRIAGE DISSOLUTION

Although the main interest of these studies was the work effect, they also looked at some other variables which will be of interest to many considering a guaranteed income. One of these variables was the effect on marriages. The authors of this part of the study conclude:

> Our results indicate that the experimental NIT plans increased the rate of marital dissolution. We believe that a permanent national NIT program would have a similar effect, although we doubt that the magnitude of the effect can be estimated. We can say nothing about the desirability (or undesirability) of such effects. . . The dissolution may make the partners better or worse off. An NIT plan might improve the situation for wives who are caught in unsatisfactory marriages by economic circumstances.[39]

I agree with Funiciello when she says:

> To reject guaranteed income as a means to enforce marital vows would be to argue that families ought to be kept poor.[40]

EFFECTS ON MIGRATION

I have argued that a benefit of a guaranteed income would be that movement of the labor supply would be facilitated. The question of whether this would indeed occur was the subject of part of the study, and one author concluded:

> This model suggests that an NIT would induce people to move to locations with better environments and lower real wages and would induce persons to reduce their hours of work. Thus, one likely impact of a nationwide NIT program would be a redistribution of the low-income population to regions with better environments and lower wage rates.[41]

DIFFERENCES BY ETHNIC GROUP

An analysis was also done of the effects by ethnic group. Part of the reason for this interest was the disparate number of minorities in the sample. Using one model, the researchers found "no firm evidence of differences in response by race," but with a second model there were "significant differences by race . . . for husbands but not for wives or single female heads of families. White husbands had a smaller response than black or Chicano husbands."[42] According to one writer:

> The effects for demographic groups follow no clear pattern. Interracial variations, for example, appear to be only a result of random statistical error.[43]

Notes

1. For most of the life of this idea, the initials GAI have stood for "guaranteed *annual* income." I have eliminated the *annual* because it is preferable to pay the benefits more frequently. I use the word *adequate* because it provides an indication of the level of benefit being recommended.

2. John Maynard Keynes, "Economic Possibilities for Our Grandchildren," *Essays in Persuasion* (New York: W. W. Norton & Co., Inc., 1963), pp. 369-370.

3. Socioeconomist Robert Theobald also provides a notable sound bite: "The guaranteed income therefore involves a major shift in rights and obligations. Today we demand of an individual that he find a job, but we then provide him with the right to 'pursue happiness.' Tomorrow we will provide him with the right to receive enough resources to live with dignity, and we will demand of him that he develop himself and his society." Robert Theobald (ed.), *The Guaranteed Income: Next Step in Socioeconomic Evolution?*, p. 103.

4. "The most important reason for the acceptance of the concept [guaranteed income] is that it might drastically enhance the freedom of the individual. Until now in human history, man has been limited in his freedom to act by two factors: the use of force on the part of the rulers (essentially their capacity to kill the dissenters); and, more importantly, the threat of starvation against all who were unwilling to accept the conditions of work and social existence that were imposed on them." Eric Fromm, "The Psychological Aspects," in Theobald, *The Guaranteed Income*, p. 183.

5. The character Julian West in the novel by Edward Bellamy, *Looking Backward: 2000-1887*, equates this concept to "true life insurance," pp. 321-322.

6. According to Clarence E. Ayres, "Security is the key to the enigma of poverty, as it was to the impasse of feudal serfdom. With the guarantee of a subsistence income, so that come what may they could feel assured that they would not starve to death, most of the present victims of poverty would make the effort of reorienting themselves in the industrial economy." "Guaranteed Income: An Institutionalist View," in Theobald, *The Guaranteed Income*, p. 176.

7. Many originally opposed the passage of Social Security because of anticipated negative effects on savings. In a story about a long-time life insurance agent, the agent was quoted: "The advent of Social Security scared the living daylights out of many agents, who thought the government program would curb the demand for private insurance. Instead it merely whetted the public's appetite for insurance. It made everybody conscious of a retirement income." "At 88, D. M. Life Insurance Agent Has Seen Changes in Business," *Des Moines Register*, January 30, 1994, p. 42.

8. Theresa Funiciello, *The Tyranny of Kindness*, p. 24. (The author is a former welfare recipient.)

9. Ibid., pp. 35-36.

10. Tara Smith provides a good review of the people and arguments supporting the claim that liberty rights require welfare rights. The author takes issue with these arguments. She argues they reflect an erroneous notion of what it is to have a right, noting that the source of one's inability to exercise a right is crucial. She also suggests they confuse freedom with ability—one can be free to do something without actually having the ability to do it. "On Deriving Rights to Goods From Rights to Freedom," *Law and Philosophy*, 11 (1992): 217-234.

11. Theobald, *The Guaranteed Income*, p. 17.

12. Jon N. Torgerson, "Taking Economic Rights Seriously," *Contemporary Philosophy*, 13(5): 20-24.

13. Bellamy, *Looking Backward: 2000-1887*, p. 97.

14. Tom Wicker, "The Right to Income," *New York Times*, December 24, 1967, p. E9.

15. Robert Theobald puts it this way: "For me, therefore, the guaranteed income represents the possibility of putting into effect the fundamental philosophic belief, which has recurred consistently in human history, that each

individual has a right to a minimal share in the production of his society.''
Theobald, *The Guaranteed Income*, p. 19.

16. A similar point was made by Thomas Paine in 1796. He proposed a
bounty be paid to each citizen upon reaching age twenty-one. This was to be
done as part of a goal to ''restore the right of every man to share in the natural
endowment of all mankind, naturally his,'' *Agrarian Justice* (Philadelphia), as
cited in Henry Phelps Brown, *Egalitarianism and the Generation of Inequality*,
p. 141.

17. This idea is also put forward in Bellamy's *Looking Backward: 2000-
1887*. In the novel, the character Julian West (who went into a trance in 1887
and awakened in 2000) asked how a person's shares were determined in the new
social system: ''By what title does the individual claim his particular share?''
''His title,'' replied [his host], ''is his humanity. The basis of his claim is the
fact that he is a man,'' p. 93. The difference between Bellamy's scenario and
mine is that he gave each an equal share; I propose only an adequate share based
on one's humanity.

18. Libertarians and many conservatives will argue that the role of
government should not include income redistribution. Although I see the merits
of their case, I side with the host in the following exchange from *Looking
Backward: 2000-1887*. Julian West comments on the increased role of
government: ''In my day [1887] it was considered that the proper functions of
government, strictly speaking, were limited to keeping the peace and defending
the people against the public enemy, that is, to the military and police powers.''
His host replies: ''And in heaven's name, who are the public enemies? Are they
France, England, Germany, or hunger, cold and nakedness?'' p. 59.

19. Brown, *Egalitarianism and the Generation of Inequality*, p. 526, also
makes the case for the use of the government mechanism, concluding, ''This
leads naturally to the organization of relief by government, which lays the
obligation to fund it fairly on all taxpayers.''

20. Brown, *Egalitarianism and the Generation of Inequality*, p. 176.

21. There are obviously a large number of people so concerned. ''The
Negative Income Tax (NIT) promise of improving efficiency and increasing
equity appealed to both conservatives and liberals. However, the political
feasibility of a nationwide NIT program rested on its ability to put to rest fears
that such a program would cause massive reductions in work effort.'' Robert G.
Spiegelman and K. E. Yeager, ''The Seattle and Denver Income Maintenance
Experiments: Overview,'' *Journal of Human Resources*, 15 (Fall 1980): 463-
464.

22. One additional published analysis of the work effects of a theoretical guaranteed income was published by the Chamber of Commerce, prior to the conduct of the massive studies. This provided the results of a simulation, conducted by economists Alfred and Dorothy Tella, as a response to the Family Assistance Plan proposal. Their conclusions were that the plans would discourage work by low-income family heads; male family heads would work fewer hours; and female family heads, in large measure, would withdraw from the labor force. A significant aspect of their findings is that 70 to 80 percent of the work disincentive would be caused by the high "tax rate" on earnings (67%). This is one reason my proposal includes the lower tax rate. Alfred and Dorothy Tella, *The Effect of Three Income Maintenance Programs on Work Effort* (Washington, D.C.: U. S. Chamber of Commerce, 1970).

23. One economic consequence of the guaranteed income was not addressed in the study. To some extent the money brought into a community by the guaranteed income payments would have stimulated the economy through an increased demand for services. This would have increased the total amount of work in the community. This point is also noted by Funiciello, *Tyranny of Kindness*, p. 305.

24. "We Won't Buy New Car, Winners Say," *Des Moines Register,* August 7, 1993, p. 3A.

25. My proposal is to eliminate *all* other public assistance programs.

26. cf. John Cobbs, "Egalitarianism: The Corporation as Villain," *Business Week,* December 15, 1975. After noting how egalitarianism would make it impossible for the capitalist system to work, he notes: "It might be possible to go a fairly long way toward equality with a simple transfer system that guaranteed every family a minimum cash income, paid for by progressive taxes on the upper and middle tax brackets. This would narrow the spread of incomes, but it would still leave differentials wide enough to mollify the unions and to motivate workers at all levels. The total cost would be lower because there would be no need for a massive administrative apparatus," p. 88.

27. Charles Murray, *Losing Ground*, p. 65.

28. Robert G. Spiegelman and K. E. Yeager, "The Seattle and Denver Income Maintenance Experiments: Overview," *Journal of Human Resources*, Fall 1980, p. 471.

29. David Kershaw, "Find Grants Didn't Hurt Work Ethic," *Des Moines Register*, March 26, 1973., p. 7. Kershaw is a private researcher who coordinated the experiment for the Office of Economic Opportunity. He noted that the reduction in work hours "probably was the result of two factors. Wives and

children who had to work before the grants came in were now able to leave their jobs. Heads of households receiving assistance were now taking more time to look for better jobs."

30. Ibid., p. 478.

31. Ibid., pp. 478-479.

32. Charles Murray, *Losing Ground*, pp. 153 and 288 (his footnote 21).

33. Charles E. Metcalf, "Making Inferences from Controlled Income Maintenance Experiments," *American Economic Review*, June 1973, p. 481.

34. Philip K. Robins and Richard W. West, "The Seattle and Denver Income Maintenance Experiments: Program Participation and Labor-Supply Response," *Journal of Human Resources*, Fall 1980, p. 542.

35. The research of one author suggests that U.S. workers are in the process of substituting leisure for work income, even in the absence of a GAI. Frank P. Stafford, "Income-Maintenance Policy and Work Effort: Learning from Experiments and Labor-Market Studies," in Jerry Hausman and David Wise (eds.), *Social Experimentation* (Chicago: University of Chicago Press, 1985), pp. 95-143.

36. Philip K. Robins, Nancy Brandon Tuma, and R. E. Yeager, "The Seattle and Denver Income Maintenance Experiments: Effects of SIME/DIME on Changes in Employment Status," *Journal of Human Resources*, Fall 1980, p. 563.

37. Robert A. Moffitt, "The Negative Income Tax: Would it Discourage Work?" *Monthly Labor Review*, April 1981, p. 25.

38. Robins, Tuma, and Yeager, "The Seattle and Denver Income Maintenance Experiments," pp. 566-567.

39. Lyle P. Groeneveld, Nancy Brandon Tuma, and Michael T. Hanna, "The Seattle and Denver Income Maintenance Experiments: The Effects of Negative Income Tax Programs on Marital Dissolution," *Journal of Human Resources*, Fall 1980, p. 672.

40. Theresa Funiciello, *Tyranny of Kindness*, p. 305.

41. Michael C. Keeley, "The Seattle and Denver Income Maintenance Experiments: The Effect of a Negative Income Tax on Migration," *Journal of Human Resources*, Fall 1980, p. 706.

42. Philip K. Robins and Richard W. West, "Labor Supply Response of Family Heads Over Time," in Philip Robins, Robert Speigelman, Samuel Weiner, and Joseph Bell (eds.), *A Guaranteed Annual Income: Evidence from a Social Experiment* (New York: Academic Press, 1980), p. 99.

43. Moffitt, "The Negative Income Tax," p. 25.

7

The History of Guaranteed Income Plans

Although I would like to take credit for it, the idea of a guaranteed income is not something I dreamed up. By now there is a substantial conceptual history behind it. There follows an overview of some of the conceptual parents of my plan. Each of these plans deserves more space than I can allot in this book. I'll try to give you a sense of each.

SPEENHAMLAND SYSTEM

Often cited as the first attempt at a guaranteed income, this late-eighteenth-century program in eighteen English counties guaranteed to each person an income equal to at least the price of two loaves of bread a week. It was essentially an income supplement plan. Its great shortcoming was the one-for-one offset (or 100 percent tax rate) for earned income just above the guarantee level. Since low-income workers were guaranteed a minimum income by the government, employers had little incentive to pay adequate wages (in those days there were no minimum wage laws). Eventually most of the pay for low-income workers was provided by the government. This system did not last long.

EDWARD BELLAMY'S FORWARD LOOK

In his 1888 novel *Looking Backward,* Edward Bellamy projected a society which would provide an absolute guarantee to "abundant maintenance." His views, which became fairly influential at the time and are still regarded as seminal on this issue, were founded on the notion that society can and must retreat from the economic theories of scarcity. He suggested that men would look back from the late twentieth century and wonder how a society could have for so long been based on some of the worst characteristics of man—selfishness and greed.

BRITISH PROPOSALS OF THE RHYS-WILLIAMS

A social dividend plan was proposed by Lady Rhys-Williams in Britain in the 1940s. It would provide a payment equal to the poverty amount to every citizen. This would be payable without regard to income. A flat income tax rate of perhaps 33 1/3 percent would be used to fund the plan. In some ways, this plan is closest of all to the one I promote in this book. It is very simple in concept and fair in application.[1]

Recently, Sir Brandon Rhys-Williams MP proposed a basic income of some 20 percent of average earnings for a single householder, around a third of average earnings for a couple, and about a half for a couple with two children. He would have financed this with a basic tax rate of 42 to 50 percent on all income.[2]

FAMILY ALLOWANCES

These systems, in effect in a number of European countries including Great Britain for many decades, provide a small guaranteed income to families with children. The amount may vary with the numbers and ages of the children. There is commonly no means test associated with the allowance. The major drawbacks to these plans are their limitation to families with children and their meagerness.

GEORGE STIGLER'S BRIEF MENTION

The economist George Stigler may have been the first prominent American to go into print with the basic argument for a guaranteed income. In a 1946 article in which he primarily criticized minimum wage legislation, he noted that there are preferable options for dealing with poverty.

> There is great attractiveness in the proposal that we extend the personal income tax to the lowest income brackets with negative rates in these brackets. Such a scheme could achieve equality of treatment with what appears to be a minimum of administrative machinery.[3]

FRIEDMAN NEGATIVE INCOME TAX

The economist Milton Friedman is generally credited with developing thie idea of a negative income tax (NIT).[4] His plan focused on the unused exemptions and deductions of those whose income is very low. Just as these deductions can be used by those paying a positive tax, so should they be of benefit to those with very low or no incomes. The benefit would be calculated as follows:[5]

Total allowable exemptions and deductions minus income = negative income

.5 * negative income = negative income tax

The negative income tax is the amount to be paid to the family. As can be seen, this amount is reduced by 50 cents for every dollar earned. In effect, this results in a 50 percent tax rate. Although he realized this was a relatively high tax rate, he felt it was necessary in order to avoid paying benefits to middle-income persons. He regards this plan as a replacement for other welfare programs,[6] and argues that it is much more in keeping with conservative economic positions. Friedman recognizes but defends the limited nature of this plan.

By varying the break-even income and the negative tax rate, by adding the negative income tax to present programs rather than substituting it for them, it is possible to go all the way from the rather modest and, I believe, eminently desirable plan just outlined to irresponsible and undesirable plans that would involve enormous redistribution of income and a drastic reduction in the incentive to work. That is why it is possible for persons with a wide range of political views to support one form or another of a negative income tax.[7]

My plan is consistent with his views in my desire to replace the current welfare programs and in the provision for an even greater work incentive (a 35 percent tax rate rather than his 50 percent rate), but I do provide for a substantially greater breakeven income.[8]

SCHWARTZ FAMILY SECURITY BENEFIT

Professor Edward E. Schwartz of the University of Chicago promoted a plan which would provide every person in the United States with a federally guaranteed minimum income (FGMI). Receipt of benefits under the plan would be triggered by filing a declaration of estimated income. If the estimate fell below the FGMI, a check would be sent quarterly. One of Schwartz's goals was to relieve public assistance workers of the burden of determining eligibility for benefits, thus freeing them to provide counseling and other assistance to the poor. He was not particularly concerned with retaining a work incentive, believing most people would want to work to enhance the FGMI. Thus, the original plan offset the FGMI on a dollar-for-dollar basis as income was earned. However, he recognized that to be politically feasible, the plan may need to allow workers to keep some percentage of what they earned.[9]

TOBIN PLAN

Part of my reason for presenting these different plans is to note the distinction of some of the people who have proposed them. For example, James Tobin was a Yale University economics professor and a member of the President's Council of Economic Advisors. He had a guaranteed income plan which would have provided a guaranteed benefit of $750 (in 1968[10]) per family member.[11] He proposed a 33 1/3 percent tax rate, but allowed for the possibility of a progressive rate structure at the top. He demonstrated that such a plan would be affordable.[12]

LAMPMAN PLAN

The distinguishing characteristic of this plan is not so much its mechanics as the rationale behind it.[13] Professor Robert J. Lampman of North Carolina State University developed the plan for the Office of Economic Opportunity. He was primarily concerned with the inequities in our tax system. He pointed out, for example, that poor people are unable to take advantage of the tax deductions allowed higher-income people. This is primarily a function of an income which is too low to require a tax. In addition, other types of taxes, such as sales taxes, have a relatively large impact on the poor. Therefore, he suggested that the poor ought to be able to claim as a payment from the government 14 percent of their unused exemptions and deductions. In addition, he proposed guaranteed income plans based on a percentage of the poverty line and incorporating tax rates on earned income of either 50 percent (on a flat rate basis) or graduated from 75 to 25 percent on successive increments of income.

I believe a major disadvantage of Lampman's proposal is that this benefit would not replace our present welfare system, but would be a supplement.

THEOBALD'S BASIC ECONOMIC SECURITY

In his book *Free Men and Free Markets*, the socioeconomist Robert Theobald proposed a constitutional amendment guaranteeing every citizen an income "sufficient to enable him to live with dignity." He felt the amendment was necessary to provide security against the whims of the particular party in power. In his view, many people could and would come to rely on this income as their sole means of support. He felt this was perfectly acceptable because it was fast becoming necessary to break the link between jobs and income.[14] Those who were able to or chose to work to supplement this income would receive the difference between what they earned and the Basic Economic Security grant level, plus a "premium" of 10 percent of their earnings. In effect this would amount to a tax of 90 percent on earnings, although Theobald's description makes it sound more like a bonus.

FAMILY ASSISTANCE PLAN

The Family Assistance Plan was proposed by President Nixon in 1969. It came very close to being law, having passed by a wide margin in the House of Representatives and then being narrowly defeated in the Senate.[15] It had most of the earmarks of a guaranteed income with the one exception noted by its title—it was limited to families. Thus only those with children were entitled to benefit. Nonetheless, by providing a guaranteed income floor, it would have been a major piece of social legislation.

The FAP included:

• A minimum income floor. For a family of four, that was set (in 1969) at $1,600.
• A 50 percent offset for earned income. As previously described, this can be regarded as a 50 percent tax on earned income.
• A limitation to families with children.
• A continuation of the provision that recipients who did not accept work or training would lose their part of the family benefit.[16]
• A requirement for states to supplement the FAP benefit up to their previous level of welfare benefits.
• Administration through the Social Security Administration.

This plan could have provided a dramatic improvement in the situation of many low-income Americans. It is ironic that its defeat came to a great extent at the hands of those who traditionally supported programs for the poor. According to Moynihan, this was due in no small measure to their conclusion the plan did not go far enough.[17]

CREDIT INCOME TAX

According to Lee Rainwater, a "credit income tax" or "tax-credit system" was originated by tax economist Earl R. Rolph in 1967.[18,19] The idea was elaborated on by James Tobin.[20] Under this plan each individual in the country would be entitled to a tax credit of some particular amount. The personal income tax system would be changed to eliminate all personal deductions and tax income at a single rate.

According to Rainwater, a major problem with this plan (because it focuses on individuals and not families) is the redistribution from small to large families. This could be partially alleviated by giving children some percentage of the adult amount. Rainwater favors gradually increasing this amount each year. He gives as examples an initial benefit of 10 percent, increasing by 10 percent per year, 20 percent increasing by 6.75 percent, and 33 percent increasing by 4.5 percent. These would all reach 100 percent by age twenty-five.[21]

Rainwater agrees with Tobin that in one sense there is no "cost" to an internal income redistribution scheme such as this. The tax revenues from some are balanced by the benefits to others.

He suggests pegging the tax credit to some percentage of weighted (by age composition) per capita income or by picking a target guarantee and working backward to calculate the tax rate necessary to sustain that guarantee. He calculates a guarantee based on reserving 25 percent of personal income to finance redistribution (the difference between that and the actual tax rate would be used for other government needs, supplemented by other taxes.) This additional tax he puts at about 9 percent.[22]

GEORGE MCGOVERN'S 1972 CAMPAIGN PROPOSAL

During his unsuccessful bid for the presidency in 1972, George McGovern proposed a $1,000 guaranteed income. This would be paid to every man, woman, and child in the United States, and would be paid without regard to income. Individuals would pay income tax on this amount, and could earn as much additional money as possible, paying normal income tax rates on their earnings. This program would have replaced AFDC.

McGovern received substantial criticism, particularly because he did not have firm estimates of the cost of the plan.[23] He did suggest some ways in which the needed revenue would be raised: through cuts in defense spending, by eliminating the AFDC program, by eliminating the personal tax exemption (which he pointed out is of greater benefit to the wealthy than to the poor), and through reductions in Social Security costs (since these benefits would be offset by the guaranteed income).

ABLE GRANT

This 1974 plan of the Congressional Subcommittee on Fiscal Policy contained most of the elements of a guaranteed income plan.[24] It provided for both a tax credit (of $225) which could be paid to those whose liability was less than the credit and an Allowance for Basic Living Expenses (ABLE) grant ($825 for an individual), payable to everyone in the country. Notable features of the plan included:

- Benefits for everyone, not just families.
- Benefits which varied by family status, including reduced benefits per child for more than two children.
  - A very low level of income.[25]
  - Elimination of the AFDC and food stamp programs.

The report of the subcommittee thoroughly documents the basis for this plan, including indictments of our current system. Their succinct statement of the purpose of the plan is:

> The purpose of these recommendations is to replace or rationalize the many public programs offering support based on family and individual income by establishing, as a part of the income tax, a new Federal system of tax credits and allowances. This new system is designed to increase the equity, strengthen the administration, and improve the adequacy of income maintenance programs, and to restore desirable social and economic incentives to the Nation's system for income support.[26]

It also comments on alternative plans, including universal demogrants. Since my proposal is essentially a demogrant, I should in fairness note they rejected such a program because of its high cost.[27]

ALLAN SHEAHAN'S PLAN

In his book *Guaranteed Income: The Right to Economic Security*, Allan Sheahen provides a fairly generic example of a guaranteed income. His argument is not so much for the particular plan as it is for the concept of a guaranteed income. As he notes, this plan is essentially similar to a negative income tax, the only difference being that the latter is more difficult to compute. He shows the resultant benefit to be the same.

Although the basic concept of a guaranteed income is consistent among plans, there are a number of choices which must be made. Among the choices made by Sheahen are:[28]

- All U.S. citizens and those living here for more than five years will be eligible.
- All those with incomes and assets below a specified level will receive benefits. The asset level is set considerably higher than under current public assistance programs. Those with assets exceeding the maximum would not be automatically excluded, but an income would be imputed from the assets and added to other income. This makes

good sense, since a person who owns her or his own home is certainly in a better financial position than someone with the same income who is paying rent.

• There will be no adjustments for regional differences in cost of living. I agree with his contention that cost of living differences are in part a function of crowding, and that a guaranteed income would allow the population to disperse. As a result, cost-of-living differences should be reduced.

• Administration would be by the Internal Revenue Service.

• There would be no immediate change in other public assistance programs, but benefits under the other programs would decline (apparently because the guaranteed income would be included in their benefit calculations). This is a major point on which I take issue with his plan. The guaranteed income makes much more sense as *the* government income maintenance plan.

For those who would like a succinct description of the rationale for a guaranteed income, Sheahen's book makes excellent reading. He has written it in a question-and-answer format, responding to the questions commonly asked by those who are contemplating a guaranteed income for the first time.

PROBLEMS WITH PREVIOUS PLANS

The primary problems with previous plans, strange as it may seem, is that they were not radical enough. Three problems are common:

• By incorporating a work requirement, they continue to require a substantial bureaucracy to oversee the operation. They also perpetuate the notion that there must be a tie between work and income.

• By utilizing a high percentage income offset (or tax on income) they perpetuate the very high work disincentive evident in current welfare programs. I argue we should not force people to work in order to survive, but we should provide them with an adequate economic incentive to improve their condition. Most of the previous plans impose a 50 percent or higher tax rate on persons receiving the guaranteed income. When one considers the job alternatives commonly available to those in low-income brackets, it is apparent this significant reduction in work incentive is undesirable.

• By utilizing an income qualification requirement, many of these plans perpetuate the "them versus us" nature of public assistance. I argue it is important to stipulate that everyone is eligible for benefits. I suggest a means by which we minimize the actual level of transfers taking place.

In the next chapter I detail my proposal.

APPENDIX

RELATIVE PRICE AND POVERTY LEVELS

Table 7.1

Consumer Price Indices and Purchasing Power of the Dollar-Selected Years

Year	Consumer Price Index	Purchasing Power of the Dollar (Consumer Prices)
1960	29.6	3.373
1965	31.5	3.166
1970	38.8	2.574
1975	53.8	1.859
1980	82.4	1.215
1985	107.6	0.928
1990	130.7	0.766
1991	136.2	0.734
1992	140.3	0.713

Source: Bureau of the Census, *Statistical Abstract of the United States: 1993*, 113th Ed. (Washington, DC.: U.S. Government Printing Office, 1993).

Table 7.2

U.S. Government Poverty Levels-Selected Years

Year	One Person	Four Person Household
1959	$1,467	$2,973
1968	$1,742	$3,531
1970	$1,954	$3,948
1975	$2,724	$5,500
1980	$4,190	$8,414
1985	$5,469	$10,989
1990	$6,652	$13,359
1991	$6,932	$13,924

Source: Bureau of the Census, *Statistical Abstract of the United States,* various eds. (Washington, DC.: U.S. Government Printing Office).

Notes

1. A major drawback to the plan would be the tremendous initial transfer costs. I will reduce these costs by requiring a declaration of estimated income so that an individual's transfer payments can be offset by anticipated tax obligations.

2. As described in A. B. Atkinson, *The Economics of Inequality*, p. 275. Atkinson comments on various approaches to dealing with the welfare problem. He concludes: "It is clear that new initiatives in the field of income maintenance are required. . . . To say that the solution lies in substantially increased transfers of income, coupled with measures to create employment, is politically unfashionable—but it is clear that the nettle needs to be grasped."

3. George Stigler, "The Economics of Minimum Wage Legislation," *The American Economic Review*, June 1946, p. 365.

4. Friedman is generally regarded as a conservative economist. He was Senator Barry Goldwater's economic advisor when Goldwater ran for the presidency. Friedman's primary objective was to develop a plan which would have a minimal impact on the working of the free market.

5. As described in Milton Friedman, *Capitalism & Freedom*, p. 192.

6. I consider the negative income tax a form of guaranteed income. There are, however, some who prefer to consider it separately. "The idea of a guaranteed income went beyond subsistence. It envisioned a level of payment sufficient to maintain a reasonable, if low, standard of living. A negative income tax would provide just such a guaranteed income. In this sense they were identical proposals. In another sense, however, they were profoundly different. The guaranteed income was an idea of the left; the negative income tax, an idea of the right." Daniel Moynihan, *The Politics of A Guaranteed Income*, p. 127.

7. Milton Friedman, *An Economist's Protest*, pp. 133-134.

8. One unfortunate consequence of Friedman's plan is the discontinuity in the tax rate at the breakeven income. Those below this level are in effect paying the 50 percent rate, but once they exceed the level they revert to the minimum regular income tax rate of 14 percent. This point is discussed by George H. Hildebrand in *Poverty, Income Maintenance, and the Negative Income Tax*, p. 19.

9. A description of this plan is in Edward Schwartz, "An End to the Means Test," in Robert Theobald (ed.), *The Guaranteed Income*, pp. 126-128.

10. For those readers who would like to compare the dollar values of various proposals with current values, I have provided some comparative information in an appendix to this chapter.

11. The actual amount of the proposed benefit in each of the plans is not particularly relevant because of changes in purchasing power since they were drafted. In addition, I believe it is fair to say that for each of the proposers, the actual amount was a relatively minor point. The essence of the plan was the important element.

12. cf. James Tobin, "An Exchange of Views: McGovern's Economics," *The New Republic*, July 22, 1972, pp. 30-31. Specific proposals were provided in "Raising the Incomes of the Poor," in Kermit Gorden (ed.), *Agenda for the Nation*.

13. cf. R. J. Lampman, "Approaches to the Reduction of Poverty," *American Economic Review*, 55 (May 1965): 521-529.

14. I argue this same point in Chapter 4.

15. Its principal architect, Daniel Moynihan, has provided an in-depth insight into its conceptualization and political progress in his *Politics of a Guaranteed Income*. Demonstrating how the idea can transcend political orientation, he notes: "It is perhaps the ultimate irony that the Nixon proposal for a negative income tax was drafted by Democratic advocates who not months earlier had had the same proposal rejected by the Johnson administration," p. 131.

16. According to Moynihan, this requirement was made to appear more rigorous than it actually was. Mothers with small children were exempt and the mandatory nature of the training was deleted. Ibid., p. 141.

17. Moynihan puts an interesting spin on this, however. "Liberal votes defeated Family Assistance, but this in the main was the triumph of conservative strategy." Ibid., p. 534.

18. Lee Rainwater, *What Money Buys*.

19. Rolph's idea was later explained in his article "A Credit Income Tax," in Theodore R. Marmor, *Poverty Policy*, pp. 207-217.

20. In "Raising the Incomes of the Poor," in Gordon, *Agenda for the Nation*, pp. 77-116.

21. Rainwater, *What Money Buys*, p. 224.

22. Ibid., p. 226. I propose to supplement the income tax revenues with a value added tax (VAT).

23. Columnist Tom Wicker provided an equivocal evaluation of the plan in his editorial "McGovernomics: Iffy Scheme," *Cedar Rapids (Iowa) Gazette*, June 7, 1972, p. 2. He seemed to applaud the elimination of the welfare bureaucracy

and the reduction in migration between states to get higher welfare benefits. However, he was concerned about the accuracy of the revenue estimates.

24. The membership of this subcommittee, chaired by Representative Martha Griffiths of Michigan, demonstrates once again the prominence of those who have supported some form of guaranteed income. Members were Proxmire of Wisconsin, Ribicoff of Connecticut, Bentsen of Texas, Bolling of Missouri, Widnall of New Jersey, Schweiker of Pennsylvania, and Javits, Carey, and Conable of New York.

25. According to the committee report: ''Benefit amounts are not designed to provide 'adequate' levels of living for several reasons. First, comparatively few families have no income or income-producing opportunities. . . . Second, the basic Federal allowances will help those with little capacity for self-support [SSI benefits were retained]. . . . Third, costs and caseloads rise rapidly as levels of allowances and/or credits are increased.'' Report of the Subcommittee on Fiscal Policy of the Joint Economic Committee, Congress of the United States, p. 157.

26. Ibid., p. 155.

27. Ibid., pp. 135-136. They note, however, that their refundable tax credit is in effect a demogrant, albeit at a low level. They cite a study by Benjamin Okner which concludes that a $5,000 grant (in 1974) for a family of four would require a 50 percent marginal tax rate. They note, however, the important administrative advantage because it could be administered by the Internal Revenue Service.

28. Allan Sheahen, *Guaranteed Income: The Right to Economic Security.*

8

The Guaranteed Adequate Income Proposal

So, reader, I suppose about now you're saying: "Enough why's. It's time for how." OK. It's time to suggest how this theoretically appealing idea is to be implemented. I do so under three headings. First, there is a listing of the nonnegotiable elements; second, a discussion of the other variables which can be the subject of democratic debate; and finally, a description of just how the GAI is to operate.

THE NONNEGOTIABLES

When I refer to some components as "nonnegotiable" it is not because I have a desire to dictate. Rather, it is because without these elements, the plan loses its raison d'être. This will become clearer as I discuss the components themselves.

A Share, Not a Gift

This is the basic premise of the guaranteed adequate income. Those who have control of the wealth of the country commit themselves to share it. Those who receive a payment are neither getting a gift nor are they on welfare or public assistance. They are simply receiving their share.

Universal Entitlement

Who is entitled to receive this share? *Everyone*! I cannot emphasize this too strongly. This includes you, it includes me, it includes disabled persons and able-bodied, it includes mothers of small children, fathers of older children, the children themselves, criminals, mentally retarded, lazy geniuses, street people, managers, owners of businesses, doctors, patients—everyone. I've left many categories off this list, but the GAI must leave no one off.

This is important for two reasons. First, a fundamental argument for the program is that there are no worthy or unworthy people—only people. Each and every person is equally entitled to some measure of the means of existence. Only with such a philosophy can we have a truly *effective* program—one which reaches all. Second, by eliminating the categorical approach which characterizes our current welfare system, we eliminate the overhead costs of administering the system. By doing this we can have a truly *efficient* system—one which accomplishes its goals with a minimum of wasted resources.

Administered Through the IRS

There is no need for a separate governmental agency to administer this program. The same agency which collects the money must be responsible for distributing it. The same form on which we determine how much we must pay is the form which is used to determine how much we receive.

Not only does this significantly reduce the administrative costs associated with the system, it also eliminates any stigma associated with being a recipient. Those who are net recipients deal with the same agency and people and forms as those who are net payers. As one moves from one status to another, one continues to file the same forms and deal with the same agency.

Proactive Payments

Payments are made as much as possible before the period in which the money is needed. This is accomplished through the filing of anticipated-income forms. These forms, similar to those currently used by the self-employed to determine their quarterly tax liability, will be filed by everyone. These will provide the basis for transfer payments to those whose income is expected to fall below the predetermined level.

Benefits in Money

Love may make the world go around, but money makes the economic system operate. In today's economy, the absence of money is the essence of poverty. There were times when this wasn't so—when food, clothing, and shelter could be obtained directly. No longer. Money can't buy happiness, but it can buy survival.

Our present welfare programs often attempt to override this fact of our economic lives by artificially providing in-kind benefits such as food stamps and subsidized housing. I have noted two problems with this: (1) there are significant administrative costs required, and (2) the economic lives of recipients are dictated by the choice of benefit. The most effective and efficient means of alleviating poverty is to provide money.

Elimination of Welfare Programs

Please take note of the fact I did not say "other" welfare programs. The GAI is not a welfare program; it is a replacement for welfare. Its existence will obviate the need for welfare. Granted, the level of benefit may be less than what is currently received by some welfare recipients. While I am not unsympathetic to the cries of those whose benefits will be reduced, I know we have to make tradeoffs in our political policy. My choice is to broaden the scope of income distribution, even if it is at the cost of lessening the depth in some instances.

I discuss below some of the programs which can and should be eliminated. Because of the welfare reform act of 1996, some of these programs will now be called by different names and the provisions of some may have been changed by the states. However, the essential features which I discuss and argue against will probably have been retained.

Among the programs to be eliminated is Aid to Families With Dependent Children(AFDC). When the subject of welfare arises in conversation, this is usually the target of most of the wrath. Although I have discussed this program in a previous chapter, a few words are in order at this point. It is important to separate two targets of the criticism of AFDC—the recipients and the program itself. Criticism of the recipients is ill-founded. It is based on an assumption that these welfare mothers are somehow different from the rest of us. If you believe they are, you will be fearful of any program which will continue to pay benefits to "them." I argue that they are people like the rest of us— responding rationally to the system. This brings us to the second source of criticism.

The primary drawback to this program is its categorical nature—the fact that benefits are paid only if you are a (generally single) parent. Thus, in order to qualify you must have children. I agree with the case made by Charles Murray that this program has led to the disintegration of families.[1] It must be eliminated.[2]

Also to be disbanded is the Supplemental Security Income (SSI) program. Another "categorical" program, this pays benefits to those who qualify by virtue of their disability or age. To become a recipient, one must prove the existence of a sufficiently disabling condition or meet the arbitrary age requirement. Recipients must also prove they are poor— in terms of both income and wealth. The cost of administering this program, including the need to monitor the disability status of recipients, is very high. It, like most of the other current welfare progams, is very inefficient and bureaucracy-laden.

Food stamps must go. Not only is this program inefficient because of the high administrative costs, it also is cursed with the "we know what's best for you" characteristic. Recipients can use this benefit only in a manner prescribed by the rules. For example, the stamps cannot be used to purchase toothpaste or cleaning supplies. If these happen to be the primary need at a particular time, tough! A simple income program such as the GAI allows the recipient the dignity of making these decisions for her or himself.

We can eliminate unemployment compensation. This also is a categorical program, paying benefits only to those who qualify by having been in the work force for a required period of time. To the extent the unemployed have a GAI benefit available to them, the need for unemployment compensation is mitigated.[3] The cost of this program is borne currently by consumers. Since employers pay a tax, this tax is added to the cost of goods. The elimination of this tax will mitigate the impact of the value added tax (VAT) which I propose to help fund the GAI.

All housing subsidies will also be eliminated. It's time we stop acting through government to decide where and how people live. With a GAI, everyone will have an opportunity to purchase his or her own housing. A market will be created for relatively inexpensive housing, and private industry will compete to provide the most attractive facilities at the lowest price. Since recipients will be free to move about the country, they will be able to select from a wide range of geographical and housing conditions. The tenement-style housing, with its accompanying deterioration in living conditions, generally favored in government programs will blessedly become a remnant of the past.[4]

Farm price supports will go. The original intent of these programs was to enhance the income of small farmers. The bulk of the benefits no longer serve this purpose. Small farmers, like everyone else, will receive the GAI. This will enhance the ability of families to survive on small farms, but it won't guarantee it. We cannot continue to specifically support a particular way of life for just certain of our citizens.

The welfare aspect of the Social Security program (OASDI) can also be axed. This aspect of OASDI is an enigma. In a program designed to be insurance, we include an income redistribution feature. With a GAI, the need for this aspect will be eliminated. Benefits can be computed as a straight percentage of income. I am not advocating the complete elimination of Social Security at this time, but it would certainly be reasonable to phase it out. With the GAI, people would have a basic level of protection against the poverty of old age; if they wish to supplement it they could do so through a private program. Social Security is socialism—it is a government-run insurance program. There have been many good reasons for this deviation from our basic opposition to socialism in the past. With the GAI these reasons become less compelling.

While I'm on the subject of socialism, I'll mention our system of public education. I am not among those who feel this system is a failure. Those who do, however, might regard the GAI as an opportunity to step up the campaign for a change to privately run educational facilities. We must recognize one of the primary reasons for publicly run education is the inability of many people to afford education. With a GAI, this reason would lose some of its lustre. The purported benefits of competition and the profit motive could be returned to the sphere of education.[5]

No Work Requirements

This proposal is the antithesis of the currently popular workfare programs and proposals. I have dealt with those proposals elsewhere in this book. They all involve tremendous levels of government bureaucracy in adminstration, and impose significantly on the freedom of the individual. The GAI retains an incentive factor for those who wish to improve their income level, but incorporates no penalties for not working. If the jobs are there, wages will adjust to encourage people to fill those jobs. If they are not there, we adequately provide for those who are unable or unwilling to work.

The Grant Is Paid in Frequent Increments

At a minimum, the grant should be paid monthly, just as Social Security is now. A number of people have expressed concern to me about the possibility of the grant being spent early in the month and the recipient having nothing for the balance of the period. This problem could be ameliorated, but never completely eliminated, by more frequent payments. With the increasing availability of electronic funds transfers, weekly payments should become quite feasible. While the same problem exists, albeit to a lesser degree, it should be quite modest.

The Grant Is Not Adjusted by Family Status

It is essential that the program not impose family-status decisions on people. There should be neither a marriage penalty nor a divorce penalty. Because the grant is available to everyone, we have certainly eliminated the present folly of divorce-inducement built into our welfare system. In addition, by not adjusting the grant as a function of family status, we will neither encourage nor discourage marriage. There will be an incentive for people to obtain communal living arrangements, but that will be more a function of the cost of alternative accommodations than of the grant provisions.

Level Throughout the Country

Since the cost of living is higher in some parts of the country, there is a natural temptation to suggest that the benefit level should be made higher there also. This we should not do. The grant system should not create an inducement to move. Rather, by keeping the grant levels equal, we allow the economic conditions to create the incentive to move. Recipients will have an incentive to move to those parts of the country where the cost of living is lower; they will also have the economic wherewithal to do so. Once this migration begins, the increase in demand in the lower-cost areas will drive up costs. At the same time, the reduction in demand in the higher-cost areas will induce a lowering of prices. As a result, cost differences will be reduced. Ultimately, the most desirable places to live will become relatively more expensive. Those living in warm climes will trade some ability to obtain material goods for the nonmarket goods—sunshine, for example.

We should also take note of the impact of this migration on the value of labor. As the supply of labor increases in a particular area, the wage rates will decline. This compounds the point made previously—not only will those in the sunny climes have higher costs of living, they will also have lower incomes.

I recognize these factors are already at work in our economy, but the advent of the GAI will significantly increase the rate at which this occurs. Currently, most people are reluctant to move without a sizable nest egg and/or the promise of a job in the new area. With the security of a GAI, an unprecented amount of migration will take place.

On a National Level

Usually my motto when regarding governmental activities is "the closer to the people, the better." The closer the governing body is to the people being governed, the greater the degree of perceived, and in some cases actual, control we have over our own lives. Nonetheless, the GAI must be an exception. It can never be instituted on a state-by-state basis. The provisions must be consistent nationwide. Without this those states with benefits, or with more generous benefits, would subject themselves to massive interstate migration. No state would dare pass such a law without significant limitations on the right to move to that state, and such limitations are unacceptable.

THE NEGOTIABLE ELEMENTS

Invariably a proposal such as this meets opposition from some who are philosophically in favor of it. That is because one or more specific elements are not to their liking. The most likely source of such opposition will be the amount of the grant.

The Grant Amount

I suggest $6,000 a year for an adult and $2,000 for a child. You say too much? I agree. You say too little? I agree. At this level the total amount received by a family of four would be $16,000. That seems to me fairly high. On the other hand, an individual will find it hard to live on $6,000 a year in many of our big cities. The point is there is *no right amount*. We will need to arrive at a figure by consensus.

The Relation to Family Size and Composition

A significant dilemma is the issue of grant size and number of children. There are many who believe the present welfare system provides an economic incentive for women to have additional children. I agree that there is unfortunately a strong inducement to have the first child. However, the economic benefit of additional children is more than outweighed by the cost of raising those children. Nonetheless, there may be many who do not correctly make this calculation. We do not want to create a system which rewards this miscalculation. From an ecological standpoint, we should argue for a stronger economic *dis*incentive. On the other hand, we must consider the child as well as the parent. To penalize the parent is to penalize the child also.

We also want to minimize the extent to which persons with small families are asked to subsidize those with large families. One alternative which may provide a compromise solution is to make payments directly to families for only two children. If there are any additional children, the additional benefits are paid into a trust fund which will be available to the children upon reaching age eighteen. This trust fund would be split among all the children in the family, just as the GAI would presumably be spent equally for all the children while they are living with the family.

Method of Considering the Value of Assets

Although this is primarily an income-based program, it is probably necessary to account for differentials in assets. Even a substantial redistribution of income will leave untouched the primary source of inequality in this country—wealth.[6] Consider two persons with zero or very little income. If one of them owns her or his own home and has no mortgage, that person is certainly in a better economic position than the one who does not. Not only is her or his wealth greater, but that individual's need for income is less since the person does not have to pay rent.[7] Even those whose assets provide no "use value" (such as stocks and bonds) are in a better financial position because of the security those investments provide.[8]   This difference should be reflected in the level of GAI to which one is entitled.[9]

Amount of the Grant Varies with the State of the Economy and the Population

I don't have a fixed view of how large the grant should be. I tend to believe, however, that the amount should fluctuate with the state of the economy. A basis for the grant is the notion of sharing in the wealth of the country. As such, the amount shared should change as the economy changes. However, it must also be a function of the population of the country.[10]   The measure to be used should be the gross national product or some other macro-economic figure per capita.

The mechanism for making this change can be quite simple. Once the amount of the initial grant is established, subsequent years' grants can be determined by a ratio of per capita gross national product in the two years.

There are, however, cogent arguments against making this adjustment. A macro-economic argument is that we would be reducing benefits during periods of depression, when what the economy probably needs is an influx of spendable money rather than a reduction. In addition, it has been pointed out to me that such a reduction would impose a "double whammy" on the poorer citizens. Since they are the ones who would most likely lose their jobs during a depression, and they are also the ones who will depend most heavily on the GAI, it is argued that we should not reduce their benefits at this time.

THE MECHANICS OF THE PLAN

Who Is "Everybody"?

I noted one of the nonnegotiable elements of the plan should be universal eligibility. Well, there are limits. I envision coverage for all citizens of the United States. At this point, some necessary selfishness must operate. Although we presently provide some welfare benefits to noncitizens, I would not include them under this plan. I do not consider them to be any less worthy human beings, and I do not feel there is any justice in excluding them from the plan. However, I recognize the limitations on our wealth. The United States is a wealthy country, but it is not presently capable of supporting the entire world.

It will become increasingly difficult to control the physical movement of people who want to come to this country. It will be much easier to control the access to the wealth.

Population control is of increasing concern. To the extent the people of the United States recognize the exigency of this, but those in other countries do not, our efforts could be overwhelmed if immigration, legal and illegal, is not curtailed. Just as the GAI must not create an incentive for an increased birth rate, neither must it be an incentive for increased immigration.[11] Perhaps by the twenty-second century the idea can be expanded to a worldwide community. It makes sense to do so eventually. But not now.

How Is the Payment of the Grant Triggered?

Everyone will have the option of filing a declaration of estimated income. If that declaration shows, for example, an expectation of zero income, checks will begin arriving as soon as the form is processed.[12]

The estimate must include a declaration of the individual's wealth. This includes the equity in a home, stocks and bonds, cash, automobiles, home furnishings, boats, and all other items of value. The burden of filing this information will be eased in two ways. First, persons who are quite certain their income (including imputed income from their assets) will make them ineligible for the GAI do not need to provide this information.[13] Second, people can choose to use a "standard" asset assumption. This amount will be set quite high; those who claim fewer assets will of course be subject to verification.

Those economic strategists among you are probably already thinking "Why wouldn't everyone deliberately underestimate his or her expected income in order to receive the grant?" I'm ahead of you on that one. Just as we now have penalties for those self-employed persons who understate their income and thus reduce their quarterly tax payments, so will there be penalties for underestimating income for purposes of GAI calculations. That penalty can be the same as is now imposed on underwithholding. Unfortunately, this penalty must also apply to those who inadvertently understate income; however, this is unavoidable since we cannot determine which instances are inadvertent.

Payments to Prisoners and Other Wards of the State

I noted earlier in this chapter that even prisoners would be eligible for this grant. This is in keeping with the goal of eliminating the notion of deserving and undeserving people. However, there is no reason the counties, states, or federal government cannot charge the prisoner for at least a part of the cost of incarceration. Since the cost of providing the "service" is surely considerably greater than the GAI level, the entire grant must be turned over to the relevant government agency.[14] The care of mental patients who are in state institutions could also be partially funded with this benefit.

This same procedure can be followed in those instances where a child is a ward of the state. The author Charles Murray has suggested we need a major increase in the use of orphanages in this country.[15] He based this assertion on the extent to which many of our young people (particularly young men) are not being adequately socialized in this country (generally because they are being raised without a father figure).[16] Were his suggestion to be adopted, the GAI to which the child is entitled could be used to help defray the costs of providing the care.

THE COST

I recently had the pleasure of discussing my proposal with some family members who have been slow to recognize its merits. The conversation, typical of so many I've had on the subject, went something like this:

"But who's going to pay for it?"
"You and I."
"How much will it cost?"
"$1 trillion."
"No way!"
"How about $0?"
"That's much better."

Perhaps, reader, you're wondering how I could provide such different estimates. Well, as the old saying goes, it depends on how you look at it. First, the $1 trillion figure. Assume we provide a GAI of $6,000 per adult and $2,000 per child. Multiplying these numbers by the total number of people in the country yields a figure of right around $1 trillion.[17]

On the other hand, it is easy to defend the position that the program costs nothing. For every dollar paid in in taxes, $1 is paid out to someone in benefits.[18] Thus the program costs "us" virtually nothing if by "us" we mean all of us. For those who consider "us" to be those who will be paying in more than they will be getting back, the following figures will be more relevant.

FUNDING THE PROGRAM

There are two elements to my proposed funding method—a 35 percent flat income tax, with a value-added tax (VAT) to supplement if necessary.

HYPOTHETICAL DEMONSTRATIONS

In October 1999, Gaby Ann Irisimo is in her last semester of college. Although her economics degree is from a prestigious university, she has thus far been unable to obtain suitable employment. She has therefore decided to spend a year doing volunteer work. Calling up Form 1997G on her personal computer, she inserts a $0 in the "Anticipated Income for 2000" box,[19] and dispatches the form via the information highway to the Internal Revenue and Income Service (IRIS).[20]

Upon receipt of Ms. Irisimo's form, the IRIS computer calculates the amount of benefit to which she is entitled. With a $0 anticipated income, the calculation is extremely simple. The GAI level for 2000 had already been computed on October 1, 1999, to be $7,235.[21] Since Gaby has no accumulated assets there is no imputed income to be considered. Therefore, she will receive a weekly funds transfer into her checking account of approximately $139.

As long as she has no additional income during the year, the GAI will continue to flow to her account. At the end of the year, she will file her Form 1040EZ, showing the GAI as her only income. Since everyone has a tax exemption to the extent of her GAI, she will incur no income taxes. If at some point during the year she obtains employment, or for some other reason has a significant increase in income, it will be in her best interests to file a revised 1997G form—otherwise she may incur a penalty for having accepted the GAI while in receipt of too much income.

Also in October 1999, I decide to retire from my teaching job to write another book describing how well the GAI has been working and suggesting some changes. I indicate on my Form 1997G an anticipation of zero earned income for the year 2000. However, since I have some savings, I will have some unearned income. Most of the assets are in my retirement account. Prior to the introduction of the GAI, income in this account had accumulated tax free.[22] Now, however, even if all earnings are just added to the value of my savings, I must report them as income. With a retirement account of $600,000, I anticipate additional accumulation of $48,000.[23] In addition, I must report an attributed income of $3,500 for the $50,000 equity in my home, $1,400 for the $20,000 equity in my automobiles, and $2,100 for my other $30,000 of assets.[24] Thus I have a total attributed income of $56,000. Since the tax on this income (at 35 percent) of $19,600 exceeds the GAI level of $14,470 for a couple, I will not be sent a GAI check. At the end of the year, when I figure my final taxes, I will owe 35 percent on the $48,000 or $16,800 less the GAI of $14,470, or $2,330.[25]

PHASING IN

It should be administratively relatively easy to phase this plan in while phasing out our other welfare programs. The GAI could be introduced incrementally, starting for example with $1,500 per adult and $500 per child. This amount would then be deducted from any other public assistance or Social Security benefits to which the person was entitled.

Notes

1. Charles Murray, *Losing Ground.*

2. Where the other Murray and I disagree is on what should be done after it is eliminated. He would have those in poverty rely on private aid and place the children in orphanages. I argue for the guaranteed adequate income.

3. If the GAI benefit is less than what employers wish to provide as unemployment benefits they could supplement it. This supplementation would be through a private program, however.

4. Unless it turns out that it provides the best quality housing for the money, in which case recipients will choose to live there. This is a major difference.

5. I say "purported" benefits because I am not convinced competiton can work in the area of education. As in the case of health care, the consumer is not in a very good position to select the best quality service at the lowest price. Unless the consumer can do so, the major source of regulation of the market is lost. Nonetheless, in both cases I am open to the possibility a mechanism can be developed for aiding consumers in this decision.

6. According to Lester Thurow, "Why Are We so Reluctant to Redistribute Wealth?," *New York Times*, printed in *Des Moines Register*, April 18, 1976, pp. B1-2, "Most of those we normally think of as rich are rich in wealth rather than income." He notes that redistribution of wealth could be accomplished by higher inheritance taxes, higher taxes on capital gains, or perhaps a wealth tax such as that used in Sweden. I recognize the merits of his argument, but am not proposing an overall tax on wealth. In my plan, wealth is only considered to the extent it affects eligibility for the GAI payment.

7. Granted, they have utilities, insurance, and taxes, but this is generally less costly than rent.

8. Of course, to the extent these investments are generating an income, that income will be included in the GAI calculation. On the other hand, some investments do not produce current income, but do increase in value (non-dividend-paying stocks or idle land, for example).

9. Unlike our present welfare system which denies eligibility to those with assets above a certain level, wealth causes no loss of eligibility for GAI.

10. Conceivably, the use of the per capita figure could have an impact on population growth. Might individuals change their procreation decisions knowing an additional child will reduce the overall level of the grant?

Admittedly, the actual impact of one additional child will be infinitesimally small. Nonetheless, there might be a psychological impact. It almost surely will have some impact on immigration policy making. The recent arguments about whether immigration has a postive or negative effect on per capita gross national product will take on even greater importance.

11. There is disagreement about the extent to which our present welfare system contributes to immigration. Charles Wheeler of the National Immigration Law Center, in testimony before Congress, said: "There is no evidence that access to federal programs acts as a magnet to foreigners." However, Donald Huddle, economics professor at Rice University, estimated that state, county, and local governments spent $42.5 billion on immigrants who have settled here since 1970. *Des Moines Register*, December 20, 1993, p.1.

12. Again, because of the availability of electronic filing and funds transfer, the delay could be only days.

13. For example, with a GAI of $6,000 and a flat tax of 35 percent, an individual earning in excess of $17,142 would not be eligible for a GAI payment. If the imputed income from assets is 7 percent, an individual with no income would be entitled to a transfer unless the assets exceeded about $245,000 (7 percent of $245,000 is $17,150).

14. Alternatively, it may be desirable to allow the prisoner to retain some portion of the grant to build a nest egg to provide some security for transition back into society.

15. *20/20*, ABC television show aired April 15, 1994.

16. Not as in socialism, but as in the orientation to the norms of society.

17. Give or take $100 billion or so. If you're looking for a more precise number, how about $978,282,000,000? I calculated this number using the population distribution provided in the U.S. Bureau of the Census, Current Population Reports, Series P60-184, *Money Income of Households, Families and Persons in the United States: 1992* (Washington, D.C.: U.S. Government Printing Office, 1993), Tables 6 and 18. This report uses figures from the 1990 census. I will be basing most of my subsequent calculations on this number because the available family income data is for that same period. For comparison, however, I have also calculated the cost using 1992 population figures. This number is $1,237,421,000,000. Population figures are from U.S. Bureau of the Census, *Statistical Abstracts of the United States: 1993*, 113th ed. (Washington, D.C.: U.S. Government Printing Office, 1993). More details are shown in Chapter 9.

18. True, there will be some cost of administering the plan. However, as I have argued elsewhere in the book, this cost will be inconsequential because of electronic funds transfers and the use of the already existent IRS mechanism.

19. At this point in her life she has not accumulated any assets which would provide her with imputed income.

20. Naturally, some have criticized the name change as "too flowery."

21. Since its inception in 1997 at $6,000, the GAI amount had been increased each year as the gross national product per capita increased.

22. This was a reasonable provision at a time when it was necessary to encourage citizens to save for retirement. After passage of the GAI, this is no longer necessary since a base income is guaranteed to everyone. It is also not desirable since the primary benefit of this tax provision, like so many, had flowed to higher-income citizens.

23. Assuming I earn 8 percent on my account.

24. At the attributed income rate of 7 percent.

25. An alternative would be to consider the attributed earnings even above the GAI level, continuing to impose a tax on them.

9

Cost and Funding Calculations

I'm not an economist. Are you relieved or disappointed? I hope you're pleased, because it means you're not likely to be overwhelmed with the jargon and mathematics favored by economists. On the other hand, it means the calculations I present in this chapter will lack some of the sophistication which could be introduced by one more conversant with econometrics.

My goal is to provide some numbers in a manner which can be understood by the vast majority of my readers. I want you to be able to recognize the assumptions I have made and decide for yourself whether you agree or disagree with them. I want you to be able to understand the sources of my statistics and perhaps look them up for yourself. You could even check my calculations if you are somewhat handy with computer spreadsheet technology. In short, I intend that you, the reader, follow my reasoning and come up with your own numbers if you desire.

This is important because of the frequency with which we encounter conflicting statistics. So often it becomes a case of "Who ya gonna believe?" In this chapter I make an effort to avoid presenting any number without clearly stating the underlying assumptions. If you disagree with the number, it should be because you disagree with the assumptions. That's OK. The important thing is that we understand and agree on the basis for our different conclusions. Let's have a go at it.

THE TOTAL POTENTIAL OUTLAY

As I noted briefly in the preceding chapter, my proposed GAI plan (with a guarantee of $6,000 per adult and $2,000 per child) would make U.S. citizens eligible for around $1 trillion in transfer payments. The actual figures I calculated ranged from $978 billion (using 1990 family income data) to $1,237 billion (using 1992 population data). Of course, as I also noted previously, this really isn't a cost, since the payments will be going to all members of society.

There are two factors which will reduce the impact of the figure. The first is a revised tax structure, and the second is the elimination of other public assistance programs.

The Revised Tax Structure

Naturally, it would be neither reasonable nor possible to transfer this much money out of government without some offsetting income. I propose two sources of additional income: a revised income tax structure and the possible introduction of a value-added tax (VAT).

The Flat Income Tax

The GAI provides an excellent opportunity to revise our exceedingly complex personal income tax structure. I attribute the complexity in our current system primarily to three factors: (1) attempts to mitigate the burden on low-income earners (e.g., with the earned-income tax credit); (2) attempts to mitigate the burden on high-income earners (e.g., with the deduction for home mortgage interest[1]); and (3) a desire to tax high-income earners at a higher rate (thus the progressive rates).

It is important to note that the availability of itemized deductions mitigates to a great extent the effect of the progressive taxes. These deductions inure primarily to the benefit of higher-income earners. Currently, mortgage interest is a major contributor. Higher-income taxpayers can afford larger homes and thus they incur greater interest costs and are entitled to greater deductions. They also benefit more from the deductibity of contributions, since they can afford to give more. Finally, there are millions of taxpayers who, like myself, are able to take advantage of business or professional deductions. Travel, meals, and even recreation can be deducted from business income when a business purpose can be shown.[2] The fact that there is also considerable pleasure derived from the activity does not affect the deduction. The problem is that these deductions are disproportionately available to higher-income earners.

The GAI will provide an income boost which will primarily be of benefit to low-income earners. Therefore, the need to assist them and place a higher burden on high-income earners through the tax structure will be reduced. It will enable us to introduce a very simple income tax system—a flat tax (i.e., the same rate for all) with no deductions. I will be using a 35 percent tax rate in my calculations. This is less than the highest rate currently applied to the highest incomes, but it will generate more revenue because it applies to all income. For comparison, Table 9.1 provides the 1993 tax rates for a single individual.[3]

Table 9.1

1993 Income Tax Rates

TAXABLE INCOME	RATE
$0 - $22,100	.15
$22,101 - $53,500	.28
$53,501 - $115,000	.31
$115,001 - $250,000	.36
$250,001 - OVER	.396

For a sample of the effect of these tax rates, Table 9.2 shows a calculation of the taxes to be paid by a single individual earning $52,500 and a married couple (with two children) earning $22,500,[4] assuming the use of the standard deduction.

Table 9.2

Effect of 1993 Tax Structure on Two Sample Taxpayers

	Married Couple With Two Children	Single Person
Gross income	$22,500	$52,500
Standard deduction	$6,200	$3,700
Exemption	$9,400	$2,350
Taxable income	$6,900	$46,450
Earned-income tax credit	$73	$0
(Tax)	($962)	($10,133)
Net income	$21,538	$42,367
Average tax (or equivalent flat tax)	4.3%	19.3%

Note: Many persons in the higher income tax brackets have higher than the standard deduction. If we assume a deduction of $7,400 (twice the standard deduction) for the single individual, the tax becomes $9,097, equivalent to a flat tax of 17.3 percent. Aggregate calculations later in the chapter will incorporate the higher deductions.

The higher-income single person (assuming the use of the standard deduction) is currently paying income taxes equivalent to a 19.3 percent flat tax, whereas the lower-income family has an equivalent flat (or average) tax of 4.3 percent. In Table 9.3, I show the flat tax equivalents for various income levels and family status. Calculations are shown using

Table 9.3

Flat Tax Equivalent of Current Income Taxes (Selected Family Situations)

Income Range Midpoints	Married- No children (%)	Married- Two or More Children* (%)	Head of Household- No Children (%)	Head of Household- Two or More Children* (%)	Non-Family Household (Single) (%)
Assuming Standard Deductions					
$2,500	0.00	-18.68	0.00	-19.68	0.00
$7,500	0.00	-18.56	0.00	-19.56	2.90
$12,500	1.92	-11.13	5.64	-11.73	7.74
$17,500	5.66	-0.53	8.31	-2.12	9.81
$22,500	7.73	5.86	9.80	4.78	10.97
$27,500	9.05	7.77	10.75	6.90	11.70
$32,500	9.97	8.88	11.40	8.15	13.95
$37,500	10.64	9.70	11.91	9.06	15.82
$42,500	11.15	10.32	13.81	9.76	17.25
$47,500	11.56	10.82	15.30	11.15	18.39
$52,500	13.05	11.80	16.51	12.75	19.30
$62,500	15.44	14.39	18.35	15.19	20.83
$72,500	17.17	16.27	19.68	16.96	22.24
$82,500	18.49	17.69	20.69	18.30	23.30
$92,500	19.51	18.80	21.75	19.39	24.13
$125,000	22.32	21.74	24.15	22.41	26.08
$175,000	25.49	25.01	27.24	25.79	28.91
$225,000	27.82	27.45	29.19	28.06	30.49
$300,000	30.34	30.03	31.40	30.47	32.39
Using a Multiple of Standard Deductions at Higher Incomes#					
$52,500	10.11	8.10	13.60	9.84	17.33
$57,500	11.33	8.70	14.86	11.42	18.26
$62,500	12.66	9.51	15.91	12.75	19.04
$67,500	13.80	10.88	16.80	13.88	19.89
$72,500	14.78	12.06	17.58	14.85	20.65
$77,500	15.63	13.09	18.25	15.70	21.32
$82,500	16.38	13.99	18.84	16.45	21.91
$87,500	17.05	14.79	19.36	17.11	22.43
$97,500	18.17	16.14	20.49	18.25	23.31
$125,000	19.24	17.50	21.45	19.70	24.08
$175,000	22.94	21.49	25.00	23.55	27.39
$225,000	25.84	24.71	27.45	26.32	29.30
$300,000	28.70	27.77	29.96	29.03	31.42

* Assuming three children.
# Double the standard deduction from $50,000 to $100,000 and triple the standard deduction above $100,000.

the standard deduction; and using the standard deduction up to $50,000, twice the standard from $50,000 to $100,000 and three times the standard for incomes of $100,000 and above.

One can observe the significant range of present tax rates, from a negative 19.7 percent for very low income earners who are able to take advantage of the earned income tax credit to a high of 32.4 percent for single persons earning $300,000 and taking only the standard deduction.[5] In all cases, then, the 35 percent flat tax will be higher than the average tax presently being paid. However, with the addition of the GAI, many people will have an effective tax lower than their current tax.

PROJECTED IMPACT OF THE NEW SYSTEM

I expect there are two questions on the minds of readers at this point: "How will it affect me?"and "What will be the total impact on government revenues?"

Impact on Individuals and Families

The individual effect depends upon one's income and family status. I present this information in two parts. First, an indication of the net income or outgo under the GAI/flat tax system. Second, a comparison of this result with the tax payable under the present tax structure.

Results Under the GAI/Flat Tax Structure

Table 9.4 presents the results under the proposed GAI/flat tax system for our two demonstration taxpayers, using wealth data shown in Table 9.5. This calculation includes an accounting for my proposal to offset the GAI by a tax on imputed income from assets. In the operation of the plan, this tax will be based on the actual assets owned by the taxpayer. For this example, I assumed the family had net assets totaling $20,000 and I imputed income from that at 7 percent[6] This $1,400 in imputed income was taxed at the 35 percent rate, yielding the $490 shown in the table. Since the taxes for the single person were already greater than the GAI benefit, the tax on imputed income was not charged.[7]

In Table 9.6 I provide a summary of the net transfers under the proposed program (by income level and filing status). To help in the interpretation of this table, I'll first point to what some may regard as the most alarming result. A married couple with two or more children and earning $42,500 will receive a net payment after taxes.[8] In other words, the positive effects of the GAI are greater than the tax due.

This observation requires some comment. One of the differences between my GAI proposal and those which preceded it is my use of a

Table 9.4

Effects of GAI and Flat Tax on Two Sample Taxpayers

	Married Couple With Two Children	Single Person
Gross income	$22,500	$52,500
Flat tax at 35	$7,875	$18,375
GAI	$16,000	$6,000
Net GAI (or tax)	$8,125	($12,375)
Tax on imputed asset income*	$490	$0
Net income transfer (or tax)	$7635	($12,375)
Net income	$30,135	$40,125
Effective average tax	-33.9%	23.6%

* This number is based on assets of $20,000 at an income level of $22,500. That number was derived from the figures shown in Table 9.5.

Table 9.5

Median and Mean Net Worth by Household Income Quintile

Income Quintiles	Mean	Median
Lowest quintile	$35,420	$5,224
Second quintile	$62,280	$19,191
Third quintile	$80,419	$28,859
Fourth quintile	$104,416	$49,204
Highest quintile	$228,398	$123,166

Source: T.J. Eller, *Household Wealth and Asset Ownership: 1991*, U.S. Bureau of the Census, Current Population Reports, P70-34 (Washington, D.C.: U.S. Government Printing Office, 1994), medians from Table 1, p. 2; means from Table 5, p. 8.

single tax rate to apply to all income earners—those receiving the guaranteed income and those not. As a result, I incorporate a much lower tax rate on incomes earned by GAI recipients than do the other plans. The figure we are discussing is the primary negative result of this decision. Families earning ''middle-class''incomes will effectively pay no income tax under this proposal. The authors of other plans have either not been personally willing to accept this outcome or have been influenced by the potential political opposition. How can I come to such a contrary conclusion? There are three reasons. First, the simplicity and fairness of the plan are sufficiently compelling as to overwhelm this consequence. Second, I continue my tax rate at all income levels, thus recovering some of the income lost at lower levels. Third, I propose elimination of all our other welfare programs. And fourth, I propose to make up any lost revenue with the introduction of the value-added tax

(VAT). This tax has much to recommend it. Its primary drawback is its regressive nature. As a tax on consumption, it tends to fall relatively most heavily on lower-income taxpayers.

Table 9.6

Net Transfers Under the Proposed GAI/Flat Tax Structure

	Household Composition[#]				
Midpoint of Income Range+	Married Couple-No Dependent Children	Married Couple- Two or More Children	Head of Household- No children[@]	Head of Household- Two or More Children[*]	Non-family Household (Single)
$2,500	$11,125	$15,125	$5,125	$9,125	$5,125
$7,500	$9,253	$13,253	$3,253	$7,253	$3,253
$12,500	$7,380	$11,380	$1,380	$5,380	$1,380
$17,500	$5,508	$9,508	($125)	$3,508	($125)
$22,500	$3,635	$7,635	($1,875)	$1,635	($1,875)
$27,500	$1,763	$5,763	($3,625)	$0	($3,625)
$32,500	$0	$3,890	($5,375)	($1,375)	($5,375)
$37,500	($1,125)	$2,018	($7,125)	($3,125)	($7,125)
$42,500	($2,875)	$145	($8,875)	($4,875)	($8,875)
$47,500	($4,625)	($625)	($10,625)	($6,625)	($10,625)
$52,500	($6,375)	($2,375)	($12,375)	($8,375)	($12,375)
$57,500	($8,125)	($4,125)	($14,125)	($10,125)	($14,125)
$62,500	($9,875)	($5,875)	($15,875)	($11,875)	($15,875)
$67,500	($11,625)	($7,625)	($17,625)	($13,625)	($17,625)
$72,500	($13,375)	($9,375)	($19,375)	($15,375)	($19,375)
$77,500	($15,125)	($11,125)	($21,125)	($17,125)	($21,125)
$82,500	($16,875)	($12,875)	($22,875)	($18,875)	($22,875)
$87,500	($18,625)	($14,625)	($24,625)	($20,625)	($24,625)
$92,500	($20,375)	($16,375)	($26,375)	($22,375)	($26,375)
$97,500	($22,125)	($18,125)	($28,125)	($24,125)	($28,125)
$125,000	($31,750)	($27,750)	($37,750)	($33,750)	($37,750)
$175,000	($49,250)	($45,250)	($55,250)	($51,250)	($55,250)
$225,000	($66,750)	($62,750)	($72,750)	($68,750)	($72,750)
$300,000	($93,000)	($89,000)	($99,000)	($95,000)	($99,000)

[#] These categories are those used in the income distribution data which will be subsequently used in the calculation of aggregate costs.

[+] I arbritrarily chose the final value of $300,000 for the midpoint of the category $250,000 and above.

[@] This category receives the same benefit as does the single category; they are shown separately because they are treated differently under the *present* tax structure.

Note: Calculations include a tax for imputed income from assets, but only on those persons receiving a net GAI benefit.

However, were a VAT adopted at the same time as the GAI, the two would tend to offset each other. The net effect would be a reduced reliance on the personal income tax structure as a source of revenue and the fiscal ability to adopt a GAI plan. At a later point, I indicate the potential aggregate revenue effects of this proposal. It is my intention that this plan be introduced on a revenue-neutral basis—that is, that it not contribute to an increase in the national debt.

Now, back to the observations on the table. For a single person the tax payable exceeds the GAI at incomes above $17,500. Each reader can find her or himself on the table and see how it affects her or him. For myself and my wife, with no dependent children and annual earnings in the vicinity of $92,500, our net tax liability would be $20,375.

Effective Tax Rates in the Proposed Plan

Although the GAI proposal ostensibly carries with it a 35 percent tax on income, the *effective* tax will be lower than that because of the cash benefit from the Guaranteed Adequate Income. How much lower depends upon one's income and family status. Table 9.7 provides the effective tax rates. The numbers in this table are simply the dollar values from Table 9.6 divided by the relevant income. With the addition of the GAI, no one pays a full 35 percent. At the highest incomes used in the calculations, the effective rate is about 33 percent.[9] At the lowest income levels, the effective tax rate is a very high negative number. Readers should bear in mind that many of those in these categories are now receiving welfare benefits and so also have effectively a very high negative tax rate.[10] A comparison of the new effective rates with the old rates is shown in Table 9.8. As expected, those in the low income brackets will experience lower rates, some substantially lower. However, the higher effective rates in the higher brackets are not substantially greater.[11]

The impact of this difference as measured in dollars is shown in Table 9.9. What is Table 9.9 telling us? Again referring to our family of four earning $42,500, we find that under the proposed system they are $3,828 better off than under the current system. Families of four in general will be better off under the proposed system at incomes up to $67,500. For the single person (whether a head of household with no children or in a nonfamily household) the new system is worse at incomes above $27,500. Two person households in the same income bracket as I and my wife, given the assumed level of deductions, will be $4,410 *worse* off under the proposed system.[12] Most readers should be able to place themselves on this table and thus determine the impact of the changes on their own situation. I hope, however, that this will not be the primary factor in determining whether one favors or opposes the plan.

Table 9.7

Effective Tax Rates Under the Proposed GAI/Flat Tax Structure

Midpoint of Income Range	Household Composition				
	Married Couple-No Dependent Children (%)	Married Couple-Two or More Children (%)	Head of Household-No children (%)	Head of Household-Two or More Children (%)	Non-family Household (Single) (%)
$2,500	-445.00	-605.00	-205.00	-365.00	-205.00
$7,500	-123.37	-176.71	-43.37	-96.71	-43.37
$12,500	-59.04	-91.04	-11.04	-43.04	-11.04
$17,500	-31.47	-54.33	0.71	-20.05	0.71
$22,500	-16.16	-33.93	8.33	-7.27	8.33
$27,500	-6.41	-20.96	13.18	0.00	13.18
$32,500	0.00	-11.97	16.54	4.23	16.54
$37,500	3.00	-5.38	19.00	8.33	19.00
$42,500	6.76	-0.34	20.88	11.47	20.88
$52,500	12.14	4.52	23.57	15.95	23.57
$62,500	15.80	9.40	25.40	19.00	25.40
$72,500	18.45	12.93	26.72	21.21	26.72
$82,500	20.45	15.61	27.73	22.88	27.73
$92,500	22.03	17.70	28.51	24.19	28.51
$125,000	25.40	22.20	30.20	27.00	30.20
$175,000	28.14	25.86	31.57	29.29	31.57
$225,000	29.67	27.89	32.33	30.56	32.33
$300,000	31.00	29.67	33.00	31.67	33.00

Notes are the same as those in Table 9.6.

The consequences appear to peak in the vicinity of incomes of $175,000. The values get smaller at higher incomes because of the 1993 maximum tax rate of .396. I have chosen to retain the single rate even at these higher incomes, partly for simplicity, partly to help avert cries for special tax breaks, and partly for equity.[13]

The fact that those with very high incomes are actually better off under my system is not inconsistent with the intent of the Guaranteed Adequate Income. It is in no way designed to penalize those with high incomes, nor is it designed to make the incomes of all persons equal. Rather it focuses on the goal of insuring that the lowest incomes are not too low. Although I recognize that very high income persons could afford to pay more taxes without reducing substantially the quality of their lives, I don't feel it is necessary for them to do so in order to make this program work.

Table 9.8

New Effective Tax Rates Minus Old Rates

Midpoint of Income Range	Household Composition				
	Married Couple-No Dependent Children (%)	Married Couple-Two or More Children (%)	Head of Household-No children (%)	Head of Household-Two or More Children (%)	Non-family Household (Single) (%)
$2,500	-445.00	-585.32	-205.00	-345.32	-205.00
$7,500	-123.37	-157.15	-43.37	-77.15	-46.27
$12,500	-60.96	-79.31	-16.68	-31.31	-18.78
$17,500	-37.13	-49.94	-7.60	-17.92	-9.10
$22,500	-23.89	-36.64	-1.47	-12.04	-2.63
$27,500	-15.47	-26.17	2.44	-6.90	1.48
$32,500	-9.97	-18.68	5.14	-3.92	2.59
$37,500	-7.64	-13.20	7.09	-0.73	3.18
$42,500	-4.39	-9.01	7.08	1.71	3.63
$47,500	-1.82	-8.02	7.07	2.80	3.98
$52,500	-0.91	-5.35	7.06	3.20	4.27
$57,500	-0.22	-3.74	7.06	3.53	4.51
$62,500	0.36	-2.88	7.05	3.81	4.57
$67,500	0.85	-2.15	7.05	4.05	4.52
$72,500	1.27	-1.52	7.04	4.25	4.49
$77,500	1.64	-0.97	7.04	4.43	4.46
$82,500	1.97	-0.49	7.04	4.58	4.43
$87,500	2.26	-0.06	6.92	4.72	4.40
$92,500	2.51	0.32	6.77	4.80	4.38
$97,500	2.74	0.66	6.62	4.76	4.36
$125,000	3.08	1.63	6.05	4.59	4.12
$175,000	2.65	1.82	4.33	3.49	2.66
$225,000	1.84	1.19	3.14	2.49	1.85
$300,000	0.66	0.26	1.60	1.20	0.61

Notes are the same as those in Table 9.6.

Aggregate Impact

In this section, I present figures showing the overall impact of the new plan on federal personal income tax revenues, and compare this with personal income tax revenues under the present system. I then provide figures on the savings to be realized through the elimination of present welfare programs.

Readers should note that I am not considering in these calculations the potential effects of the GAI and the flat tax on the economy. Whether the change in work incentives will have a deleterious effect on the economy

Table 9.9

**Comparison of Net Income Under Present Tax Structure
with Net Income Under GAI/Flat Tax System**

Midpoint of Income Range	Household Composition				
	Married Couple-No Dependent Children	Married Couple-Two or More Children*	Head of Household-No children	Head of Household-Two or More Children*	Non-family Household (Single)
$2,500	$11,125	$14,633	$5,125	$8,633	$5,125
$7,500	$9,253	$11,786	$3,253	$5,786	$3,470
$12,500	$7,620	$9,914	$2,085	$3,914	$2,348
$17,500	$6,498	$8,739	$1,330	$3,136	$1,593
$22,500	$5,375	$8,245	$330	$2,710	$593
$27,500	$4,253	$7,195	($670)	$1,898	($408)
$32,500	$3,240	$6,073	($1,670)	$1,273	($842)
$37,500	$2,865	$4,950	($2,657)	$273	($1,192)
$42,500	$1,865	$3,828	($3,007)	($728)	($1,542)
$47,500	$865	$3,808	($3,357)	($1,331)	($1,892)
$52,500	($1,065)	$1,878	($5,233)	($3,207)	($3,278)
$57,500	($1,610)	$878	($5,583)	($3,557)	($3,628)
$62,500	($1,960)	$66	($5,933)	($3,907)	($3,978)
$67,500	($2,310)	($284)	($6,283)	($4,257)	($4,201)
$72,500	($2,660)	($634)	($6,633)	($4,607)	($4,401)
$77,500	($3,010)	($984)	($6,983)	($4,957)	($4,601)
$82,500	($3,360)	($1,334)	($7,333)	($5,307)	($4,801)
$87,500	($3,710)	($1,684)	($7,683)	($5,657)	($5,001)
$92,500	($4,060)	($2,034)	($7,948)	($6,007)	($5,201)
$97,500	($4,410)	($2,384)	($8,148)	($6,333)	($5,401)
$125,000	($7,694)	($5,880)	($10,937)	($9,123)	($7,648)
$175,000	($9,109)	($7,647)	($11,497)	($10,035)	($7,320)
$225,000	($8,609)	($7,147)	($10,997)	($9,535)	($6,820)
$300,000	($6,898)	($5,690)	($9,120)	($7,912)	($4,754)

*   For the purpose of calculation of present income taxes, these familes are assumed to have three children. Only two children are considered in the GAI calculation because that is the maximum for proposed benefit.
Notes: 1. Income taxes under the current system are computed using the standard deduction for incomes up to $50,000, twice the standard for incomes between $50,000 and $100,000, and three times the standard for incomes over $100,000. 2. Calculations for the proposed system include a tax for imputed income from assets, but only on those persons receiving a net GAI benefit.

is not known. Remember that my tax rate of 35 percent is considerably less than that used in the guaranteed income studies; therefore, the work effect should be less. Since my tax rate is lower than the marginal rate on very high incomes, if the theory is correct, people earning those incomes should work more. Finally, the additional transfer payments to persons with lower incomes will provide a demand-induced stimulus to the economy. Which of these effects will be greatest is open to debate.

Now to my numbers. The aggregate calculations are made using data as shown in Tables 9.10a and 9.10b.

Table 9.10a

Distribution of Incomes in the United States (Total and Married Couples)

Income Range	Total	Married Couple-No Related Children	Married Couple-One Child Under 18	Married Couple-Two or More Children
		Numbers in Thousands		
Total	96,572	27,437	9,911	15,800
Less than $5,000	4,737	405	124	206
$5,000 to $9,999	9,886	987	216	431
$10,000 to $14,999	9,195	1,864	440	756
$15,000 to $19,999	8,519	2,165	606	931
$20,000 to $24,999	7,842	2,213	571	998
$25,000 to $29,999	7,467	2,131	726	1,128
$30,000 to $34,999	6,774	2,067	708	1,199
$35,000 to $39,999	6,184	1,986	734	1,275
$40,000 to $44,999	5,367	1,720	750	1,244
$45,000 to $49,999	4,812	1,527	692	1,237
$50,000 to $54,999	4,271	1,507	630	1,083
$55,000 to $59,999	3,606	1,316	582	957
$60,000 to $64,999	3,003	1,100	544	793
$65,000 to $69,999	2,426	908	441	638
$70,000 to $74,999	2,024	847	349	468
$75,000 to $79,999	1,553	658	315	379
$80,000 to $84,999	1,346	582	212	347
$85,000 to $89,999	1,130	512	173	270
$90,000 to $94,999	1,034	434	189	232
$95,000 to $99,999	755	339	112	190
$100,000 to $149,999	3,232	1,510	555	722
$150,000 to $199,999	790	369	136	177
$200,000 to $249,999	314	147	54	70
$250,000 and over	305	143	52	68

Source: U.S. Bureau of the Census, Current Population Reports Series P60-184, *Money Income of Household, Families and Persons in the United States: 1992* (Washington, D.C.: U.S. Government Printing Office, 1993), Tables 6 and 18.

Notes: 1. Does not include 708,000 unrelated subfamilies in family columns. 2. Row and column totals have been changed to coincide with cell values (necessary because of slightly different figures in Tables 6 and 18). 3. Values for incomes above $100,000 were calculated from data obtained by phone from the Income Division of the Bureau of the Census. 4. Head of household numbers are the sum of male and female from the original tables.

Table 9.10b

Distribution of Incomes in the United States (Non-Married)

Income Range	Head of Household- No Related Children	Head of Household- One Child	Head of Household- Two or More Children	Non-Family Household (Single)
	Numbers in Thousands			
Total	5,196	5,013	4,968	28,247
Less than $5,000	158	797	950	2,097
$5,000 to $9,999	444	800	1,094	5,914
$10,000 to $14,999	510	701	684	4,240
$15,000 to $19,999	567	572	521	3,157
$20,000 to $24,999	511	604	436	2,509
$25,000 to $29,999	470	371	354	2,287
$30,000 to $34,999	461	312	262	1,765
$35,000 to $39,999	381	238	159	1,411
$40,000 to $44,999	357	183	131	982
$45,000 to $49,999	254	113	134	855
$50,000 to $54,999	277	76	60	638
$55,000 to $59,999	195	62	27	467
$60,000 to $64,999	111	60	23	372
$65,000 to $69,999	106	32	32	269
$70,000 to $74,999	82	14	13	251
$75,000 to $79,999	40	5	7	149
$80,000 to $84,999	43	16	9	137
$85,000 to $89,999	35	13	12	115
$90,000 to $94,999	51	9	13	106
$95,000 to $99,999	22	6	10	76
$100,000 to $149,999	84	20	26	314
$150,000 to $199,999	21	5	6	77
$200,000 to $249,999	8	2	3	30
$250,000 and over	8	2	2	30

See notes in Table 9.10a.

Although these are the most recent data available, they are based on a 1990 survey, so all aggregates will be as of that year. The result of applying this distribution to the individual data is shown in Tables 9.11a and 9.11b.

In the aggregate, households earning less than $30,000 would have received a net income while those earning more than $35,000 would have made a net payment into the program (this ranges from about $15,000 in the case of single-person households to about $45,000 for familes with two or more children). In the aggregate, the payments into the system would have exceeded the outgos by slightly over $325 billion.

Table 9.11a

Aggregate Transfers by Income Category (Total and Married Couples)

Income Range	Married-No Children	Married-One Child	Married-Two or More Children	Head of Household-No children
	Figures in millions ($)			
Less than $5,000	4,506	1,628	3,116	810
$5,000 to $9,999	9,132	2,431	5,712	1,444
$10,000 to $14,999	13,756	4,127	8,603	704
$15,000 to $19,999	11,924	4,550	8,851	(71)
$20,000 to $24,999	8,044	3,218	7,620	(958)
$25,000 to $29,999	3,756	2,732	6,500	(1,704)
$30,000 to $34,999	0	1,338	4,664	(2,478)
$35,000 to $39,999	(2,234)	13	2,572	(2,715)
$40,000 to $44,999	(4,945)	(656)	180	(3,168)
$45,000 to $49,999	(7,062)	(1,817)	(773)	(2,699)
$50,000 to $54,999	(9,607)	(2,756)	(2,572)	(3,428)
$55,000 to $59,999	(10,693)	(3,565)	(3,948)	(2,754)
$60,000 to $64,999	(10,863)	(4,284)	(4,659)	(1,762)
$65,000 to $69,999	(10,556)	(4,245)	(4,865)	(1,868)
$70,000 to $74,999	(11,329)	(3,970)	(4,388)	(1,589)
$75,000 to $79,999	(9,952)	(4,134)	(4,216)	(845)
$80,000 to $84,999	(9,821)	(3,153)	(4,468)	(984)
$85,000 to $89,999	(9,536)	(2,876)	(3,949)	(862)
$90,000 to $94,999	(8,843)	(3,473)	(3,799)	(1,345)
$95,000 to $99,999	(7,500)	(2,254)	(3,444)	(619)
$100,000 to $149,999	(47,958)	(16,512)	(20,040)	(3,181)
$150,000 to $199,999	(18,175)	(6,407)	(8,009)	(1,137)
$200,000 to $249,999	(9,799)	(3,493)	(4,404)	(596)
$250,000 and over	(13,269)	(4,771)	(6,071)	(788)
	(151,023)	(48,331)	(31,785)	(32,593)

This number can be compared with federal government income from individual income taxes. This figure was somewhere in the vicinity of $500 billion in 1992.[14] There would have thus been a revenue shortfall of some $175 billion. However, since my proposal includes elimination of welfare programs, the federal government outlays will also be reduced. In 1992 the country spent, through the federal government, $198.1 billion for "income security."[15] So with the elimination of these expenses, we would be about $23 billion to the good.

I have not included in these figures the savings generated by elimination of the unemployment compensation program. Since that program is separately funded by Federal Unemployment Tax Act (FUTA) taxes, the savings in outgo will be offset by the reduction in income. It should be noted, however, that this will be a reduced cost to businesses which will be passed along to consumers in lower prices.[16]

Table 9.11b

Aggregate Transfers by Income Category (Non-Married)

Income Range	Head of Household-One Child	Head of Household-Two or More Children	Non-Family Household (Single)	All Households
	Figures in millions ($)			
Less than $5,000	5,679	8,669	10,747	35,153
$5,000 to $9,999	4,202	7,934	19,235	50,090
$10,000 to $14,999	2,369	3,680	5,851	39,091
$15,000 to $19,999	862	1,827	(395)	27,549
$20,000 to $24,999	0	713	(4,704)	13,932
$25,000 to $29,999	(603)	0	(8,290)	2,391
$30,000 to $34,999	(1,053)	(360)	(9,487)	(7,376)
$35,000 to $39,999	(1,220)	(497)	(10,053)	(14,134)
$40,000 to $44,999	(1,258)	(639)	(8,715)	(19,201)
$45,000 to $49,999	(975)	(888)	(9,084)	(23,298)
$50,000 to $54,999	(789)	(503)	(7,895)	(27,550)
$55,000 to $59,999	(752)	(273)	(6,596)	(28,581)
$60,000 to $64,999	(833)	(273)	(5,906)	(28,579)
$65,000 to $69,999	(500)	(436)	(4,741)	(27,210)
$70,000 to $74,999	(243)	(200)	(4,863)	(26,581)
$75,000 to $79,999	(96)	(120)	(3,148)	(22,511)
$80,000 to $84,999	(334)	(170)	(3,134)	(22,064)
$85,000 to $89,999	(294)	(248)	(2,832)	(20,596)
$90,000 to $94,999	(219)	(291)	(2,796)	(20,766)
$95,000 to $99,999	(157)	(241)	(2,138)	(16,352)
$100,000 to $149,999	(722)	(870)	(11,856)	(101,139)
$150,000 to $199,999	(263)	(323)	(4,240)	(38,555)
$200,000 to $249,999	(139)	(172)	(2,183)	(20,784)
$250,000 and over	(185)	(231)	(2,937)	(28,253)
	2,479	16,090	(80,159)	(325,322)

I have also not shown any savings from reductions in state and local welfare expenditures, which amounted to $130 billion in fiscal year 1990-1991.[17] Some states may wish to continue to supplement the federal benefit. This may be particularly true in the case of those persons whose benefit under the GAI will be lower than what is currently available to them under the present myriad public assistance programs. On the other hand, states will certainly benefit to the extent that they are supporting persons not now eligible for federal assistance but who would receive an income under the GAI.

State and local expenses will also be reduced in the area of institutional services. Those currently being housed at public expense can be asked to spend their GAI to offset the cost of the service. This can include the cost of incarceration of prisoners (including federal costs).

A final federal expenditure which could be reduced under the new plan is the cost of education, training, employment, and social services. My preference is to limit the federal government's role to this one income redistribution program (the GAI) and get government out of the social services business. These services should be somewhat less needed under the GAI at any rate. However, since there will probably be considerable sentiment for retaining these programs, I have not considered the savings which might be generated by eliminating them.

As an aside, note that I have not argued for a reduction in national defense spending to help fund the program. While I personally believe reductions are in order, that issue is best left separate. By the way, we spent about $289 billion on defense in 1992.[18]

SUMMARY

It looks to me as though we can do it. You and I may quarrel over some of the details. You may feel that the GAI amount I used is not high enough or is too high. You may feel the 35 percent income tax rate is too high or too low. However, as long as you don't insist on decreasing the tax rate while increasing the GAI benefit, or vice-versa, we should still be able to make the plan work.

Notes

1. Ostensibly, this deduction is provided to help enable low-income earners to purchase a home. Its primary benefit, however, accrues to higher-income earners.

2. This is a difficult area with which to deal in the income tax structure. It is certainly reasonable to allow business owners deductions for the cost of doing business, prior to calculating their net income. Nonetheless, greater pain should be taken to limit these deductions to those involving a genuine business necessity.

3. The figures used in all my calculations are from the period 1990-1993. This is the most recent period for which all of the needed numbers were available as of this writing. By the time the book is read, some of the numbers will be out-dated. Nonetheless, the results will still be relevant because they provide primarily a *comparison* of two systems at one point in time. Just what time period is chosen is not particularly important.

4. These are arbitrarily chosen income figures. Here and in other places in this chapter, I use an apparently "odd" number, rather than some round figure

like $50,000, for a reason. The aggregate calculations I will be making are computed using income statistics which are provided in ranges (e.g., $50,000 to $54,999). My calculations will be based on the midpoint of these ranges. Hence, in this instance, $52,500.

5. Two points about this figure: (1) very few persons earning this income level will only have the standard deduction; (2) this is obviously not the highest income bracket in the United States; it is used here as the median of the highest earnings category ($250,000 and above) available for the income distribution.

6. The basis for this figure is shown in Table 9.5. Relying on the median values, I assumed assets of $5,000 at the lowest income level ($2,500) and increased by $5,000 in assets for each $5,000 increase in income.

7. A feasible alternative would be to consider *everyone's* assets in calculating the taxes, thus increasing taxes even for those well above the GAI level. This would actually yield a simpler to understand tax structure and could allow a reduction in the tax rate itself. (If this were the policy, the sample individual would pay a higher tax. Assuming assets of $50,000 at this income level, the imputed income would be $3,500, the additional tax $1,225, the total tax $13,600 and the effective tax rate 25.9 percent).

8. Although I refer here and elsewhere to a "married couple," it should be remembered the GAI benefit does not depend upon marital status. It is paid to the individual. Any two adults and two children would be entitled to the $16,000 benefit. The reference to married couples is primarily for purposes of comparisons with the present system, which does make that distinction.

9. As incomes actually exceed the $300,000 figure, the tax rate will more closely approach 35 percent.

10. Although I do not demonstrate the present effect of these benefits on individuals, I recognize them in the calculation of the aggregate relative cost of the new plan.

11. Note, however, that the current rates are based on assumed levels of deductions. To the extent certain taxpayers have higher than the assumed levels of deductions, their effective tax rates will be lower than those calculated.

12. Since our deductions were considerably higher than those assumed in the calculations (primarily due to home mortgage interest and property taxes), our actual 1993 taxes were only $11,200. Thus we would be about $9,000 worse off under the new system. Hmmm! Since I haven't figured out how to make these consequences apply to everyone but me, this really "taxes" my commitment to the GAI. Oh well, the political reality is that the plan will be very difficult to pass, so I will probably continue to enjoy my nice lifestyle undiminished.

13. A higher rate could be introduced at higher incomes without doing any signficant damage to the proposed plan.

14. According to U.S. Bureau of the Census, *Statistical Abstract of the United States: 1993*, 113th ed. (Washington, D.C.: Government Printing Office, 1993), Table 510, individual income taxes as a source of federal receipts were $515.3 billion in 1992. The figure shown in *Economic Report of the President* (Washington, D.C.: Government Printing Office, 1993), Table B-75, p. 437, is $476.5 billion. When I calculate the total taxes using the 1990 income distribution and 1993 tax rates, with assumed levels of deductions, I get about $497 billion. Doesn't $500 billion seem like a reasonable and nice round figure to use? (The estimate for 1995 was $588.5 billion. *Statistical Abstract of the United States: 1995*, Table 518, p. 334.)

15. *Economic Report of the President*, p. 437. Of this figure only some $37 billion is genrally thought of as "welfare"—that is the cost of AFDC and food stamps.

16. Total unemployment insurance payments in 1991 were $27.5 billion. *Economic Report of the President*, Table B-40, p. 393. Although my preference is to eliminate the unemployment insurance program, a case could be made for retaining it to provide supplementary benefits to those who lose their jobs. Note, however, that the GAI payment should be offset against the unemployment benefits, thus reducing the cost of that program.

17. *Economic Report of the President*, Table B-81, p. 443.

18. U.S. Bureau of the Census, *Statistical Abstract of the United States*, Table 509. The 1995 estimate is $271.6 billion. *Statistical Abstract of the United States: 1995*, Table 549, p. 356.

10

Final Thoughts

In this final chapter, I summarize the line of reasoning which has led me to conclude that a guaranteed adequate income is the optimum alternative to our present welfare system in the United States. In addition, I present some thoughts on the issue of how much is enough. Finally, the prospects for passage of legislation are considered.

THE THOUGHT PROCESS LEADING TO THE GAI

An important, although by no means essential, step on the path to support of a GAI is agreement with the view that none of us is more worthy of economic well-being than any others of us. The path itself is made less difficult when one accepts the tenets of determinism. Those of us who have concluded that each of us is a product of factors over which we had no control recognize that we can fault no one for failure to (or even unwillingness to) earn a living.

For the same reasons that we cannot blame others for their poverty, so also can we not conclude that those with income deserve to have it. The whole notion of deserving as a basis for a just economic system is without merit for those who accept the cause-and-effect explanation for human behavior.

An alternative basis on which to found a system of justice might be a notion of rights. Although a substantial case can be made for the position that all have a right to at least a minimum economic status, I have not chosen to advocate that position. The concept of a right is subject to so much debate that it would be almost impossible to convince anyone who did not accept it intuitively. My only attempt to invoke the notion of a right was in pointing out the extent to which we no longer have ready access to certain means of survival which were throughout history so taken for granted (and thus regarded as something to which we had a right).

The next major observation on this path is a recognition that our economic system of choice—capitalism/private enterprise—does not contribute well to a just economic distribution. Although it is the best system we know of for accumulating wealth and fostering economic growth, its rewards are not distributed in a manner consistent with the notion of justice I have put forth. This is primarily because the system virtually requires a cadre of unemployed. Even those who do not accept the tenets of determinism and thus wish to fault people for their behavior will recognize that for many persons unemployment is beyond their control.

In addition, our economic system rewards those whose contributions are valued by society, without regard to the efforts that were needed to make those contributions or the sacrifices that were or were not necessary. Many are rewarded highly for such pleasurable activities as playing games or being creative, while others receive little compensation for risking life, limb, and sanity in unrewarding work.

In order to partially offset the undesirable consequences of our economic system, we have gotten involved through government. However, our welfare system itself is founded on the notion that some members of society are deserving of help while others are not. This notion of worthy and unworthy poor people is inconsistent with a concept of justice founded on the common worthiness of all members of society.

Additional problems with our current welfare system include the significant extent to which it requires that government interfere in individuals' lives and with the workings of the free market. Efforts to reform this system with workfare-type systems only exacerbate these problems.

If neither the market system nor our current welfare system nor recent attempts at welfare reform provides a just distribution, what alternative is there? One option which was considered but rejected was an egalitarian distribution of wealth. Certainly if no one deserves to have more than anyone else, it would logically follow that a just system would be one in which all had the same. However, this is unworkable for two reasons. First, there is still a need to provide some incentive for people to be productive. Second, any attempt to impose an equal distribution will quickly be thwarted by those who can find ways to gather some of the shares from others.

If there is no justice in some having more than others, but it is impractical to try to provide everyone with the same, what then? The only alternative that is consistent with the dictates of justice as developed in this book is a system in which everyone gets at least something. How much that something should be is a debatable point, but it certainly seems it should be adequate. My goal is a guaranteed income that is at least adequate to provide everyone with the economic opportunity to enjoy life.

Having opted for this alternative, one must be prepared to deal with the most common criticism. What will this do to the work incentive? One can continue to support this alternative only if this concern does not overwhelm the advantages. For me it does not. There are two primary reasons it does not. First, I am not all that concerned about everybody working. I argue that it is neither necessary from the viewpoint of societal well-being that everyone work nor essential for the intrinsic sense of self-worth for the individual. The first conclusion is founded on the recognition that technology can be our slave labor force, providing all the necessary goods with a minimum of human contribution. The second conclusion is based on a recognition that it is not an intrinsic part of humanity to work. Rather, work is a cultural phenomenon promoted and enforced to the extent it is necessary to survival. Now that it has become no longer necessary, with a just distribution of incomes, people will be freed from the slavery of the workplace.

The second reason I am not so concerned about the impact of the GAI on work is that my system retains a definite work incentive. With a 35 percent flat tax, everyone will be able to keep a high percentage of each additional dollar he or she earns. This incentive is much greater than what exists in our present welfare system. At the other end of the income spectrum, we have observed for years evidence that people keep working even in the face of marginal tax rates this high and higher (and these are people who already have substantial incomes).

Well, if you're one of those readers who starts with the summary, and you're not convinced, I hope you'll take the time to look at the more extensive arguments presented in the book.

HOW MUCH IS ENOUGH?

In the chapter on costs, I used figures of $6,000 per adult and $2,000 per child to make calculations of the total cost of a GAI program. I noted at the time that the figures were somewhat arbitrary (and were chosen to be more relevant to the early 1990s since that was the period for which other needed data were available). I also noted that the actual amount of the grant was a negotiable item in the plan, and that it could vary from year to year. However, for many people the amount is a touchy point. This is particularly true for those who are inclined to use the government mechanism to assist the poor, and are thus attracted to this plan but for their concern that the amount might be too low.

Just how much is an adequate amount? For some, of course, there seems to be no amount which qualifies. No matter how much they have, they seem to spend more and need more.

Our primary concern with a GAI, however, should be to at least provide enough to cover the costs of necessities such as food, clothing, and housing. It is hoped that we could also afford to make the grant generous enough to provide funds for some additional expenses such as entertainment.

My stated goal is to provide everyone with enough to give her or him an opportunity to enjoy life. In this regard, there are two points I wish to make. First, we as a society need to emphasize those nonmaterial blessings which contribute to the enjoyment of life. We would do well to rejuvenate the pleasures of life of which Henry David Thoreau wrote a century ago. Of course, we need to recognize that he had access to Walden Pond. Nonetheless, his basic advice that we should learn to enjoy the contemplative life is valuable.

Second, we need to recognize the joys of some material blessings which we tend to take for granted. So many of us have gotten so used to such conveniences as running water and water pressure and window screens and electricity that we forget to marvel at how comfortable they make our lives.

In my judgment, a grant in the neighborhood of $6,000 per adult should enable most people to enjoy the "significant and vital" experiences of life, as well as some of the luxuries which are often taken for granted.

POLITICAL PROSPECTS

Can this proposal become law? Not in today's political climate. Two changes need to take place before it can become politically feasible. First, we need to go through a few years of experience with the current "welfare reform." I have noted in the book why I don't believe that this reform will be successful. In particular, I feel that it will lose favor with the very people who had ardently supported it. They will come to see how much government interference in people's lives and with the working of the free market is necessary to make it operational. That is why I subtitle the book "Welfare Reform for the 21st Century."

The second required change is a widespread acceptance of two of the positions taken in this book. First is the recognition that no one is undeserving of a stake in the economic wherewithal of the country. The second is an acceptance of the view that it is no longer essential that everyone work, neither for the sake of the individual nor for the sake of society.

As I write the final words to a project that has spanned more than two decades, I pause to contemplate the potential impact. Will I have changed anyone's mind? Will I have caused some to think more rigorously about the issues? Will I have reinforced the views of others? Probably not, hopefully so, and probably are the answers I come up with to these questions (in the order asked).

Among those who read all or a substantial portion of the book, I hope there are at least the following. First, those who tend to disagree with my positions, but who have occasionally responded "That's something I hadn't considered. He may have a point there." Second, those who have been predisposed in the directions I argue, who now know there is someone else who shares their views and thus feel reinforced in their position.

Finally, my hope is that we will all recognize that these are points on which reasonable people can reasonably disagree, and be willing to continue a civil discussion.

References

Albert, Michael and Robin Hahnel. *Looking Forward: Participatory Economics for the Twenty First Century*. Boston: South End Press, 1991.

Atkinson, A. B. *The Economics of Inequality*, Oxford: Clarendon Press, 1983.

Bellamy, Edward. *Looking Backward: 2000-1887*, New York: Houghton Mifflin, 1888.

Berofsky, Bernard. *Determinism*, Princeton, NJ: Princeton University Press, 1971.

Branden, Barbara. *The Passion of Ayn Rand*. Garden City, NY: Doubleday, 1986.

Bridges, William. *Job Shift*. Reading, MA: Addison-Wesley, 1994.

Brown, Henry Phelps, *Egalitarianism and the Generation of Inequality*. Oxford: Clarendon Press, 1988.

Friedman, Milton. *An Economist's Protest*. Glen Ridge, NJ: Thomas Horton, 1972.

——. *Capitalism and Freedom*. Chicago: The University of Chicago Press, 1962.

Funiciello, Theresa. *Tyranny of Kindness*. New York: The Atlantic Monthly Press, 1993.

Gilby, Thomas. *St. Thomas Aquinas, Philosophical Texts*. London: Oxford University Press, 1951.

Gordon, Kermit. *Agenda for the Nation*, Washington, DC: Brookings Institution, 1968.

Harrington, Michael. *The Other America.*. Baltimore, MD: Penguin Books, 1971.

Heilbroner, Robert. *21st Century Capitalism*. New York: W.W. Norton, 1993.

Hildebrand, George H. *Poverty, Income Maintenance, and the Negative Income Tax*. Ithaca, NY: New York State School of Industrial and Labor Relations, 1967.

Kaus, Mickey. *The End of Equality*. New York: Basic Books, 1992.

Knebel, Fletcher. *Trespass.*. Garden City, NY: Doubleday, 1969.

Lewontin, Richard, Steven Rose, and Leon Kamin. *Not In Our Genes : Biology, Ideology, and Human Nature*. New York: Pantheon Books, 1984.

Lutz, Mark and Kenneth Lux. *The Challenge of Humanistic Economy*. Menlo Park, CA: The Benjamin/Cummings Publishing Co., 1979.

Marmor, Theodore R. *Poverty Policy*. Chicago: Aldine Press, 1971.

Miller, David. *Social Justice*. Oxford: Clarendon Press, 1976.

Morgenbesser, Sidney and James Walsh (eds.). *Free Will*. Englewood Cliffs, NJ: Prentice-Hall, 1962.

Moynihan, Daniel. *The Politics of A Guaranteed Income*. New York: Vintage Books, 1973.

Murray, Charles. *Losing Ground*. New York: Basic Books, 1984.

Nozick, Robert. *Anarchy, State, and Utopia*. New York: Basic Books, 1974.

Orwell, George. *down and out in Paris and London*. New York: Berkley Medallion Books, 1959.

Phillips, Derek L. *Toward a Just Social Order*. Princeton, NJ: Princeton University Press, 1986.

Rainwater, Lee. *What Money Buys*. New York: Basic Books, 1974.

Rawls, John. *A Theory of Justice*. Cambridge, MA: Harvard University Press, 1971.

Report of the Subcommittee on Fiscal Policy of the Joint Economic Committee, Congress of the United States. Washington, DC: U.S. Government Printing Office, December 5, 1974.

Sadker, Myra, and David. *Failing at Fairness: How America's Schools Cheat Girls. New York:* Charles Scribner's Sons, 1994.

Sandburg, Carl. *The Complete Poems of Carl Sandburg.* New York: Harcourt Brace Jovanovich, 1970.

Sheahen, Allan. *Guaranteed Income: The Right to Economic Security.* Los Angeles: Gain Publications, 1983.

Sidgwick, Henry. *The Methods of Ethics.* London: Macmillan Ltd., 1930.

Skinner, B. F. *Walden II.* New York: Macmillan, 1948.

Soloman, Robert C. *A Passion for Justice.* Reading, MA: Addison-Wesley Publishing Company, Inc., 1990.

Theobald, Robert. *Free Men and Free Markets,* Garden City, NY: Doubleday,1965.

Theobald, Robert (ed.). *The Guaranteed Income: Next Step in Socioeconomic Evolution?* Garden City, NY: Doubleday, 1967.

Trusted, Jennifer. *Free Will and Responsibility.* Oxford: Oxford University Press, 1984.

Vonnegut, Kurt. *Player Piano.* New York: Dell Publishing, 1988.

INDEX

Michael L. Murray is a professor of insurance in the College of Business and Public Administration at Drake University in Des Moines, Iowa. He holds an MBA and a Ph.D. in insurance from the University of Oregon, and a bachelor's degree in sociology from the University of Iowa. He has taught at Drake University for eleven years, having previously taught at the University of Iowa for nineteen years. His work experience also includes two years in an insurance agency and two years as a United States Army Infantry officer.